TOAD SUCK REVIEW #4

toadsuckreview.org

*Named for the Toad Suck region of Arkansas
where we view the world and offer
the following flashes of luminous lit,
avant-garde art and cutting-edge
commentary.*

TOAD SUCK REVIEW #4

EDITOR IN CHIEF
Mark Spitzer

ASSOCIATE EDITOR
John Vanderslice

ASSISTANT EDITORS
Douglas Luman
Jobe

EDITORIAL ASSISTANTS
Audrey Carroll   Rebecca Hawkins
TJ Heffers   Benjamin Sneyd

SOCIAL MEDIA ED
Chris Hancock

Copyright © 2014 Dept. of Writing
University of Central Arkansas

ISSN 2158-1088
ISBN-10: 0983760764
ISBN-13: 9780983760764

Toad Suck Review
Department of Writing
University of Central Arkansas
Conway, AR 72035

Please address all correspondence for *Toad Suck Review* to toadsuckreview @gmail.com. Submissions can be sent to the address above and should include an SASE. Submissions can also be sent to toadsucksubmit@gmail. com. Generally, we read in the summer. Publishers: send books for review to address above. To order copies of *Toad Suck Review #4* send a check for $15 per issue made out to "UCA" to address above or go to ordering page at toadsuckreview.org. To order back issues, see ads in the back of this issue. Lifetime subscriptions are $75. If you'd like to make a tax-exempt contribution, write to us at toadsuckreview@gmail.com.

Printed in USA

#4

TOAD SUCK REVIEW #4

TOAD SUCK CONTENTS

FROM THE TOADSTOOL

O LOST SUCK OF TOAD!!!
By Mark Spitzer 1

TOADMAIL 4

WILLIAM S. BURROUGHS FEATURE!!!

LOST BURROUGHS!!!
By William S. Burroughs, Davis Schneiderman
and Editors 8

HIGH-OCTANE POETIX

THOUSANDS OF DEAD RATS
By Christopher Citro and Dustin Nightingale 15

FUNNY BUSINESS
By Kyle Flak 17

SPIKE LAVENDER IN DEATH
By Claire T. Feild 21

EXCERPTS FROM *WORLDS LINGER*
By klipschutz 23

COVERED IN HASHTAGS
By Billy Cancel 27

ASTER RISKS
By Simon Perchik 30

AN AUDIENCE OF DEMONS
By Jeffrey Zable 32

NONFIXION

WALK IT OFF
By JD Iripino 34

THE LOST ISSUE!!!

TOAD SUCK CONTENTS

THE GOOD CHRISTIAN KID
By Jennifer McGaha......................41

HOT AIR
By M. John Fayhee........................47

TRANSLATIO

LOST RIMBAUD!!!
*By Arthur Rimbaud, Akakia-Viala Prasteau,
Nicolas Bataille, Daryl Spurlock and Editors*...............54

NAME THE QUIET EYES
*By Vicente Aleixandre
Translated by Stephen Kessler*..........................64

ARKANA

THE CARPET WON'T LIKE US BACK
By Matthew Henriksen......................67

SIREN SQUAWKS JIVE TALK
By Seth Pennington........................69

THE FORGOTTEN RIVER
By Charles Portis..........................71

CRITICAL INTEL

STRAIGHT-UP BOOK REVIEWS
By Tom Lavoie...........................87

NO B.S. REVIEWS
By C. Prozac............................90

RACIST LIKE ME
By Joshua D. Bellin........................95

WHAT WOULD DICKINSON DO?
By Greg Graham..........................102

TOAD SUCK REVIEW #4

TOAD SUCK CONTENTS

POSTCARD POINTERS FOR PERFORMERS
By Bob May 105

REBEL WITH A CAUSE: RADHA BHARADWAJ'S
MAVERICK MISTRESSPIECE
By Bob Mielke 108

FIXION

VERY BLONDE HAIR, VERY BLUE EYES—
VERY WHITE SKIN!
By Radha Bharadwaj 114

AN EAR WHERE MY HEART SHOULD BE
By Sean Rabin 119

STANTON'S GRIEVANCE
By Jacqueline Doyle 129

SO MUCH UNCOLLECTED GARBAGE
By Michael Cuglietta 135

ARTISTS IN RESIDENCE

THE TOAD INTERVIEWS DAMIEN ECHOLS & LORRI DAVIS
By Arkansas Writers MFA Workshop 142

THE TILTED WORLD OF TOM FRANKLIN
AND BETH ANN FENNELLY
By Tom Franklin, Beth Ann Fennelly and Kelvin Krill 150

ECO-EDGE

LOVERS SPELUNKING
SMOKE SCREAMING
By Doug Luman 157

EARTH DAY, TEXAS
By David Taylor 162

THE LOST ISSUE!!!

TOAD SUCK CONTENTS

FLOAT: A TEASER
By JoeAnn Hart. 164

WALKING TO LAOS
By Scott Ezell. 170

LAST WRITES

YOU'RE KEEPING MY OXYGEN IN YOUR OXYGEN TANK,
BUT EVEN THIS BORES ME TO TEARS
By Daniel Banulescu
Translated by Adam Sorkin and Lidia Vianu 185

CONTRIBUTOR BIOS

TOAD SUCK BIOS 187

ARTWORK

LOST ANDY WARHOL PHOTOGRAPH CUT-UP
By JJ Cromer 14

PHOTO
By Sarah Katharina Kayß 16

PHOTO
By Sarah Katharina Kayß 22

THINGS TO DO TODAY
By JJ Cromer. 68

TOAD SUCK REVIEW #4

O LOST SUCK OF TOAD!!!
By Mark Spitzer

Welcome Toad Nation, to the fourth *Toad Suck Review,* in which the concept of *lost* is the binding theme. A recently discovered image of the legendary poet Arthur Rimbaud, lost in Abyssinia, proudly (& in Warholian Splendor) announces what we've unearthed from the gone annals of literary history. Our Rimbaud feature includes the first-ever English translations of two questionably lost Rimbaud poems. We also have a feature on William S. Burroughs, wherein a letter to Allen Ginsberg, lost for over fifty years, envisions the Great Beat Junky's now-famous cut-up method. On the back cover, you'll see a mural by the mysterious underground artist Banksy, who leaves his mark on the public domain by playing with a refaced/defaced fresco of Christ, recently "restored" in Italy. The question here, however, isn't whether something was lost in Jesus' makeover; it has to do with the toad in the corner, which doesn't appear in other photos of this wall. Hence: Is that toad legitimately Banksy's, or is it another bastardization? Then there's the fine prose of Charles Portis, whose work is currently being rediscovered, especially in the lost classic "The Forgotten River," an essay of true grit, straight out of Arkansas. We also have an interview with Damien Echols, the infamous "Ringleader of the West Memphis Three," who was scapegoated into a false conviction, which led to eighteen years of lost life flushed away just like that.

Our poetry section contains work by the iconic Simon Perchik, whose "nothing, nothing—a rain / with no one to take hold" defines the epitome of loss. Outlaw poet klipschutz also takes a stand, writing in a lost semi-Baudelarian form crossed with a soon-to-be-lost Dada logic. Jeffrey Zable, on the other hand, celebrates loss, when "little in this life / happens on our own terms." Claire T. Feild addresses a sullen loss of life and actually ascribes it a color. The verse of Kyle Flak, Billy Cancel, Christopher Citro, and Dustin Nightengale intentionally loses track of conventional expectations, thereby creating sense from non-sense.

In Nonfixion, JD Iripino's comic portrait of our ridiculous selves concludes with the assertion that not all is lost. Meanwhile, Jennifer McGaha steels herself to a world in which the loss of property becomes the ephemeral-but-empty gain of a good Christian kid lost in the Flux of Mendacity. As for John M. Fayhee's hilarious narrative of losing altitude in a couple of disastrous hot air balloon rides, the proof is in the pudding and the pudding's in his pants.

Translatio, of course, features France's most mythical boy-genius *enfant terrible*, as mentioned above, whose greatest lost forgery has been masterly translated by Daryl Spurlock. The research and Toad commentary in this feature was mainly the product of Scotty Lewis, Assistant Editor from last year. But wait! Nobel Laureate Vicente Aleixandre is also translated in this section through an art in which sacrifice is imminent, except when exquisitely rendered by Stephen Kessler.

Our Arkansas focus leads off with Matthew Henriksen, whose elusive "Forgiveness as an act of theater / on the meat hooks" suggests a desperation propelled by the driver of loss. Seth Pennington's vision of the homeless (home-loss) in the San Francisco Library is, in a sense, a sophisticated exposé of "pink potted meat" just trying to survive another day.

The luminaries in Critical Intel include Tom Lavoie reviewing Portis, C. Prozac commending Ed Sanders, Joshua D. Bellin on racism, Greg Graham extrapolating Emily Dickinson, Bob May providing pointers on directing drama, and Bob Mielke exploring the imagination of Indian filmmaker Radha Bharadwaj. What these scholars have in common is their loss of seconds and minutes and years compiling their thoughts into this exact micro-second, in which you, dear reader, stand at the gates of their labor, where their rays of insights beckon you to enter.

And O the lowly losers in Fixion! Not the writers, but their characters. Eg, Radha Bharadwaj's delusional romantic whose quest for an American blonde ends in disaster. Witness also Jaqueline Doyle, whose loser professor lodges a grievance in an academic parody of denial in action. Or Michael Cuglietta, whose protagonist loses his respect for life. Don't worry, though, this story is hardly a bummer in the end. Sean Rabin, however, breaks from the mold of profiling losers in this section. His "liner notes" of a lost cult-classic album envision the aesthetics of a disquiet mind.

Beth Ann Fennelly and Tom Franklin appear in our Artists-in-Residence feature, spotlighting an excerpt from their collaborative novel *The Tilted World*. This tale of murder and moonshine framed by a literal flood of loss is then reviewed by Kelvin Krill.

Now we arrive at the Eco-Edge, where Doug Luman's historical approach to verse looks at a tragic loss of life aflame in the wilderness. (As an aside, we'd like to note that it is not the Toad's policy to publish its own editors, but after we accepted Doug's work, he applied to the Arkansas Writers MFA Workshop, and with qualifications such as his, there was no way we couldn't accept his technical wizardry and artistic sensibility. Hence, he is now our Assistant Editor.) The other environmental visionaries in this section are David Taylor, reminding us of what we have to lose; Scott Ezell, lost in Laos; and JoeAnn Hart, whose story of a beaten boss results in an epiphany that can't accept an eco-loss.

Of course, we also have some artwork in here by JJ Cromer and Sarah Katharina Kayß. JJ's collage methodology is definitely postmodern in that it tells all prior movements to get lost. As for Sarah's whimsical photographs, there's a kind of loss inherent in each that declares a certain freedom of expression.

Finally, there's the Romanian writer Daniel Banulescu, expertly traduced by Adam Sorkin and Lidia Vianu. This semi-absurd knee-slapper of a poem ends this issue on a humorous note in which loss can actually be a bonus.

Speaking of this issue, you might notice that we've lost some inhibitions. When we started this publishing project as the *Exquisite Corpse Annual* six long years ago, we assured the Provost that we'd avoid graphic words and provocative commentary that might freak out the good people of the Toad Suck environs. That Provost, however, is long gone, and we're ready to start taking some risks with the risqué, or language and content that we might've self-censored before. I'm not saying that we've metamorphosed into an in-your-face literary journal; I'm saying that we're finding our voice, and our voice is yours, and we're glad to be part of your strut upon this stage, if only for a flash in Toad Time.

So adios, friends, and may the Toad be with you!

4 FROM THE TOADSTOOL TOAD SUCK REVIEW

TOADMAIL

TO: TOAD SUCK REVIEW
FROM: JEFFREY D. PRATTE
SUBJ: SUBSCRIPTION INQUIRY

Hi. I am a Little Rock native serving a life sentence in Florida's Department of Corrections for robbery. More than a convict I am a hearty reader.

Our institution has a small library supported by donated books from our inmate population. I have worked there myself through the years and am ever trying to raise the reading profile of its patrons. Your publication caught my attention in an ad running in the *Oxford American* which I am subscribed to.

I would like to sample a current or archival edition of your publication if you would be gracious enough to provide one, complimentary. Please also summarize your publication's mission, focus, and vision of its place in the literary world. And finally, send subscription information, terms, etc., also submission guidelines, too.

Thanks so much for your time, consideration, and your anticipated response.

> Yours truly,
> Jeffrey D. Pratte, DC# R35337
> Central Florida Reception Center
> East Unit, B-2, 130 S
> 7000 H.C. Kelly Road
> Orlando, FL 32831-2518

Dear Jeffrey D. Pratte:

Thanks for your letter and your interest. Enclosed is an issue of the *Toad Suck Review*, gratis. We see ourselves as a quirky avant-garde forum which embraces a mainstream audience. Our mission is to publish the most cutting-edge works in the Universe. In addition to the usual genres of creative writing, we make an effort to focus on aspects of the Beat legacy, environmental subject matter, translations, weird art, and a dose of scholarship while showcasing artists from around the world—and especially from Arkansas. You'll get a better idea of what we're about when you open this baby up. You'll also find subscription and submission info in there, though we now read in the summer. Like it says on our website, "our guidelines are very open and ambiguous. Don't send us too much and don't make it too long." It might take us a few months to get back to you. That said, we'd love to receive a submission, and we'd also love to print your letter. If you are agreeable, we'll sign you up for a free lifetime subscription including all back issues. Please pardon the pun, but the Toad loves a captive audience.

Hope to hear from you soon, and thanks for promoting the literary imagination.

Sincerely, Mark Spitzer

Dear Mr. Spitzer:

Thank you indeed for the issue of the *Toad Suck Review* that you graciously provided. Read it—loved it! So did those who have since had the good pleasure; many, many will enjoy it here!

You certainly have my permission to print my previous letter and, I certainly would accept the "Free Lifetime Subscription including all back issues" that you appeared to offer—gladly I would!

I anticipate more good writing from y'all. I also anticipate submitting in the future. Thanks for opening our literary windows just a little wider here in this murk institution.

Very truly yours,
Jeffrey D. Pratte

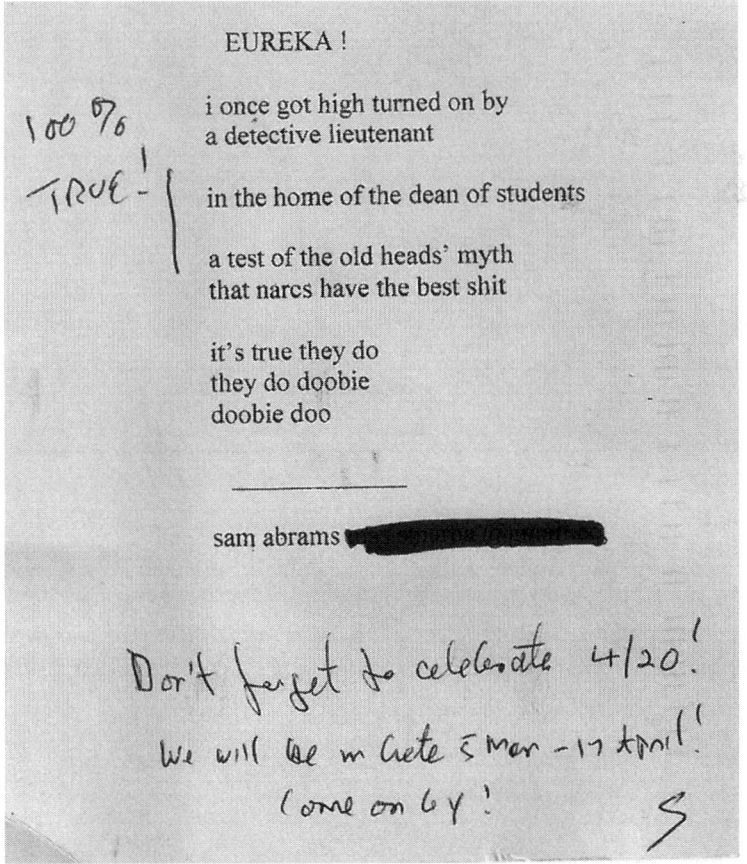

—Sam Abrams

Dear TOAD SUCK,

With that last issue, the Toad went psychedelic. Reading Lew Welch's essay brings to mind sucking psychotropic off the lips of a chin-stroked toad. The same could be said for the Ed Sanders poetry gracing #3D's pages. I'm sure I heard, in my mind's ear, batrachian lips being sucked in the background during Mr. Sanders' interview.

    I truly want to thank you folks for hopping out into the public eye Welch's "Language Is Speech." A brilliant essay that puts into words ideas and imagery lurking at the edges of my brain since that unreliable organ first learned how to use me. On an even more personal note, the work brought back the only time I was ever privileged to see the man himself in action:

    It was mid-January of 1971. The place was the Faculty Office Building at Reed's Fine College. Reed was then in the midst of UIS: Unstructured Independent Study. A daring concept brought about by the late sixties that loosely translates to: Hey, let's suspend all classes for six weeks of pure fuckoff, starting with the onset of Xmas vacation and ending on January 31st.

    Lew had been invited to give a reading during UIS. The reading was attended by two dozen straightback chairs and roughly eight disheveled stoned-out hippies legally disguised as Reed students.

    Lew arrived joyfully drunk, garbed in jeans, Redwing boots, red-and-black-checked flannel lumberjack jacket and black sweatshirt. His face was so scarlet and glistening with booze sweat, I'm sure if we'd doused the overhead incandescents we could have read a newspaper by the glow.

    He made friends with us at once. Cordially invited the audience to board Spaceship Welch and boldly go wherever the poetry of the moment would take us. First we went to a few of Lew's scenic hermit poems. Then he started to read the vulture poem, his signature piece, but stopped in the middle, looked up and asked if anyone present had yet figured out what is the sound of one hand clapping?

    Shrugs, embarrassed giggles, stoner stares. Lew let the silence settle in. Then solemnly pronounced: "Well, I have the answer to this age old koan. I cannot of course put the answer into anything so crude and inexact as words. But I am prepared to demonstrate."

    All eight sat up straight. Tossed long hair out of eyes. Desperately shook off acid flashes, pot blearies, benzedrine audios. This guy was enlightened. He had lived in the woods with his own mind and little else. He had come down from the mountain to reveal the Secret.

    "OK—here it is:"

    Lew, without getting up from his chair, raised his right hand to the level of his head. Presented palm to audience. Snapped the wrist briskly. SLAP! His fingers banged against the inside of his upper forearm. Snapped again. SLAP! And so on: SLAP! SLAP! SLAP!

White teeth gleamed as he laughed hugely and his red face shook: "I'm double jointed! Nobody else I've ever met can do this!"

As we all automatically held up our hands and tried in vain to replicate the feat, laughter swept over our modest gaggle of pre-Bob, post-Manson slacker-bodhisattvas. We, too, in that moment, were all enlightened. We saw God's face in that grinning Red Monk—and the face was none other than each his own.

Five months later, the poet went on his date with the vultures.

Thanks Daddy Lew, Professor Welch, your Monkship. Whenever my own life looks like shit, whenever I think I might myself just say fuck it, take my pistol off into the woods and let nobody but the buzzards ever find me… I just hear that SLAP! SLAP! SLAP! and see my own face grinning, sweating, suffused with good hearty oxygenated point-two-five blood.

—Raid Kills Bugs Dead, Willie

Dear Beloved Cherished Devoted Toad Suck
Submitters Who Didn't Quite Make the Cut:

We scrutinized it all—your fabulist fixions,
        your articulate articles, your ingenuous essays—
while picking for our limited space.
        (Hardest to deny was your electric verse.)
In the end, we chose as we chose and so chose to send (*désolé*!)
to too many of you our regretful, belated,
        never-nice-to-read send off message.
We're writers—we know how much it hurts—
        we've given and gotten
too many in careers that seem even longer than
        our cumulative age,
and because we have we know that you'll do
        what we'd do once rejection is forgotten:
You'll submit again!
    We welcome that (as long as what you throw us isn't too long) (oh—and as long as you only throw once for each
        Toad's round of reading).
We'll be jumping back into the submit box soon,
        reveling in the throng,
perhaps sending some of you better-feeling notices.
        Meantime, we have a lot of bleeping
business to get to. (We're not only writers but the workiest
        professors you've ever seen.)
Bottom line: Despite your blunted aspirations, we hope you like
        the magazine.

—John Vanderslice,
Assoc. Ed.

LOST BURROUGHS!!!

This year the Toad was lucky enough to get its hands on William S. Burroughs' letter to Allen Ginsberg, in which the infamous Beat junkie explains his postmodern cut-up philosophy, then enters into other matters. We're grateful to Ecco Press for granting us exclusive permission to print this letter, and we're glad to provide a shout-out to the new Burroughs book Rub Out the Words: The Letters of William S. Burroughs, 1959-1974, *which recently debuted this important epistolary document lost to the American consciousness for more than half a century. This book is on sale right now, so get it while it's hot!!!*

WSB [London] to Allen Ginsberg [New York]
Sept 5 1960
Cargo American Express
London England

Dear Allen:

The cut up method is a tool which I am learning to use after a year of intensive experiments. There is no reason to keep cut up material that is not useful to the purpose. Often from a page of cut ups I will use one or two sentences. It depends on the material cut and the purpose in cut. In *Minutes To Go* and *The Exterminator* I was using cut up material intact. At the time had not learned to select. Also was more concerned with using the cut ups as fact assessing instrument. When used for poetic bridge work procedure is different. Like I write a page of prose or prose poem straight. Then cut once or twice or more. And select from all sections what I find most valuable. A sifting panning process. The enclosed selections will give you idea of potentials in the method. There is no reason why classic sonnets or any other poetic form could not be so reduced. I find cut ups most immediately workable on poetic prose image writing like Rimbaud, St. Perse and your correspondent. Use of cut ups of course increases ability to cut with the eyes, that is to make "natural cut ups" whatever that may mean and what is an unnatural cut up? Whatever abilities Gregory [Corso] may possess logical thought is not one of them. That is having cut with the eyes there is always extension of awareness possible with scissors cut. I repeat, no necessity to retain any material not pertinent.

Letter of September 5, 1960 to Allen Ginsberg [pp. 44-6] from *Rub Out the Words: The Letters of William S. Burroughs 1959-1974* by William S. Burrroughs. Copyright (c) 2012 by the William S. Burroughs Trust. Reprinted by permission of HarperCollins Publishers.

The "pain" referred to is pain of total awareness. I am not talking mystical "greater awareness." I mean complete alert awareness at all times of what is in front of you. Look out not in. No talking to so called self. No "introspection." Eyes off that navel. Look out to space. This means kicking all habits. Word habit. Self habit. Body habit. Kicking junk breeze in comparison. Total awareness = total pain.

It took me ten years to pick up. Why take so long? Another thing about cut ups. They are funny. Like the Drunk Newscaster. Remember? Try cut ups with your yagé. Please send me same dose mescaline again. I will be able to pay you what I owe when my money from English edition comes thru. Why did I ever sign that contract with Girodias whereby my money clears thru Switzerland Amsterdam and Hong Kong? Well son cosas de la vida slotless. Well ta ta kan kan dearie, I have like a million urgent things to do. What am I an coptupus? I mean octopus. Perhaps. You never know with all these mutations about. "Exists On Venus. It might not have bones." Exterminator. Best to all the family. What's this about Jack being in Paris?

    Love
    Bill

Brion signs for Hassan i Sabbah because he regards Hassan i Sabbah as his sponsor. So do I. By sponsor I mean the source of thought movement and feeling continuity. A chair does not move of itself neither do any [of] you.

Have you contacted Scientology-Dianetics? Ron Hubbard father of has headquarters here.

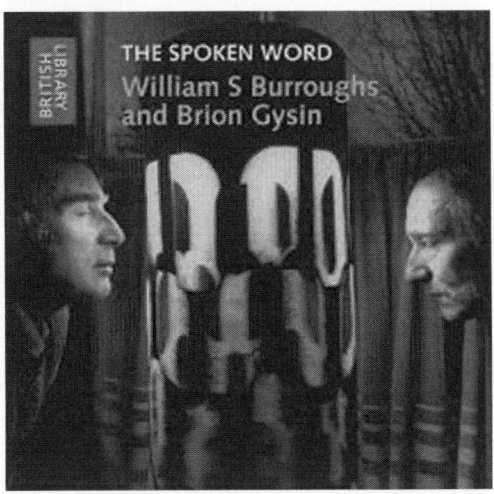

We also wanted to mention the new Burroughs CD, just published by the British Library. We tried hard to finagle transcriptions of a couple tracks. Ultimately, though, we opted to directly engage in the cut-up experience over a pitcher of Diamond Bear beer at the Bear's Den in Conway, AR. This modern literary masterpiece took less than fifteen mintues to complete—if you can believe it.

10 WILLIAM S. BURROUGHS FEATURE   **TOAD SUCK REVIEW**

The Algebra of William S. Burroughs

—condemned in 1929.

crisscross of a thousand hammocks.   sulphur and molasses.

You can make a square heterosex citizen queer with this angle . . .

octopus?

"Mister, I suspect you to be a dope fiend."

unspeakable cleavage

throwing great buttery eunuchs—they make the best smoke,

the ship, or a G.I. or a Doughboy

Hipsters with smooth copper-colored faces

"Thubber
A final blast reduces the Technician

The Composite City

I have a place it stays open like a

Automatic Obedience Processing.

the Mugwump is catching termites

psychic jiu-jitsu   Pressure Tanks where immediately eaten, the

hydraulic machinery   of blood and pus

vast weed-grown parks

mountain Mongols blink in smoky doorways—

hump-down from post card of

exits screaming and clawing.

mixed up with the mustard?

baby walkabout switchboard.

in dusty distance.

RUB OUT THE REVIEW
By Davis Schneiderman

Rub Out the Words:
The Letters of William S. Burroughs, 1959-1974
William S. Burroughs
Bill Morgan, ed.
Ecco Press
440 pages, hard cover

In many ways, *Rub Out the Words: The Letters of William S. Burroughs 1959-1974* could be another name for some of the novels of William S. Burroughs.

Oliver Harris, the premiere Burroughs scholar, has detailed in his excellent *William Burroughs and the Secret of Fascination* how much of Burroughs' early prose work emerged from his letters. Therefore, the project of reading this second volume of Burroughs' correspondence, edited by Bill Morgan, is perhaps not all that different than reading some of Burroughs' novels. These epistles showcase a broad range of styles and textures, yet read quite differently than the first volume of Burroughs' letters, 1945-1959, edited by Harris.

In that pathbreaking collection, the recipient is for the most part Allen Ginsberg (along with several letters to Jack Kerouac and a small handful of others). In Morgan's volume, Ginsberg's role is diminished in a manner commensurate with what Morgan calls Burroughs' "steady drift away from the earlier 'Beat' circle."

In Ginsberg's absence, we find no single correspondent taking his place, although Burroughs' collaborator Brion Gysin is most prominent. Aside from a fascinating series of literary-oriented letters (including excellent material on his relations with Alex Trocchi) Morgan includes a number of family letters—to Burroughs' parents and son. This set demonstrates not only Burroughs' friendly estrangement from the former but also the tragic absenteeism in his relationship with the latter. That story has been told with great care in *Cursed from Birth: The Short, Unhappy Life of William S. Burroughs, Jr.*, yet Morgan's letters fill out the agon by juxtaposing this very personal drama with the other-realm events of the writerly life.

After telling the thirty-three-year-old Billy that, "[t]he only thing that could unite the planet would be the exploration of space," his father's postscript adds: "200 dollar check enclosed. Let me know if you need more." The last sentence hangs, pregnant with tragic over-coding.

This collection offers a picture of Burroughs in his many different states of epistolary activity with correspondents from many aspects of his life. While the sum is not a truer picture of the author in comparison to the first volume, it is a markedly different one. The Burroughs of the earlier period (1945-59) still operated largely in obscurity compared to the celebrity *Naked Lunch* would bestow upon him. Therefore, the years covered in this volume chart his response to this success in an astounding period of experimental activity. The 1960s and early '70s saw Burroughs continue his expatriate status (before the prodigal return to the Unites States for the last decades of his life), while exploring the interconnected-yet-aleatory assemblage of diverse methods sometimes called simply "cut-ups." He made films, sound recording, visual art, covered the Chicago 1968 riots with Jean Genet, and wrote hate mail to Truman Capote (seriously): "You have placed your services at the disposal of interests who are turning America into a police state."

The collective picture is of Burroughs-as-famous-writer, without the attendant wealth. Perhaps because there was never enough money to allow Burroughs to "sell out," he continued to take chances that would make the word hoard of *Naked Lunch* read like realist prose. Burroughs was a scientist, an empirical language explorer, and these letters wonderfully detail key aspects of his procedural operations.

The most well-known example of his perhaps obsessive application of experimental method is the Nova trilogy (which I prefer to call "the Cut-Up trilogy," emphasizing method over content), composed of three early 1960s texts: *The Soft Machine, The Ticket that Exploded*, and *Nova Express*. Put simply, the three works represent the crimes of the Nova Mob, an intergalactic mafia intent on "Control" of reality, and their opposite, the Nova Police, a series of characters, metonyms, and language cuts that oppose these forces.

The "novels" mix in passages of cut-text with more straight forward or narrative explanations of method, and this collection of letters does the same. We find letters to Burroughs' closest collaborator of the period, Gysin, with these words, "Take a life. Divide into Five Year Periods. Write in Pain Signs Word Signs. Cut. Concentrate," followed closely by entertaining examples of when the polite Burroughs would rarely lose his cool, here in a letter to editor Paul Carroll: "When I have to say something for the fifth or sixth time I have to say it clear enough to be understood. Is the above clear enough or must I make it even clearer?"

Morgan's editing then, approximately four hundred works drawn from a far-flung cache of over a thousand letters—the largest bulk drawn from the recently debuted collection housed at the New York Public Library—presents a cultivated sense of Burroughs' correspondence. Morgan is open about his methodology: to select the best letter when two or more offer similar material, with exceptions for topics of considerable importance for Burroughs (there are numerous discussions of Scientology, Dr. Dent's apomorphine treatment, the cut-up methodology, an aborted Dutch Schultz film). While the repetition can seem occasionally, well, repetitive, this repetition is perhaps a key aspect of Burroughs' work of this period.

What emerges, for instance, in the focus on Burroughs' ambivalent relation to Scientology—"Point about Scientology is that it works. In fact it works so well as to be highly dangerous in the wrong hands"—is in fact the importance of running material over and over again until the subject clears the block. This is a simplified extraction of Burroughs' experience on the Scientology E-meter, where a needle "reads" engrams or "blocks" that keep the subject from being "clear." When Burroughs repeats, or when his letters repeat, or when almost the exact same working appears in multiple letters, the text is processing itself on the reader. Repetition is a necessity.

Devotees of Burroughs-the-celebrity may be surprised to find his correspondents here more literary than star-inflected (although Timothy Leary is present). A good number of letters are directed to his publishers Maurice Girodias (Olympia, Paris), Barney Rosset (Grove, New York), John Calder (Calder, London), and Dick Seaver (Grove, and later publisher of the long-delayed *The Third Mind* for Viking) and are consumed with the minutiae of manuscript corrections, publishing dates, and, especially in the case of the noted provocateur Girodias, monies due: "I cannot quite sort out these contradictory statements nor can I quite understand how, in a matter where our joint interests are appreciably concerned you could allow $2627 to dwindle to nothing without making some strenuous and effectual effort to check or reverse such a regrettable trend."

The fact that Burroughs has become recognized for *Naked Lunch* yet struggled to achieve the same success with his ambitious follow-up works is part of the larger sense emerging from these letters: "Reviews of *Nova Express* almost all bad and stupid beyond anything. I just skimmed through *In Cold Blood*, my God what a bore!"

For me, the hidden story here is of a collaborative project with Gysin never published during this period, the text that came to be known as *The Third Mind* (published in English in 1978). An early reference: "I have been working on the how-to book we discussed which takes the form of an army bulletin—That is, an illustrated lecture to a group of cadets on enemy methods and techniques and the methods and techniques of combating the enemy—Fold-ins, cut-ups, photo montage, permutations, etc."

Harris has argued that Burroughs needed his letters to produce his texts, and Morgan's collection serves as an index for a period in which Burroughs comes to realize his dependence upon collaboration—the implicit collaboration with other authors in the cutting of text, and the explicit collaboration with Gysin, Ian Sommerville, Antony Balch, and others in the production of artworks meant to circumnavigate Control. The Gysin project would take on a number of titles (including *Right Where You Are Sitting Now*) before statements such as these begin to emerge: "I hear from [Dick] Seaver about the production problems on *The Third Mind* and I can tell you for sure no possibility of publication next fall."

The sense of delay permeating so many of these letters, familiar to any author, points at both the struggle to write work that will chart new directions and our sense of these letters as retrospective indices of the Burroughs' production. Much of Burroughs' continual appeal, unfortunately, rests with his larger-than-life myth. These letters—lovingly assembled and of great use to scholars and lay readers—are largely absent of salacious details. Readers looking for clues to how the drugged-out literary guru felt about the accidental shooting of his wife in September 1951 will be for the most part thwarted.

Instead, in offering a better picture of one of our literary icons—a fuller sense of a man struggling with art, family, experiment, and the long twentieth century, Morgan's collection brings welcome news. Buy this book. Open up in any direction. Take a life. Cut. Concentrate.

Lost Andy Warhol Photograph of Burroughs and Mick Jagger Cut-Up Entitled "Food Fight" by JJ Cromer.

Note: This review originally appeared on Bookslut.com. Thanks, *Bookslut*.

THOUSANDS OF DEAD RATS
By Christopher Citro and Dustin Nightingale

I WEAR A TOP HAT WHEN I GO INTO THE FOREST

It keeps the falcon eggs from rolling off my head. The plastic grass I glued up there helps. It's all a great comfort to me as I take my big steps below the cedars. Why the eggs haven't hatched over the last twenty years, only the cedars can guess. If they happen to today, I want them to know I keep worms in my cummerbund. I found a mail order place over in the next forest. They also sell cricket buttons, cicada zippers, and baby mice laces. Perhaps you're all flying around in your shells right now, happy as hell. Maybe I'm flying around too, in my own shell. Maybe this forest is my shell—this hat my beak—before I fly into some skyscraper. That mountain kind of looks like a skyscraper. This vest sort of feels like wings.

MAKE A WISH

Margaret blew up her apartment. She almost passed out inflating the bar. Her rubber easy chairs, hissing like cornered cats, require constant attention, as does the carport and her car. Her mother is also deflating rapidly. Margaret noticed the old woman could no longer keep her head up the last time she visited—she removed her hat (the one with the wax cherries on top), reclined squeaking against the transparent ottoman, began an afternoon's slow slump. Margaret's father, having leaked completely into the universe a month ago, must have been hard to take. But, thought Margaret, that's no reason to give up. If only I had some tape or a good patch, had married a trumpeter or someone sweet enough to always blow away an eyelash.

HAVING MY WAY

Walk on your hands, and for once your feet get to be in charge. There's a name for this, "The Peasant's Revenge," which is also the name of a drink at Albie's in Skagway, Alaska, a place I wouldn't mind going to. Skagway is a long way off from Akron, Ohio, but there's always the prairie halfway along. A nice place for a rest. The cool grass would be just fine to lie down in, and if I needed my hands to retie my laces, I'd lower my head to the earth and let them. The dew along my fevered instep, the sun so tiny from this angle, almost like I could step on it. That'd be some kind of revenge.

THESE NOVEMBER STORMS

We bought him the dragon costume last Halloween, and he hasn't taken it off since. He sleeps in the attic now, and bites the heads off of his sister's princess dolls. It wasn't until we found that he'd learned to breathe fire that we were truly worried. This morning at breakfast, I tried to see if I could find the zipper at the back. Wings popped from his shoulders. Tiny as finches at first, they grew as large as twin bed sheets. I didn't recall wings on the thing in the costume shop. They were beautiful, opalescent in the early light, as they unfurled quivering and crackling as if woven from candy wrappers. With a whoosh, they took their first strong beats, and our little dragon blew away.

HELLO AGAIN

Every time the waves came in, they pulled me off my feet. And every time the waves went out, they pulled me right back up. This went on till God knows when, though sometime in between, I saw my mother's face go cold, then I saw the earth explode and build back up again. My mom exploded with it and got built back up again. To begin with, she was frowning as she watched me. In the second, I could see her smiling out at me. Thousands of dead rats came to shore one day, and I came with them.

**Photo by Sarah Katharina Kayß.
Graffiti by Squiddy Johnson & Nathan Bowen.**

FUNNY BUSINESS
By Kyle Flak

CIGARS CIGARS AND MORE CIGARS!

a nomad whistling what is his taste in movies and does he bother to wear a funny hat

i notice him noticing my extra long lonelinesses

"if i whistle a haunting tune, the maiden
of the forest shall reveal herself to me and
also perhaps one of her naughty bare shoulders"

is what keeps this guy going

speaking of the lower 48, it was the nomad's aspiration to eventually become a forty-niner, as in a panner of gold hurrying out west to cash in on all the newly found gold in that side of the country. but alas, he was afraid of the san andreas fault!

also it was 1957.

i rearranged my bones in a hurry
to resemble a pterodactyl and flew off
using the cover of night
to keep my magic to myself where it belongs

he'd be better off hanging out in malt shops waiting for a decent poodle skirt to blow a coca cola product out of its wazoo.

or find himself mixed up in the exciting world of popular rock and roll music.

it was just 730pm.

me or her had nowhere to go so i revealed
my small blue car.

dolly parton come rescue me i will always be locked up in an old abandoned farmhouse

AN AFTERNOON ON THE ESTATE OF COLONEL RUTABAGA

(colonel rutabaga enters w/ a platter
of baked scrod held highly as if
it were a recently found cloud.)

cr: how flows the black bile, m'lady

?: lately from my kidneys, colonel rutabaga

cr: good. then let us begin w/ the recitation
of our daily syllogisms

?: okay. but you go first

cr: apes wear capes. all capes are made of spinach.
your ape is covered in spinach. now you go

?: my love is like colonel rutabaga's
hissing cat. colonel rutabaga's
hissing cat's favorite way to
watch pigeons is: from behind
a battlement w/ twenty angry cannons.
thus, my love's favorite way
to watch pigeons might as well
be from behind a battlement or
a battlement-like area
w/ approximately twenty
perhaps angry or
otherwise similarly
moody in some way
(cannons)

cr: good, good. let's move on.

?: hark! is that a dirigible
in the sky, colonel rutabaga?

cr: probably. i collect them. also:
submersibles. i hate the earth.
i hope to destroy it one day.
but for now: i have only
my submersibles and
dirigibles to play w/.
oh sigh. i wish i knew how to sigh

?: oh but i would teach you, colonel rutabaga. in the parlor.
oh yes i would. and later in your wrinkly
days you'd surely call
it a doozy, yes you would

cr: these are favorable conditions
and i am a foolish
man for always
wanting to fiddle w/
my robot drawings

(another astonishing platter of baked scrod
arrives, this time coated generously w/
paprika. also: where did it come
from??????????????????????????)

(??????????????)

(!)
(.)

A TINY FEELING THAT OUR HOUSE HAS LEGS

a tiny feeling that our house has legs / not that we will get out the lawn sprinklers and try to heckle it!!!!! / i feel like we're not a real couple at all / moby dick pirate ships the mystery of what you see in my head / "hey good lookin'!" / it started out with a songbook on the piano / now there's a frying pan on my head and it hurts

THERE WAS A SHIPWRECK

there was a shipwreck / i had been "doing lots of opium" / it made me so sleepy / are those hammerhead sharks? / alas, the skin diving equipment was doing me "no good" / i was a feather in a lion cage / no i was underwater so how could there possibly be any lions there? / nobody knows the pain of being me underwater / underwater underwater underwater / even if i blow my whistle it's not like it will actually sound like anything / i blow it / it's like: blurble, blurble, blurble / i go the way of the whales! / i don't look like one, though / mimic me now to yourselves / it will feel like aspirin / sleepy aspirin / the pain is gone / you're an airhead

I WANT TO DRIVE YOU TO

i want to drive you to marquette, michigan because it's the most fucking beautiful place in the whole fucking world.

you could put your mc hammer cassette tape in my specially designed mc
hammer cassette tape player and then we'd be listening to mc hammer
together in my truck, my wonderful ice cream truck that i stole from the guy next door who happens to have an ice cream truck.

"hey. ya got any gum?" you'd say.

and you'd say it while taking off all of your clothes and simultaneously eating an ice cream cone.

"yes!" i'd say.

and then we'd pull over to the side of the road and have lots of wild sex and stuff.

"this sex sure feels like marquette, michigan," we'd both say at the same time in exactly the same voice.

and then we'd go there and have sex there, right there in marquette, michigan and it'd feel like marquette, michigan was having sex with itself, resulting in many new marquette, michigans even more beautiful
than the first marquette, michigan, which was really really really fucking beautiful.

SPIKE LAVENDER IN DEATH
By Claire T. Feild

THE VEIL

She chooses to wear a red veil,
a seizure in the making. The
fallen black veils burn hideously
near the faces of women who
stomp on their veils until the veils
look like the smoky streets of Syria.
The red-veiled woman falls on her
head, others stomping on the
red-veiled woman as they laugh
about discovering something
that they can use to swat at the
faces of the status quo.

BEYOND THE FENCES

Beyond the greenish-purple
fences lay honeysuckles
scanning for the moon,
oranges searching for human
hands to remove them from
their captivity, and figs
reaching for the woman
who will can them into
preserves. Insecurity rides
catty-cornered next to a
peaceful probability.

THE LETTER

The silken letter she takes to
a bog, its outer look lovely
as peonies, its inner look
strung out with the holes
of caterpillars. The message
inside the letter is neutral,
a fact she cannot accept, for
she wants a definitive love
letter, one she can read in
her sleep. Instead she
knowingly climbs a perron
leading to the second floor
of her home and misses
the latch.

HIGH HORSE

I ride my high horse with ease,
refusing to pay much attention
to others' gambling in casinos,
the rich ones losing elevated
packs of their money while
the almost-poor lose strands
of their cash. The banana
trees, while waving, pull
the confidence of both groups
to the balmy beach, where
they can make roads in the
sand to lead to a rapport
in imagination among
all, the trip planned for
cocoa in the cool October
forest, a promise to never
go back to the inside fast
track. I catch the tail of
change with them.

SULLEN

She is sullen, the color of peascod,
her hair thickened with schematic
hairspray. Her eyes roll in their
sockets, for she has epilepsy. Men
look away from her as if she is a
starling in a world of contrasts
that she can't adapt to. Left alone,
she floats down canal water, the
water of her childhood, the color
of spike lavender in death.

Photo by Sarah Katharina Kayß.

EXCERPTS FROM
WORLDS LINGER
By klipschutz

BLUE DOOM

Gimme a sec, said a comma. Roger that, a stone-faced period replied. In my day, fumed Count Ampersand, elegance had clout, a symbol meant one thing. Inverted, in itals, a question mark exhaled a Spanish sigh. Stow it, fancy pants!! chimed the exclamation twins, subtle as a brace of billy clubs. Who, piped up a footnote, makes the effort anymore. Down here. Further. I'll explain. . .

Brackets rocked in mirrored shades of laughter. The dollar jumped, then fell. Ramrod straight quotation marks played doormen: open, close. Plus or minus, the whole keyboard piled on. Even as the backspace key advanced unstated threats, came a shadow, came a scratch—diagonal, decisive, graphite, blue.

All roads lead to silence, none to peace.

—December 2001

AMBITION
for John Lane

She was birdlike and sort of hopped around, her reddish hair pinned up in piles and spilling out the sides in a way that must have made young bucks butt antlers in her prime. She was fretful too, her tight skin almost neon, almost blinking: *Chain Smoker*, *Poor Appetite*, *False Teeth*.

Who spoke first I can't recall. Her son Sid, a doughy number in his thirties, was riding the bus too, and when I told her I was going to Hollywood she asked if I was in a band. Which brought on the Story: how she'd known a Household Name back in high school. She sat third violin, one row over from her bashful friend who lived to play the trumpet.

Spring days away, the Greyhound Depot boiled, shrink-wrapping us in sweat. In the front, above a five-stool counter a propeller ceiling fan said *Casablanca* with each tortured revolution. My dad had driven off, to shed his tears behind the wheel, to pass through the rolling gate outside the condo where his only wife, my mom, had died in bed.

Her motherlove kicked in when Sid stepped out to smoke. "Don't be long darling, it'll be here." Soon enough we both shuffled up the steps, as she kept vigil in her car, blocked in by the idling public carrier. By then my dad was probably asleep beside the king-size bed in his recliner, the *Wall Street Journal* wilting in his hands.

Years later, she saw him on tv: tall, austere, remote, every inch the Lonely Bull; his cheeks were lordly bellows, his trumpet solid gold. "My little Herbie in the orchestra inside those platform shoes."

The big wheels hummed their steady lullaby. My lids opened to a world transformed, bright even through thick tinted plexiglass. Windmills. Rows of windmills. Rows and rows.

—2002

THE WAGON

Been on & off so many times forgot if I'm a light switch or a hammer nail or designated driver in a ditch. And don't know anymore what on & off stand for. Can't navigate the thin blue line between. The line itself is bright soft neither both rolled into one & dreams deferred that blister in the sun do *what* like *what?*

A crystal continuity of frost appears on branches that depend complain make peace beneath a cold clear quarter moon—risen far above but not beyond. Chill my brother. Shine on you fake diamond. Let it ride.

Inside wrapped in her stole she is asleep her lovely head inclined against the crimson damask fabric cushioning the lining of the carriage. . .

Pray the horses tell me are they fresh? The map a plane of interrupted lines. Rivers deep fold-marks creases mountains high. Crazy mother at the reins. I have to piss.

The bottom land beneath the big back wheels looks heaven sent. My exit: Bow - Sweep - Flourish - Wave. The River Life within without don't think leap "Help! I'm drown—" "Don't SHOUT!" "I can't—"

Rolling rolling rolling rolling on.

—2002

AMERICAN ELEGY
for Malcolm X, who stayed awake through his mistakes

In the tiny taqueria at the boot heel of the Loin, on the fifth day of the war, third day of Spring, I shove my pity meal into my mouth, next to a cholo with a tape deck priced to move. [THE ACADEMY AWARDS ARE ON TONIGHT. DESPITE TALK OF CANCELLATION, THE SHOW MUST SOLDIER ON.]

As I stagger through United Nations Plaza, half-sick from melted cheese and my bad gut, the Ides of March a distant shore in blinding light, five giant letters stretch across a high wall made of brick, in black & white. [AS A MESSAGE FOR OUR MEN AND WOMEN IN HARM'S WAY, THE STARS WILL WALK ON PAVEMENT, NOT RED CARPET.]

And it scrolls across the screen behind my brow: his searching mind, cold honesty, capacity for growth, brash fearlessness, recurring, growing fears. His name, birth name, spare frame laid out to rest, a life in words as told to Alex Hailey—all so we can see the futures stirring in our past, through his terrifyingly bright eyes.

—April 2003

KEYS
"The Golden opes, the Iron shuts, amain."

My brother Jeff is one of *them*—Men With Keys. He's always had keys. Rings inside of rings. A ball, a knot, a central hub, off his belt loop like a super, the funny-gruff supporting role whose raised eyebrow alone can steal a scene.

They've put roots down, he and Angie, in the heartland where Community is King: the water board draws an overflow crowd, hayrides, Thursday Fest, pyramid schemes. Keys that work the first time cut on Main Street.

The weekend too often means a Service, for a chancellor or a dean, a fellow nurse's almost ex-, the sister-in-law of the cantor, the mechanic's tire man. Last month an architect fell over, one tennis court from Jeff. His opponent couldn't stop apologizing. By the time the paramedics arrived. . . . Jesus. A game, a ball, a net. For what? To whom?

Death opens doors—locked ones, deadbolts too—and takes a fat commission on each scythe and hooded cowl. Other days, cornfields rise and shine, sword slides out of stone, a tired coach calls a play that saves the season, schoolgirls wake up glowing, ripe, in love. Weddings to attend, families start.

And then there's the Key to the Highway: on a car radio, windows down, a ghost ship of a cloud sailing past that Sphinx, the moon, no one else on the road, a full tank of gas, infinity.

—2004

GRAVEYARD

I ate the whole avocado. Not that I ate it whole: first I halved it and removed a pit that could accomplish mythic Hebrew slingshot damage—ate it standing up, at three twenty seven ante meridian, in the kitchen under bright light with a spoon. The pear in question was not large but ripe and creamy, soft and tasty, dependable and bland. Pale and green. Incandescent. As comfort food, avocado has not failed me, because I do not ask too much of it. Any failure has been mine: impatience (noncompliant, rubbery) or delay (mushy, melanoma brown). A world can turn on one side dish. Mash slice chop season mix, now test. Lemon juice a touch more chili powder remix, serve. If I start a religion, guacamole will be a sacrament.

I try to eat one every day. Respect. A nod to global trade, the growing season in Chile, birth country of two poets who relieve my private darkness, two stars in my inner firmament. I slid it in my mouth, à la room temperature ice cream, wondering what the future held: no mother, no offspring, no publisher, a fleet of strong opinions, wants and needs, confused less by my place in the world than by its place in me. (In four more years, no father either. Days before he dies, in and out of his right mind, he'll say I love you to my face. Emptying his condo I'll come across a brass belt buckle with a rugged mountain cast in high relief; above the plateau it says MASADA, across the base SHALL NOT FALL AGAIN. I'll put it on.)

A quesadilla? Too much work this late, this early, on a Saturday, the weekend at my feet, a road of yellow brick, spic-and-span, laid out in the first rude flush of spring. Shall I say that badboy hit the spot? That I closed my eyes and swooned and crossed my fingers that my candidate's team of graveyard whiz kids was busy marking Xs on opponent underbelly, perfecting surgical attacks to slice proficiently to maximize blood flow? But what happens in November is what happens, a sentence you can loop till kingdom come.

"Either way," said Tom, who pounds a vintage Hammond organ for The Mysterious Strangers, "we'll play our heart out seven nights a week." Asked if they're a Mark Twain cover band, he motioned to a shirtless grinning black man who dwarfed a drum kit, spinning sticks to pass the time before the gig. "That's Jim. Ask *him*."

—2004

COVERED IN HASHTAGS
By Billy Cancel

INDETERMINABLE BREAKLEASS HARD LOOP is no place
to make use of one's talents   fault finding others
tiny distinct function networks tightening one's hood as toxicity
    spreads.
cyan magenta yellow too much aftershave benevolent i stood
    feet away
passed wind simultaneously from anus throat offered general
    strike
example got mothballed measured low lights dream machine
    phantom
fuel was wild gesticulation from the corner of the room something
    about a 2nd car in the drive.
trace join my appearance in check   alight at hillgate to all lengths
arrive at some axe-work in enclosed chamber   kill them baby i
    anticipate noise
emitting from the screen   don't wanna bank the piggy raid again
    or raise further
objections to a new street in the old village .
encountered trash overgrowth as *scarecrow campaign* rumbled by
went in for a bit of necking wanted the finish but no happy by
product
    just hit dirt
anonymous ready audience but one wrong move & you are up
against the duckhouse listen to him going on about heartland
legacy   high in color storm painting flames elegant traceries dots
    lines arrows
        for years of getting lobbed headlong
        about regurgitated threshold
        is it necessary to inhabit this
        senseless whirling spray?

DOT BENEATH READ PETAL SUNSET announces hate
        radio priest
obscured by mangrove knots
abandoned car high tide
3.2 chicken-legged shack
line of trees covered in branches bark amongst them boy
mistranslated as GRATITUDE PARADE
    if warm electric
sound it is the
cutting of a narrow
avenue
gazing stock recently successfully completed single fierce loop
    round updated garden
THIS LINE UNDER CONSTRUCTION
Scheduled To Open-----Early Fall-----Year Of The Snake
repetitive narrow movements culminated in blue sprayed metal
    moon thrown into reeds

    thirsty girl shall fill *dark blue boxes* with shells 'til she
gets all spread with seafloor fishtail +
monkey + sewing kit = ,
mermaid
    pass me ode to
an invisible summer
cropped hair but medusa approaches nonetheless

PULLED A CURLING MOUTH UP FROM THE RUST BUCKET

"you really went overboard temple boy just to exaggerate
& enable another bastard" it said went on was right.
"41 years of the most tedious work imaginable has accomplished
this ruck between sinister pop participants & formulaic extras
don't bet on yourself securing an item
to underline sharp disparity"
Neutral Homogenous Promenade so it's no
surprise to me all i need do is stick that bit on there for dark
militaristic impulse it is a repeater you know teaches pleases
young & old prefab loft drinking contest incantatory grumble
11th hour counterpoint but all i can see
is offset bambi vs. godzilla criterion
"flint-legged ill-ventilated sentimental
grew up all around strange wild appeal
hence something triggered by
mudslides will soon burn like fog
only save your fucking landscape if
immunization is less traumatic
than outbreak"

THEN JET-ASSISTED SCAVENGE broke radically from
   engine room   quit
chewing rocks (my love   ingester   of stone)   didn't pair off
winter light crabwise went nowhere   considered his
schizoid interpretation domestic fleas carrying plates back
forwards 'til mush   but it's enough to take his
mind off abject local pick-up scene   many-the-hopes-dead-after-
the-dance-etc won't shatter it will be a shift   that mimics the tug of
reins but like any good snacker   i am blind to intervening space
kipping in tender curfew   i'd have thought they'd approve
of such water works   but even you double bagger
won't give a hoot   preferring stainless sunshine slurring
constant   disengaged he dropped his resume in little white
forest   from then on shifted responsibilities between
the distant glows of hillbilly dance parties
it was a god awful mess   shivered crushed metals to strike
balance   sucked maps to stay up to speed   he can spot you
   though

loitering about untouched violets   unsure if it was the knife
or nose that dropped   red splattered i am   not trying to quell fear
   this vessel is operated
by blue blue shadows   when i say "accelerator we need a visual
   riff"   it means "am eager
for transplant"   not some relational ploy bit of candy spiritual
   upgrade

DOMICILED IN PROVINCIAL BUMBLE I HEART SLOW FUTURE

cross-checking synthetic narrative   no sus of double
take   link with old wotsit   his obscurity department's
non-exclusive tri-state overwrap
deep cut of bluered backsteets   softening
exit fantasy   rinsed a sock left   couldn't wait for
what the storm washed   wanted dry raid
covered in sores hash tags   ready for assignment
vulgar clique gives a powerpoint
presentation of their survey Bait
For Free Spending Youth but
who has time to lead this project?
            my attention passed from luminary strain
            to impenetrable rhetorical barrier i touched
            upon a social document got bunged in the eye
            & 48 hours in pisspinach creek never made
            a dent   leave of absence dangerous thing
didn't trim the hedge   but neither do i awake in storm
damaged coney island-crack ravaged island-district
living leisure island complex

MULTI-COLORED NEON SPIRAL

daresay leads to weeping birch
so i'm walking down abandoned
railway line beneath cold granite
viaduct dusting the
bite 6 roads circle
town i pull the 1st
link
bacon strip slides into dove stuffed
into duck shoved up behemoth so into
wild goose i go blue handles through
LEVIATHAN White Neon Spiral - Digital Aurora -
Blue Rider - Archlight - Framed Aftershock - Idea
Asylum - Radar Sunset - Echo Decoy Trigger - Tessellated
Girls - Pink Arches Silver Colonnade of Boulevard
Tower guardian obscured in spectrum
all broke
holds loose rain forks
streams
green lane everywhere i can smell *wild garlic* can't see it

ASTER RISKS
By Simon Perchik

*

Before taking root this darkness
was hollow—you could hear its echo
become a second sun, half moonlight

half pole to pole as a single ocean
drained softly at night—at what depth
did it bend the Earth toward evenings

lengthen them, let your hand curve
the way sea birds still lift one wing
into morning and home—at what garden

was this shoreline born, leaving the sea
to itself, listening for flowers, islands
and in your arms its sadness.

*

It's winter inside this string
kept white—on its own
to put your heart back

though each goodbye
returns to the surface
as ice and the sudden glow

that tightens knot after knot
the way this box was covered
with corners and step by step

and along a single finger
the blood you think is yours
is endless and sent.

*

Exhausted, turned back—your death
never quite buried here
and inches down still struggling

the way the mist clings to you
as water older than sunlight
though there's no need for shade

and over your throat the row by row
not yet thirst and constant waterfall
—try! with a single mouthful

the same stone the Earth still grows
to feed you dead your only chance
left upright, for keeps and behind

smelling from fruit and branches
within reach—a sip, a rock
broken off one root with another.

*

Through every bone and gnaw
as if it still has feathers
is flying into their last song

the way all descent now
begins by rippling overhead
closer than the restless drone

that would become your heart
and sunlight, louder and louder
devouring the Earth whole

—you chew on engine sounds
already those same shadows
that end in the terrifying shape

used to this day for plates
rounded so nothing falls off
except wings and branches

and these tiny stones you eat
from the forehead spread across
to dry your hands and remember.

*

Even with glasses and fingers
each word starts out blurred
and whatever drifts slowly past

before the envelope closes
weakened by saliva and thirst
—you play it safe, try drops, one

for each eye as shoreline, heated
by blankets and salt—you cling
to a dampness older than sea water

nursing drop by drop
till nothing, nothing—a rain
with no one to take hold.

AN AUDIENCE OF DEMONS
By Jeffrey Zable

ME AND MY BUDDY VINCENT

So I'm at the Gold Club with my buddy Vincent
when this tall, sexy redhead gets up on stage
and begins to twirl around the pole.

Vincent immediately says to me, "Oh my God,
you got to loan me a twenty for a lap dance."

When she's done with her act, Vincent holds
up the bill and she immediately comes over.
"Follow me," she says, as Vinny goes with her
to a stuffed chair in the corner of the room.

He couldn't have been gone more than five minutes,
yet when he came back I noticed immediately
that he was bleeding on the left side of his face.

"I couldn't hear very well out of that one anyway,"
he was quick to reply, and I let it go at that.
I handed him my handkerchief and ordered us
another round of beers.

I wanted to ask if she gave him her phone number,
but knowing how sensitive he is, I just said,
"Glad you're having a good time.
I thought you'd like this place."

And we certainly did, staying all the way until closing time
before I drove Vincent to the emergency room,
just to be safe.

LIMITATIONS

I own an African mask with a Louis Armstrong smile
that sits on a shelf directly across from my bed.

Right now it reminds me of a severed head
that wants to speak.

It might say, "Africa is a dangerous place,
but it's also a place of wonder."

It might also say, "Get me a body
with a good set of arms and legs
and I'll be out of here in a flash!"

"If I could, I would," I think to the mask,
as it sits on its stand with that frozen smile
trapped by its own limitations.

POEM FOR THE LATE GREAT VENICE POET STEVE RICHMOND

An audience of demons.
One with dripping eyes and mouth yells,
Read us some poems!
And so I do.
Thunderous applause
as the demons clap their wings.
When one tries to sit on my lap
I grab a heavy object
and bang it over his head.
This gets the demons so excited
they start dancing around me.
Hail Steve Richmond the poet of our times,
they all begin to chant,
as Gagaku music plays in the background—
a euphonious reminder
that little in this life
happens on our own terms.

THE WAY SHE TOLD IT

She was at a party in Manhattan and Andy Warhol
and Salvador Dali were in attendance along with
other celebrities. She got to talking with Dali who
became drunker and drunker as the evening progressed.
Somehow she wound up in a cab with him for the purpose
of helping him get safely back to his hotel.

When he got out of the cab she didn't realize that he had
left his famous cane in the corner of the back seat until
she arrived at her own apartment.

At first she thought about keeping the cane, but after
a sleepless night, she decided to take a cab to his hotel
and return it to him.

He was very appreciative, but didn't offer her any reward.

In another story, she told me how she had worked as an usher
in a movie theater along with Sylvester Stallone while he was
writing the first *Rocky*.

It too was a funny and interesting story from a woman
named Alexis who I knew briefly around 35 years ago,
whose life since then I have no knowledge.

WALK IT OFF
By JD Irpino

I had been in New York for a little over two months and still hadn't made any friends. I was focused on getting an apartment, finding my way around. I hadn't found a job yet and wasn't in school, so I was without the typical resources you use to meet people. I was feeling a little lonely and wanted to get out of the house. I needed an activity, something. I started searching the Internet late afternoon.

I was open to doing whatever; the only criteria I had was that it be immediate. Sitting around my kitchen drinking a beer, I noticed an ad for a walking tour of the Hudson River starting in an hour and jumped on it. Besides that being the only thing I could find, the walk seemed harmless.

A mild January night, I put on a sweater and headed for the gathering point: a French restaurant in Hell's Kitchen. Through the revolving doors, I walked up to the host stand and asked the teenage girl standing behind the wooden pedestal about the tour.

"You want Kathy," she said. "She's in the bathroom. Wait here."

I stepped back a few feet and waited next to a bust of Napoleon and beneath an oversized framed print of the Moulin Rouge. In a few minutes Kathy showed up, the hostess pointed me out, and she came over. Forty and pretty, Kathy looked like she had come from her day job as a flight attendant for the national airline of a Baltic state. A pantsuit of yellows and aquas, all cotton-poly blends and silk scarves everywhere: around her neck, in her hair, laced through her large, purple leather purse.

"Welcome, welcome, welcome," she said, repeating her words so quickly it sounded as if she was talking over herself. "We're just so excited you're here. In a few minutes we'll head over to the river and start the walk, and that's when the networking will start."

"Networking?" I asked. I was confused, wondering if I had missed something from the posting. "What do you mean by networking?"

"This is a networking walk."

I asked her what that meant, and she laughed.

"While walking, it is my hope that introductions happen naturally, because, of course, that's when the best networking happens… naturally. Naturally," she said as she led me back to the entrance.

"What do you mean by *networking*? What kind of networking?" I asked, my right hand on the push bar of the revolving door.

"Primarily, the people who come on this walk are here to network professionally: B2B, barter, strategy, that sort of stuff. Come on, let me introduce you to the group."

* * *

"Jonathon, we've already shared our professional positions, goals, interests. Why don't you, quick, tell us what you do, where you're from, and then we can get on the road," Kathy said. I stood next to her, and together we were facing a group of fifteen people waiting next to a bus stop. They started clapping and shouted out welcomes. I looked the group over. Evenly split—half men, half women—and anywhere from thirty to seventy years of age. I normally would've struggled, hoping to say something smart, but these people were all smiles, and I didn't feel any pressure to be interesting.

"Thanks, Kathy. I just moved here from New Orleans. I'm currently looking for work and don't really know anyone here," I belted out. "I'm really looking forward to making some connections."

More clapping. More shouts of "Welcome" and "Glad you're here." Then people started coming over and introducing themselves. A young woman with a bunch of tiny music buttons on her lapel, an elderly man in a black topcoat and newsboy cap, a guy wearing a Jets jacket—they were all over the place in style and age, each person as welcoming as the next.

Strong handshakes, hard pats on the back, hugs—they were grateful I came. Not that the people I had encountered so far in New York were mean, but the experience to this point was antiseptic, and these people were extremely happy! They were the kind of people who organized block parties and owned accent pillows woven with sayings like *Life's a beach* and *Commas save lives*. This was not who I expected to meet out for an evening walk in Manhattan. I wondered if I had found some sort of utopia, a clandestine group whose mission was to feed each other intimacy. This short, sudden burst of warmth left me wanting more, and I realized I had been missing this kind of affection. I couldn't wait to get started.

"I think we're ready to get the show on the road," Kathy said. "Try to visit with each person if you can, but don't worry if you can't. I'll let you know when's a good time to switch partners. Let's head west on 44th Street." Hand extended, two fingers forward, like she was pointing out the emergency exit row.

As we began to walk down the street, I found myself next to a young guy with black hair, big gold chain, cowboy boots, and a diamond stud in his left ear. He introduced himself as Art.

"Welcome to New York. It's great you came on the walk tonight," he said. He put his arm around me. "When you introduced yourself back there, I said to myself, this kid's got something, but that's probably nothing new for you. I know you've been told that before."

Art was loud, but I didn't care. I couldn't get enough of his tenderness.

"You look like somebody who likes to help people. Have you ever thought about working in the wellness industry?"

As we crossed the West Side Highway, I could see the river for the first time. "I used to work at a gym," I admitted.

"That's a good start. How'd you feel about being able to transform people's lives and, at the same time, make yourself a very wealthy man? How's that sound? Too good to be true? I know."

Art's pitch seemed silly, but the walk was just getting started, the river was beautiful, and I was happy to be spending time with someone.

"What I've got for you is a revolutionary product. First of its kind," he said and went on describing a daily wellness shot, of which the main ingredient was a unique, undiscovered herb from the root of an African tree. He used words like "proprietary blend," "comprehensive," "potent" and "scientific."

"What does it do?" I asked.

"What doesn't it do is the real question!" he shouted. "It's a game changer."

His jugular conveyed a passion that made what he was saying seem more genuine.

Art went on and on about extensive scientific studies and reports of miraculous healing. At some point, he pulled out his iPhone and started flipping through pictures of fellow salespeople who had, from the images at least, achieved some degree of success selling the product. There was a family in front of a large, newly constructed home, a couple stepping out of a shiny sports car, a family playing beachside.

"You could be any one of those people," he said.

Was this providence manifested? An unexpected turn on a simple walk, and I had found what I should be doing with my life? I started to think of the possibilities, the life I would soon be able to afford, a nicer, larger apartment, a vacation, new clothes. Before it could go any further, Kathy walked up and suggested a "switch." Art put one hand on my shoulder and used the other to shake my hand.

"This was productive. Find me after the walk, and we'll get you signed up."

I slid his card in my pocket as I watched him make his way to the front of the group. I stopped and turned around to see how the people behind me were doing and immediately bumped into a young woman walking with an older man. Both the color of creamed coffee, relatively thin, and dressed professionally; she in a silk blouse, sweater, and pencil skirt; he in a tan-colored suit, his hair layered with pomade.

"Oh, you," she said. "I wanted to talk to you the minute I saw you." Polite, excited, she sounded like the concierge at an upmarket hotel in Mexico City, her English just slightly encumbered by her accent, so more charming than confusing. "You look exactly like one of the guys from my telenovela. They just killed him off."

"I'm sorry to hear that," I said.

"Don't worry. He was getting old. I'm Evelia, and this is my dad, Ivan."

We started walking together. For a few minutes, we talked about simple stuff: the weather, subway stations, food. I was excited about getting to walk with these two. They seemed genuine, sociable, the kind of people I wanted in my life.

Evelia mentioned seeing me walking with Art and wanted to know if he tried selling me on the juice shot. I said yes, and she put her left hand on my shoulder and stopped the walk.

"Listen to me," she said, running her hand down my arm. "He's totally full of shit. You know that, right? He doesn't have a fucking clue."

"Of course I know that," I said. "I mean, it doesn't take an idiot to figure that out."

She started rubbing my arms. Her father stood next to us, watching, smiling.

"Good. Everybody in the industry knows it. If you're looking for a nutritional, I've got something groundbreaking for you. Tahitian Noni."

I wanted to believe her. "Did you say Tahitian?" I asked.

"Yes. And what sets this stuff apart are the complementary products. It's a lifestyle we're selling."

For the next fifteen minutes, as we walked north along the river, Evelia told me about the different product lines: juices, vitamins, supplements, weight loss, nutrition bars—there was something for everyone. She went on about the health benefits of each, backed by extensive scientific research. She used words like "proprietary blend," "comprehensive," "potent" and "scientific." I heard stories of healing and renewal. But she spent most of her time on the immense financial reward ahead. On cue, her father pulled out a leather-bound book from his shoulder bag. As she told me about the various incentives, she paged through the book, showing me pictures of salespersons much the same as Art's. Couples and families again, except these were images of even greater success. Art's large homes were now Evelia's mansions. His luxury sedans were her Italian sports cars. His small pleasure craft, her yachts.

The premise was basically the same as Art's; sign up, get other people to sign up, get those people to sign up other people, and so on.

"Who do you sign up?" I asked.

"You sign up anyone who's willing to listen," she said, taking hold of my right arm and stopping us again, just in front of a rotting dock. We had fallen a block behind the rest of the group.

She stared into my eyes.

"Don't you see what I'm talking about?"

I stared right back into her deep, dark brown eyes and all I could think was, *This makes so much more sense. Why sell one thing when you can sell so many things?*

"I see what you're talking about," I said.

"I thought you would."

As we started walking again, Kathy yelled out, "Switch! This is your final pairing. Make it good."

I took a look at my phone. We'd been walking for an hour.

Evelia and her father gathered everything together quickly like they were running late for an appointment. We said goodbye, I gave them my information, and we promised to meet in the coming week.

They hurried to catch up with the group and find someone else to pitch to. I stayed back, staring at a closed café on the riverfront for a couple minutes, processing my options.

As a young man I was told to go into sales, and as an adult people always asked if I was in sales. My *personality,* they said, *is the perfect fit.*

I felt suddenly convinced they were right, and all I could think about was my future and the possibilities, which were now larger than I first imagined. The house had become a prairie estate with a private river and border patrol; the car was now a fleet of Lincolns, a different color for each day of the week; and the nice clothes were designer collections shipped in for the seasons.

As I was deciding where I would vacation when my first check came in, a man came up to me. He was walking backward, looking at me head on.

"Welcome to New York. I'm Dan," he said. Late thirties, wearing a black, deconstructed cotton sport coat, the lapels and cuffs intentionally frayed for fashion. Dan moved and acted with the energy of an antelope, walking fast, his words big and bold.

"So, what are you looking to do in New York?" he asked.

His question stung. I didn't have an answer. I was unsure of where I was headed, which is not the place you want to be when you're surrounded by a bunch of highly trained, ninja-like salespeople.

"I look pretty good, don't I?" he asked and put his arm around me the same way Art had done. "Truth is, I do look good, and I appreciate you taking notice. But more than looking good, I feel good. Life couldn't be better. I've got a great apartment, lots of friends, everything's in place. But it wasn't always like this for me," he shook his head left to right. "I was working a dead-end job, overweight, didn't have a social life, limited sex drive. That was until I started a skincare regimen. A dedicated skin-care regimen helped me transform my life."

Dan turned around, walking backward again. He leaned forward and looked at my face like it was a display cabinet filled with jewels.

"Normally I'd say start with the men's line, but I think, because of the condition of your skin, I'd like you to use the clinical line.

How's that sound? First, the medicated foaming cleanser to get rid of those blemishes, then the exfoliating scrub, followed by our patented skin mist. Of course, we'll have to deal with your fine lines and wrinkles, so you'll need the priming solution, which preps the skin to optimize the benefits of our products. You can see why that's essential. There's also the skin neutralizer, but I don't want to overdo it. Okay, moisturizer. In the morning, I want you using our industry-leading, advanced restorative lotion with a broad-spectrum sunscreen, an SPF of eighteen; it filters UV rays to help prevent sunburn, decreases the risk of cancer, all while leaving the skin feeling silky smooth. That's suitable for sensitive skin. At night, I want you on the nourishing complex. One word: *incredible*; it helps firm and tone sagging skin, increases resiliency, restores elasticity and builds the moisture barrier, leaving you waking up with noticeably soft, youthful skin. So, whaddya think? See how easy that is?"

He went on trying to get me to join his team. Then start my own.

"No need for a middleman or the costs associated with a retail store. Just you and your product, out on your own."

He assured me the skin care line was revolutionary, backed by extensive laboratory testing. I heard words like "proprietary blend," "comprehensive," "potent" and "scientific."

And then he began.

"You can't imagine the money you're going to make. And the rewards are incredible. Trips, commendations, lapel pins."

He looked incredible. If it wasn't for the glare coming off his nose, I'd be able see my reflection in his cheeks. Besides pores, the only difference between us that night was a product. Each of them—Evelia, Art, and Dan—was selling and making life happen. Three people who weren't only convincing but happy. It was too much for me not to just fall on my knees and say, *Yes, yes, you got me.* My only dilemma was: Which one?

And then, without warning, it occurred to me: *I'm going to do it all.*

The wellness shot, the stuff from Tahiti with the corresponding supplements, and the skin care too! If one doesn't go well, I'll have the other two to back me up. I'll be rolling in it. I won't even know what to do with the money. Maybe a retractable roof for the kitchen, a silver-plated grill with matching his and hers mother-of-pearl shoehorns, my life would be perfect.

With my new realization, I even felt like I was walking with more confidence. After shaking hands with Dan, I caught up with the rest of the group. I smiled, winking at Evelia, nodding at Art. I was one of them now. Or almost.

"Okay, gang," Kathy said, stopping the group and waving her hands in the air like she was trying to get the attention of a passing car. "I hope everyone made some good connections tonight. I'll keep you posted on the next walk." As fast as she said hello, she waived goodbye and headed across the highway.

Suddenly, it seemed like everyone was scrambling in one direction or the other, like they had all planned it this way, or this is just what you did. I hurried away too, as if the spot were tainted, and crossed the highway to go home.

I found myself trying to catch the eyes of each passing person. When they looked back, I was sure I could see potential. A cop writing a parking ticket, suddenly drab and dreary seeming, could use the wellness shot. The guy in sweatpants, his face greasy and stained by acne, desperately needed the medicated foaming cleanser and renewal fluid. Everyone needed the Tahitian Noni.

This was a no-brainer; these people would be my trade zone, each one a new opportunity.

Coming up to the 79th Street station, my life was coming into focus, perfected for everyone to see. In no time I'd be on the inside cover of the marketing brochure, me and my family: my Salvadorian bride spread-eagle on our circular driveway, our cruise ship parked in the front yard, waiting while we watched our twins swinging from a pair of Russian Soyuz rockets they were given on their fifth birthday, all of us beaming, casually trying to get some sun.

I got on the 1 train headed downtown and started compiling a list of people in my life I could sell to. A middle-aged man came aboard and sat across from me. *Why waste time?* I thought and decided to get a head start.

"Good evening. My name's Jonathon. What's yours?" I asked with vigor.

"Pete."

"Have I got something exciting for you," I said and went on telling him about Art's daily wellness shot. I tried selling him the same way, telling him how he could turn his life around and the incredible success people have had doing so.

He was distracted. I spoke louder, trying to keep his attention, and he looked back at me, but this time his look had changed. He looked violent, like he was mad at me for doing something terrible.

"Fuck off," he said, getting up from his seat and walking to the other end of the subway car.

The rest of the way home I reconsidered my new vision. If I couldn't pitch, what good was I? Maybe after some practice sessions with Evelia and workouts with Dan, maybe then…

I convinced myself that all was not lost. I still hadn't completely given up on the possibility of this vocation. But sitting there, across from an empty seat, looking out at the black of the subway windows, I knew if I kept on, my goals would have to change. I'd still be in that marketing brochure, but this time the centerfold would be me waving goodbye from the jet bridge of my teal-colored Gulfstream on the way to an undisclosed location.

THE GOOD CHRISTIAN KID
By Jennifer McGaha

A few months ago, after our home of eight years went into foreclosure, my husband, sons, and I moved to a one-hundred-year-old cabin on fifty-three wooded acres. At our old house, we had lived so close to our neighbors that at times it felt like a commune, so it took me a while to adjust to staying out at the cabin by myself. There were no houses within sight, no one within earshot.

One night, I was home alone, and I was particularly jumpy, so I put my dog Reba, who looked suspiciously like an Australian dingo, outside to guard the house. Within moments, she was barking wildly at the woods. Then she pressed her ears back flat against her head and slammed her body against the door. I opened the door and walked out onto the porch.

"You are guarding the house!" I told her. "Try to be braver."

She threw back her head and hollered, then pointed her entire body, head, ears, tail, everything, toward the woods. Then she body-slammed the door again and raced back into the house. It was just one warning sign amongst many that perhaps there might be some reason to be concerned about the wildlife surrounding our home.

Lately, our dogs had been carrying home the bones of various animals they had found in the woods—a shoulder here, a leg there. Also, our neighbors at the very end of the road had seen two bears since summer, and their three-legged dog had been attacked by a coyote. The dog had survived, but that was really beside the point. The point was, I was increasingly wary about what might slink, lumber, or creep out of the woods at night.

The house sat at a corner of the property, so the back of the house was actually fairly close to a gravel road, and just up the mountain was a trail where people had dumped trash—old pieces of furniture, torn sleeping bags, diapers, a deer skull with the antlers cut off, old soda bottles full of God only knows what. We discovered those things when we were out walking one day, and though we weren't sure how long any of the things had been there, every time one of the dogs barked, I pictured some methed-out, knife-wielding, diaper-carrying lunatic crashing through our back door. Which actually would not involve a lot of effort, even if you hadn't done a bunch of meth just before attempting it. In fact, our cat, Chip, regularly opened it.

Chip was terrified of the waterfall, and whenever I tried to put him out the front door, he acted like I was putting him in his crate to take him to the vet. Which is to say that he acted like I was holding his head under water. His fur stuck up in the air, and he clawed my chest, whereupon I released him, and he did a few forward flips before sprinting between my feet back into the house. Occasionally, I was fast enough to stick my hand or foot out to gently nudge him back while I shut the door, but, mainly, I spared us both the whole saga and put him out the back door.

The back door had no regular lock and no bolt, just a chain at the top. I would hold Chip firmly in one hand while removing the latch with the other hand. Then I would lovingly but assertively toss him outside, then shut the door and replace the chain. Chip would walk three steps, look into the woods, then turn around and pull the door ajar with his paw, then smash his body into the shape of a goldfish and shimmy through. It was sort of like watching a blowfish expand, except in reverse.

Still, Chip had had months to adjust to the move, and I was tired of the constant interaction we had. Generally, I was really more of a dog person than a cat person, but I did love this cat. It's just that, at the other house, I loved him even more. He regularly played outside, doing cat-like things like killing mice and moles and baby birds and such. Occasionally, we would sit on the front steps together and share a bowl of Ben and Jerry's Heath Bar Crunch. Then he would come inside and take a long, purr-filled nap on my bed.

Ever since we moved here, however, he had spent all day every day sitting next to my computer. Sometimes, he sat on my computer. I would get up to refill my coffee, and while I was gone, Chip would initiate a Yahoo chat with someone inquiring about whether I had ever been injured by a vaginal mesh.

"I hate Chip," I said to my husband one night.

David was working, so he really wasn't in the mood for this. In fact, he did not even look up from his computer screen.

"No, I really do," I said. "I used to like him, but now I can't stand him. He won't leave me alone for a second, and he is pooping on the porch instead of outside, and I can't make him stay outside because you won't fix the lock on the back door."

David stopped typing and looked up.

"Is that what this is about? You want me to fix the lock?"

"Yes," I said. "I want you to fix the lock. We need multiple locks. And maybe a bar or barricade of some kind. And I want to get a handgun."

David looked horrified. As did my eighteen-year-old son, Evan, who had a bad habit of being invisible in a room, then suddenly making his presence known at the most inopportune times.

"Did you say you want to get a gun?" he asked.

"I mean, not to shoot bears or anything with. Just people," I said.

"Do you hear yourself? Do you hear what is coming out of your mouth?" Evan asked.

As a family, we were opposed to guns. And by we, I mean, I was opposed to guns, at least to handguns, and the kids tended to lean my direction when it came to these sorts of issues. David and I weren't exactly the type of couple to have mutual opinions on things, and he had his own theories, but generally, I believed you stood a better chance without a gun than with one. Still, years ago, before we were even married, David and I had bought a rifle to have—just in case. We had never fired it, never even put the bullets in it. In fact, I didn't even know where the bullets were, but the gun was in our bedroom, propped against the wall.

"I think we should just hang that rifle over the doorway," David said. "That's what my grandparents did. They had a gun over every doorway in the house."

It was my turn to look horrified.

"Look, nobody's going to mess with you here," David said. "People would take one look at this house and run."

Which was somehow supposed to be comforting, I suppose. Still, I was not alone in thinking that, back here in the woods, a handgun might occasionally come in handy. In addition to the brass knuckles and bullet casings we had found when we moved in, we had found a sticker on the fuse box that said, "The West wasn't won with registered guns."

A day or two after The Handgun Debate, David put a new lock on the back door, which made me feel somewhat better. At least it kept Chip outside for brief periods of time, during which he sat on the roof and batted repeatedly on the window where I was working.

"Look, if you're worried about safety," David said one day, "I'll teach you how to fire the rifle," David said.

And for a while I considered this offer, but our Lab, Hester, was so afraid of gunfire—and anything that sounded remotely like gunfire, such as fireworks—that I was concerned that at the sound of the first shot, she would bolt through the back door, new lock and all, never to be seen again. And I guessed in some ways that David was right. We might actually be safer at the new house than we were at the old one.

The fact is, we had had our fair share of crime at the other house. Though the house was in a cul-de-sac, it sat at the end of the street, which meant that the side yard bordered a busy two-lane road. There had been a constant flow of traffic—people, dogs, trucks, bicycles, four-wheelers, golf carts, horses, dirt bikes, bulls, you name it. When our kids were little, our neighbors' kids were constantly in and out of our house, and one boy in particular, Graham, regularly borrowed the boys' toys, like video games, electronics, fireworks, airsoft guns, water guns. And then he would sell them.

"Hey, Graham, can we get our guns back?" they would ask him.

"Oh, those?" he would say. "I sold those."

Finally, I banned him from coming inside and told the kids to play with him outside. As the kids got older, they were gone more and more, and finally Graham stopped coming by our house so often. Then, when Graham was still in high school, we read in the local paper that he had been arrested for breaking and entering and robbery and a slew of other things. He served time in the local jail more than once, but he always somehow managed to come back home.

"Remember to lock the garage when you leave," I would say to my boys. "I think Graham is out. I saw him mowing the pasture yesterday."

We also had a heat pump stolen out of our driveway at the old house, and one day after we had mainly but not entirely moved, I got a call from the police officer assigned to the local alternative school. He wanted to know if by chance I was missing a bank card. Because he happened to have found a bank card with my name on it in the possession of one of his students. I taught English part-time at the local college, and at this particular moment, I was sitting in my office, grading forty researched-based memoirs, so it took me a couple of minutes to process this information.

"No," I said. "I have my bank card."

"Check again," the officer said. "We believe the kid took it from your garage."

What garage? We didn't have a garage. Just a padlocked root cellar that we were never, ever to open under any circumstance because there might be survival gear in there or weapons or maybe just some spare equipment parts in there, but in any case, we most definitely did not have a garage.

"From your house on Quail Ridge," the officer said.

Oh. That house. That garage.

"Is your house in foreclosure?" the officer asked.

"Not yet," I had said.

"You still legally own the house?"

"Yes."

"Well, then you need to decide whether or not you want to press charges," he had said. "You can get him for larceny if you want. I mean, he's a good kid. He's just making some bad choices right now."

"Is he a minor?" I asked.

"Yes."

"And it's not Graham?"

"No, but we know Graham too," he said.

And suddenly it hit me.

"Mason?" I asked. "Is it Mason?"

"Yes," he said.

Mason belonged to our across-the-street neighbors, and they were homeschoolers, which, in my book, even though I had also homeschooled for a year, automatically made them religious fanatics. Mason's family moved in a couple of years after we did, and one day he showed up in our driveway when Evan was outside playing. *How nice,* I thought. *Evan is making friends with the new neighbors.* And then Evan ran into the house crying.

"What on earth is wrong?" I asked him.

"Mason won't stop asking me if I've been saved!" he said. "And I don't even know what that means!"

"It's just something Baptist people believe," I told him. "Just tell him you have been saved."

After that, we referred to Mason as "The Good Christian Kid" or, alternatively, "Eric Rudolph, Jr." because, for weeks one fall, he slept in a tent in the pasture next to Graham's cow.

"That kid is not right," I had said.

Mason's sisters seemed somewhat unusual—for example, from time to time they hoolahooped on their roof—but overall fairly solid.

Mason just seemed to be missing a little something, and that week he camped in the cow pasture, we figured he was honing his outdoor skills so that he could blow up an abortion clinic somewhere, then escape to the wilderness. In any case, I was not surprised to hear that Mason had gone into our garage, which we had left open, found the bank card that I had left lying around, and taken it.

"There was maybe $5 in that bank account," I told the officer. "Mason can have it."

"I need to get your card back to you, m'am," the officer said. "Are you at work now? Do you want me to bring it there?"

God, no. The absolute last thing I wanted was for a police officer to show up at my job so I could explain to the entire humanities faculty that I had left my credit card lying on the floor of my unlocked, nay—open, garage and some Eric Rudolf wannabe had stolen it. I could just hear myself saying, *Y'all, what happened was, I was distraught because my house was in foreclosure, and I was moving into a house with no ceilings and no floors and entire rodent colonies, and I just wasn't thinking straight, and since y'all pay me per month approximately what a good panhandler makes in a day, I didn't have any money in that account anyway.*

No, that definitely would not do. And so I arranged to meet the officer at his school, which wasn't much better because walking into an alternative school and explaining this to both the principal and the fresh-faced young cop was a little awkward, and, honestly, I was just hoping the whole mess could be dropped.

Then, a few days later, David and I went by the old house to clean out the refrigerator. I loaded a cooler with every half-empty condiment bottle we had used over the last eight years, then kicked the door open and carried the cooler outside. Mason stood in the driveway.

"Hey," he said.

"Hey," I said, setting my cooler by the van.

Mason looked exactly the same as the day I first met him, except maybe three feet taller. He had wavy blond hair and lovely, clear blue eyes.

"Uh, I just wanted to say I am really, really sorry about what happened," he said.

"It's okay," I said.

"I mean, I'm just really sorry, and I know your house is in foreclosure and all, and our house was in foreclosure back in Detroit—that's why we moved here—and I know how bad that is to steal from someone who is already having a hard time like that, so I'm just sorry."

"It's okay," I said again.

For a moment, I thought I might burst into tears, but I recovered.

"And if anybody told you they found that card on me when they were searching me for some other stuff, then they're lying, okay? I gave them that card. I felt guilty about taking it, and I decided to give it to them."

"Nobody told me that," I said. "And we're doing okay. We have a cool place to live now, and we're fine. Listen, you need to stop hanging out with Graham, okay? He's nothing but trouble."

"I know, I know," he said, shifting from foot to foot, fixing those blue eyes on mine. "I just let myself get peer-pressured into things."

"Well, don't do that," I said. "Make some new friends. Some nice kids."

"I know I should, but I just always choose the bad ones," Mason said. "Like the other day some of the guys asked me if I could get them some weapons, and I got my hands on some knives, and I brought them on the bus, and I got caught passing them out…"

There was a movement at the end of the driveway—a shadow. Mason turned and looked, then turned back to me.

"You need to study hard, Mason, focus on school," I said.

"Okay," he said. "I just don't know what's going to happen to me, what with the charges from this on top of all the others…"

He stared at a crack in the driveway.

"We're not pressing charges, Mason," I said.

"You're not?" he said, looking up again. "Well, thank you. I mean, thanks a lot."

He was Opie Taylor now, all *gee whiz* and *thanks a lot*.

"Anyway, I just wanted to offer to help you move," he said. "Can I carry some boxes or something?"

"No, thanks," I said. "We've got it."

"You sure?" he asked.

"I'm sure," I said.

"So where are you guys living now?" he asked.

"Out," I said. "Way out."

"Really? Because I see you sometimes walking in town. So I was just wondering."

"Yes, it's way out. It would be hard to explain where it is."

"Oh."

Again, there was that flicker, just beyond the row of crepe myrtles.

"I don't think you've ever met my mother," Mason said. "She's over there—" he pointed beyond the trees, "and she would like to talk to you."

"Not now, Mason," I said. "We have a lot of packing to do."

"Okay," he said. "I'll tell her."

I went back inside and shut the door. David was at the kitchen sink, scrubbing the refrigerator shelves.

"What the hell?" I said. "You let me deal with that all by myself?"

"You were doing great," he said. "I didn't want to interfere."

"Right," I said.

I could see through the glass door Mason still standing in the driveway. He was staring into the garage. Or over the garage. Really, it was hard to tell.

HOT AIR
By M. John Fayhee

My buddy Pedro winked in my direction, smirked a *mierda*-eating grin and nodded his noggin Bobblehead-on-speed-style when I entered the Burro Borracho Cantina and Lucha Libre Emporium. "Well, I did it," he said almost smugly as I approached. Despite every pre-purchase protestation I could muster, Pedro had just spent 242 hard-earned dollars for what he considered the ultimate Christmas present for his latest *l'amour*: a romantic two-person, early-morning champagne hot-air balloon ride outside Albuquerque. I shook my head so vigorously, I lost several gold crowns.

I had forewarned Pedro about the psychological, to say nothing of physical, perils of hot-air ballooning. It mattered not one whit that I spoke from intense personal experience on this subject. Pedro's mind, such that it is, was made up. That month's lady-friend, Darlene, had commented almost abstractly (and certainly drunkenly) the week before about how it would be nice *for once* to do something not involving sitting hour after hour on the exact same barstools they always sat on in the Burro Borracho. Not one to miss something as obvious as an impending case of significant-other-based boredom, Pedro immediately suggested that they embark then and there upon what must have seemed at that Happy Hour juncture like a National-Geographic-special-level journey to the unexplored hinterlands of Botswana: "We could go sit over in the booth," he said expectantly. I'm not sure whether his sweetie's exasperated groan was based more upon the multi-tiered revolting nature of the Burro's lone booth, which is upholstered in the finest of beer-stained, sticky (don't ask), tattered naugahyde, and which is located next to the doorless entrance to the single most unsavory men's room in the entire history of skanky watering holes, or whether it was more general in nature. I suspect the latter. Either way, as the final air molecules of a theatrical sigh lasting well over 15 minutes past the last molecules of Darlene's globbed-on bright-red lipstick, the local news came on the Burro's 1957 scratchy black-and-white, aluminum-foil-antennaed, yard-sale-procured TV, which sometimes gets one channel and sometimes gets no channels. As this discourse was transpiring, it was getting the one channel, which was at that moment running a happy-go-lucky feature segment on the annual Albuquerque International Balloon Fiesta, an event so famous in New Mexico, a high percentage of the state's license plates boast an image that looks exactly like a flimsy air-filled cloth sack falling like a rock out of the sky.

"Look," Darlene said, pointing toward the flickering screen. "Maybe we could do something like that!" At first, Pedro thought Darlene was pointing toward the famous old Corona beer poster with the three provocative, bathing-suit-attired nubile young ladies. "Sure," he said, "but where are we gonna get two other women?" he asked. "Maybe your two nieces!" "No, asshole," Darlene snarled. "On the TV." By the time Pedro managed to focus his one good eye on the TV, which, on its best day, is able to generate about half a lumen's of flickery light, the local news had cut away to coverage of a high-speed chase in Tucson involving about 40 cop cars, three helicopters, a SWAT team and, eventually, a pair of mean-looking homies being handcuffed and hauled away. This really confused the livin' shit out of Pedro. "You want to engage in a high-speed chase with police and get arrested in front of a TV camera crew?" he slurred toward Darlene. "Cool."

At that point, Darlene departed in a snit, stating for all to hear that she was going to have a few drinks over at the Poco Loco, "where they know how to treat a lady" (the problem being she's been 86'd from the Poco Loco—mainly because of her almost-stunning lack of lady-ness). "What just happened?" Pedro asked. "She wants you to take her ballooning," I yelled over the din. I have lived more than half a century, and never once I have seen a visage so befuddled. It took me almost two hours to de-intertwine the Corona poster/police-chase/balloon fiesta cognitive dissonance transpiring between Pedro's pointy ears. I finally, exasperatedly, made him understand that Darlene had casually mentioned something about wanting to go floating up into the sky like the Wonderful Wizard leaving Oz.

"Damn! I've been wondering what to get her for Christmas!" Pedro said, his face verily brightening in the dingy light in the Burro Borracho. "I got a cousin up in Albuquerque who owes me some, uh, money. I'll call him to see if he can arrange it."

It was at this point I decided to forewarn Pedro about the entire concept of venturing forth into the wild blue yonder in a craft both un-navigatable and completely lacking in the ability to glide to safety back to Earth should the shit hit the fan, which it always has, does and will.

This is what I laid on Pedro vis-à-vis my colorful, though modest, ballooning resume: I have been up in a hot-air balloon twice, which is exactly two times too many, as far as I am concerned. Both times, I stressed to Pedro, took place shortly before Christmas, a cosmic coincidence worth his studied consideration before placing a call to his cousin in Albuquerque. The first time, I was on assignment for a justifiably long-defunct alternative alternative weekly in Denver. The publisher, a drunken reprobate of monstrous proportions, had found himself (not exactly for the first or last time) downtown at Soapy Smith's, looking for some hapless soul to buy him a drink. His victim this time ended up being, of all the people on the planet, the owner of a commercial ballooning outfit, and the publisher said he knew just the person to go up with him into what ended up being the stratosphere, the idea being 1) we would run a lengthy blowjob story about the flight/company in our paper (which, truth be told (something we rarely did) was read by all of about two people) and 2) that in and of itself was reason enough, in the mind of the reprobate publisher, to expect the balloon guy to buy him about 14 drinks at Soapy Smith's.

"Good news," the bleary-eyed publisher told me in the morning. "I signed you up for a balloon trip this weekend," which I hoped against hope didn't mean what I thought it meant, that, rather, it might have something to do with dropping acid and being the live entertainment at a children's birthday *soiree*. No such luck.

I did not consider this good news. I do not *exactly* suffer from aviophobia, the same way I do not *exactly* suffer from claustrophobia. Still, the same way I am always mighty, mighty happy when I emerge unscathed from an MRI machine, a cave or a jail cell, I am always mighty, mighty happy when the plane or helicopter safely touches down. Though not debilitating, never once in my life have I gone up into any sort of aircraft unless there was palpable good reason— usually getting to a place otherwise not reasonably accessible via non-aerial modes of transport. The notion of voluntarily going up in a hot-air balloon for no other purpose save going up in a hot-air balloon flat-out did not, and still does not, compute. It had never entered my head, the same way parachuting has never entered my head, except as something to avoid at all costs.

But, being a professional and all, I showed up at the appointed time, which was literally just as a stunningly beauteous dawn broke upon the Great Plains southeast of Denver. Since it was mid-December, it was a bit on the nippy side, which apparently is optimum for ascension, as cold air is more dense than hot air, and, for reasons that escape me, that helps the balloon get off the ground and make its way heavenward, until it's just this little dot lucky people sitting in the warm comfort of their living rooms, sipping hot coffee, can barely see. I would be joining a young (paying) couple that had just tied the knot and were looking upon this journey into the hereafter, er, sky, as some sort of marital consummation. They were all giggly and smoochy, which made me even more uncomfortable.

The ballooning outfitter my publisher had met at Soapy Smith's was also the pilot. He was affable enough and evoked a sense of confidence, and, truth be told, once we passed the moon and started making our way toward the outer Solar System, I calmed down a bit and started enjoying the expansive, albeit frigid, view of the Front Range. "Where we headed?" I, being on the journalistic clock and all, queried. "Don't know," the pilot responded. "What do you mean?" I squeaked. "I can use the burners to make us go up and down, and I have a pretty good eye for where the wind is, but, for the most part, I have absolutely no control over the balloon. We go where Mother Nature takes us."

Ain't that an interesting little tidbit?

After seeming decades aloft, it was finally and thank-godfully time to descend. The just-married couple was cuddling and cooing and sharing a bottle of bubbly, the pilot was pointing out various mountains and I was leaning against one of the basket uprights. Suddenly, the pilot went frantic. He yelled at the top of his lungs for all hands to hold on tight. We were apparently going through some sort of high-speed meteorological anomaly taking place like 50 feet above the ground I oh-so-much wanted to be standing safely upon. "I'M NOT KIDDING!!!! HOLD ON TIGHT!!!! AAAAHHHH!!!!" the now-frenzied pilot screamed. I wrapped both arms around the support, very much like Tom Hanks did in "Cast Away" when his plane was going down (I don't know about you, but I started paying a lot more attention to those pre-flight safety briefings after watching *that* movie), and instantly became a convert to at least seven religions. Seconds later, we crashed into Planet Earth at both a 45-degree angle and at a very uncomfortable rate of speed, and we spent the next almost 400 feet (I paced it off later), getting dragged by the still-partially-inflated balloon, which was now acting like a fully unfurled spinnaker, the muddy turf zooming by just below my nose (yes, it was my side of the basket that was closest to the ground). A couple times, just for grins, the balloon pulled the basket back up into the air, just so we could smack down hard and get dragged toward Castle Rock *yet again*. By the time we finally came to a stop, the new wife was crying, and the new husband, whose visions of a nookie-laden night were dissipating before his very eyes, was trying mightily to console her. That marriage was destined to either be very short-lived or very long.

After I wrote the blowjob story for the justifiably long-defunct Denver alternative alternative weekly, I vowed to never ever even ponder the notion of setting foot in a hot-air balloon, which, you would think, would be a fairly easy oath to uphold. Well...

The very next year, the editor of Adventure Travel calls me up and asks whether I would like to go to the southernmost Appalachians to write a story about this outfitter who offers what he advertises as "Adventure Orgies," wherein clients are taken on a different type of NON-AEREAL potentially deadly recreational pursuit every day for a week (whitewater rafting, climbing, horseback riding, hiking and, I shit you not, wild-boar hunting and mako-shark fishing). Being the starving writer I was, I said sure. It was once again the very week before Christmas when I landed at Atlanta's Hartsfield-Jackson International Airport. The plan was for the outfitter to pick me up, take me to the closest bar, where I would conduct a formal interview over many pitchers of suds, and then drive me to his mountain cabin for the night. The next morning, we were set to go rafting on the famed Chattooga, the very river where some of the whitewater scenes from "Deliverance" were filmed.

"I've got great news," Adventure Orgy Guy told me as we were driving out of the airport. "I've managed to squeeze in one more adventure for you! A buddy of mine has a hot-air balloon, and he said he'll take you up this afternoon!"

Yey!

Shit!

The first thing I noticed about the man who was going to take me up into the muggy Georgia air was, unlike the guy I went up with near Denver, who actually seemed like a fairly normal schmuck, right up until the point when he started screaming for us to hold on tight because we were about to crash, this guy seemed crazy as batshit from the get-go. Something about the way he cackled like a crow at his own bad jokes and the way he kept furtively rubbing his hands together, like he was trying to get something nasty off.

Because Georgia was experiencing an unseasonably warm late fall, there was not enough in the way of vertical-lift-inducing death molecules in the air for Adventure Orgy Guy, the crazy-as-batshit pilot and yours truly to all go up together. As I was about to volunteer to man the chase car, Adventure Orgy Guy patted me on the back and, with a bemused gleam in his eye, wished me not bon voyage, but, rather good luck. So, it was me and the crazy-as-batshit pilot, and, before I could calculate a plan for changing professions, I was airborne, with nothing between me and the ground save a wicker basket, some thin balloon material and one crazy-as-batshit pilot, who, it turned out, thought the best way to amuse his guest was to buzz the tops of as many giant Southern hardwood trees as often as possible while saying things like, "I'll bet we can take some branches off the next one."

And here I am, holding on for dear life, feeling like Sigourney Weaver in "Aliens," like all I had to do was stay back on Earth, and I wouldn't be here getting chased by deadly, drooling carnivorous creatures yet again. And, of course, just like my first time up in a hot-air balloon, we came down hard—hard enough that I bit my tongue almost clean in two. Then we tipped over so violently that my nose literally hit the dirt. Then, the wind caught the balloon and we got dragged through a field for a couple hundred feet. And that was the best part. Matter of fact, some hours later, as we were being detained by several local Southern redneck police officers straight out of bubba central casting, I looked back with fondness upon the those relatively pleasant moments when we hit the ground with a back-breaking thud and my mouth was suddenly filled with blood and my nose was smacked into the dirt so hard, I had to breathe through my mouth, which was filled-to-brimming with spit-laced tongue-wound blood.

What happened was this: The field that we thudded down in was home to endless vistas of waist-high dry grass. When we tipped over, the flamethrowers that are part and parcel of every hot-air balloon caught the grass on fire, which spread fast, far and wide, right before my very eyes. The crazy-as-batshit pilot started freaking and yelling for me to exit the basket and stomp the fire out. Try though I might, the only thing I managed to do was to gouge a seven-inch-long wound into my shin, which got caught up on one of the wing nuts holding the basket to the balloon frame.

Finally, through no fault of my own, I found myself ejected and lying dazed on my back in a north Georgia field that was pretty much by this point totally ablaze. There would be no stomping this fire out. The only thing to do was get up and run, except for the fact that we had a big balloon to deal with. Thing is, it damned sure wasn't my balloon. Fuck the balloon, and definitely fuck the crazy-as-batshit balloon pilot. Just as I was getting ready to high-tail it into the woods, a pick-up truck came careening toward us, and, before it came to a complete stop, two very agitated, overall-wearing, African-American men jumped out and pointed their double-barrel shotguns at the crazy-as-batshit balloon pilot and, well, poor, innocent me.

"Ya'll ain't goin' nowhere," I was told in no uncertain terms by my personal gun-bearer as I started eyeballing a potential escape route toward the closest trees—and as those famous banjo notes from "Deliverance" started playing in my head. "We done already called the poe-leece."

So, there we were, standing with hands up, like we were being robbed by banditos in an old Western movie, when, suddenly, a large white van pulls up. It was not the poe-leece or the fire department or even a representative of the local loony bin looking for an escaped crazy-as-batshit balloon pilot. No, par for my karmic course, that van bore a Chattanooga TV news crew arriving on the scene so quickly they seemingly were parked in the very field we set ablaze on the off chance that an errant hot-air balloon might fortuitously fall out of the sky and crash at their very feet, a news story from God, if ever there was one. And, worse, since the crazy-as-batshit pilot was still running around trying to stomp out a conflagration, which by then, could have been accurately classified as a "wildfire," the cute young on-air personality sprinted up to me and shoved a microphone the size of a baseball bat right into my face. Only then did she notice I had a bloody bandanna hanging limply out of my mouth and two nostrils completely caked with dirt.

"So, uh, what happened here?" she asked me, clearly flustered.

My brain was sending a red-alert message to my vocalization apparatus to unambiguously cast all blame at the feet of the crazy-as-batshit balloon pilot, but the only sound that sprang forth from my wounded maw was a series of unintelligible, pitiful moans and groans. I removed the bandanna in hopes of increasing my articulation factor, which caused a torrent of blood to dribble down my chin and onto my shirt. The reporter recoiled in abject horror, as though she had just in the flesh witnessed a man in the last stages of death-by-ebola. She shrieked and retreated to her van and, despite the best efforts of her cameraman, could not be persuaded to re-interface with the contagious pestilence standing there in the middle of the burning field with blood gushing forth from his most-obvious orifice.

About 20 minutes later, the poe-leece and the fire department arrived, sirens blaring. It took more than an hour to douse the flames, during which time the two shotgun-bearing African-American men, the poe-leece, several firefighters and the crazy-as-batshit balloon pilot realized that they all knew someone who knew someone else somewhere sometime. If memory serves, there were several "y'alls," "all y'alls" and maybe even a reference to hominy grits with redeye gravy. Basically, a meandering, drawl-laden verbal journey through Southern social inbreeding that resulted in the crazy-as-batshit balloon pilot eating a modest-sized bucket of shit and promising to pay for the damage and make a small donation to the poe-leece/fire-department retirement/drinking fund. We were let go and I, bloody tongue, gashed shin and smelling like smoke, was left with Adventure Orgy Guy to continue upon our merry way.

Despite the fact that I had related all this to Pedro, he still felt compelled to go forth and procure that $242 romantic two-person, early-morning champagne hot-air balloon ride outside Albuquerque. It dawned on me later that all of the mishaps I had described, Pedro considered to be plusses. I realized, once he finally took Darlene up into the stratosphere, he would be disappointed, maybe even to the degree of wanting his money back, if he did not get to experience a crash landing, setting a field on fire and having shotguns leveled at him.

I wished him all the best.

A few days later, Pedro called. Darlene had left him, and he asked, "You want to go ballooning with me, bro? I already got the tickets. After all, this was your idea. Merry Christmas, amigo!"

Note: This excerpt from *Smoke Signals: Wayward Journeys through the Old Heart of the New West* by M. John Fayhee was provided courtesy of Raven's Eye Press in Durango, CO. Thanks, Raven's Eye!

LOST RIMBAUD!!!

INTRO TO *LA CHASSE SPIRITUELLE*
By Editors

On May 19, 1949 members of the Parisian literary scene rushed to buy copies of the leftist newspaper *Combat.* The literary page of that issue was dedicated entirely to the discovery and impending publication of the lost literary masterpiece *La Chasse spirituelle* by the legendary boy-genius poet Arthur Rimbaud. Rumors of this poem had been circulating since 1888, a decade after the poem had supposedly been composed. Paul Verlaine claimed that he had abandoned the manuscript with some other personal possessions when he separated from his wife Mathilde. She ignored Verlaine's repeated request to recover the works of Rimbaud that he had abandoned. Though Verlaine is likely the only reader ever to cast a critical eye on the material, discussion and speculation over the contents of the *La Chasse* evolved into myth in the imaginations of the Parisian literary circle long after Verlaine's death. However, by 1949, most critics were resigned to the idea that *La Chasse* would likely never reappear. The sudden re-emergence of the lost manuscript thrilled Rimbaud scholars. They were eager to see how it compared to Rimbaud's other masterworks. The promise of this literary discovery would be shattered only two days after its release by Jean Prasteau's article in *Le Figaro*. Conveying the content of his interview with Mlle. Akakia Viala, Prasteau was the first to publicly challenge the authenticity of the poem. In the interview, Akakia Viala confessed that she and her acting partner Nicolas Bataille composed the poem that the publisher Mercure de France was selling as Rimbaud's missing masterpiece. Moreover, she told Prasteau that Maurice Nadeau, the literary editor for *Combat,* and Maurice Saillet, the editor for Mercure, knew about the forgery's origins. Indeed, Viala and Bataille composed the forgery to dupe and embarrass Saillet. They wanted retribution for Saillet's harsh criticisms of their theatrical interpretation of Rimbaud's *Une Saison en enfer.* In short order, the critics agreed that the newly released *La Chasse spirituelle* was a fake. Even so, the publication of the forgery reinvigorated Rimbaldian scholarship. According to Bruce Morrisette, author of *The Great Rimbaud Forgery* (Washington University Studies, 1956), scrutiny of the forgery ushered in a new emphasis on the concepts of comparative criticism, the art of pastiche, which Rimbaud often practiced himself, and the critical immersion and dedication required for creating a convincing imitation of a poet's work. The following translation of this forgery is the first to be published in the English language, and the Toad is proud to debut it. Moreover, we hope it might spark renewed interest in the search for the authentic *La Chasse spirituelle*.

THE SPIRITUAL HUNT
By Akakia Viala and Nicolas Bataille
Translated from French by Daryl Spurlock

I. VAUDEVILLE

I wept once for vain attachments. I do not believe in family, in duty, in the happiness guaranteed by esteem. Rancid soup, flavorless sweets and angelic perfumes of sanctimonious cupboards. Rejecting moods, mismatched playthings—accepted sentimentalities—and not forgetting those early afflictions. Nor complacent attitudes, nor meditations, nor prudent glory. Neither heroism nor repaid honor. Hide away your wisdom and your science, your treasure—your detestable wounds.

I brooded over your scorn, your excuses, your meaningless patience. Still, I appreciated the pleasant delicacies. Not so long ago I, too, could court the good and great, full of severity and principles. No longer can I laugh at these splendid things of old.

I depart from the memory of those childhood communions, of those inventive fairylands. Holidays. The country parsonage smelled of laundry, and I encountered the man concealing the schemes of his indifference in marvelous frescoes. Dear disease! I retrace my way up to the boulevards teeming with empty people. Pleasures vain and soft. The smell of our urban angels make the suburban milkmen swoon.

Our fleets will sail again for distant islands, future fields of honor. Catarrhal emperors will spit on the sleeping masses. Pirates, murderers will be immortalized. What will we dream of? Barracks pour out their stream of sickly heroes on sanitary fields, dead from tedium. Women await the invalids with gratitude.

Magic of nauseating colors, trumpeters copper-plating palms and mouths with abscess blue in the middle of the filthy, systematic bloodbath. Generations of communicants again whitewash their sincerity. Hideously docile nature, rich and comfortable city, accessible arts, miserable, out-of-tune pianos.

Mornings of misfortune…

Frenzied, epileptic hours, you will experience common dangers, arms thick with blood, legs spread, lewd, face down, in nights of extreme human freedom.

In the exercise of daily movements, from the transportation of weapons and flags, to the collapse of the glorious apotheosis, you may be a little tired, in the gloomy dawn of fatherlands authentic like mothers.

II. PAGAN HOLIDAY

That day, denied, lost, dead to the hope of destinies, positions, advantages, decay from the glimpsed abyss—it was yesterday, without a doubt—I discovered the meaning of choices born of debauched deceptions.

I will forget the taste of anathema, the easy insult—for once—all the savageries, the grotesque frenzies, the cruel gestures, as well as the vain blasphemies of childhood. I see with these eyes deserts cracked like crusts, crushed by sky. A forest of silk and amber, perhaps, but farther away. I listen, why then this silent treason in which I enter like a prince, shameful melodies. Must I suffer to be dragged so far? I can drink no more, but what exquisite rewards beyond the boundaries of this impoverished flesh. I will flee the boorish day, the familiar snares, the lights of lying, suffocating evenings, the customary digestions, the quiet rustling behind the door, the exhausted city.

I want to babble about the desertion of our unchangeable systems, of our cultures, the wealth of our memories. To learn henceforth to forget accepted fictions, I speak of easy and fatal hours, of friendship, of practical recognition.

I venerate the indifferent animals, splendid and wandering like the ancient gods, pitiless in the heavens.

It is abolished, forgotten, feeling the skin dry out under the arid and envious gaze of childhood curiosities and—shamelessly—devoured in the deepest dreams. Time: the madness of others! I will not cry out for you, sated by the wisdom of logicians. You will ignore these forbidden revelations, the rhythms of this savage orchestra, my patience, my obstinacy, my coarse royalty, my strength.

Floods devour superior peoples, and only a couple of maniacal idiots and prigs can see on the bulwarks of a crimson sumptuousness the messengers burned up by their duties.

The old shores blur in the wind; the fraternal rustling meadows of insects' delights.

I see straightaway some cliffs of quartz, guardians of the black and russet valleys, without rivers. I batter the ordinary dream with cunning, science, bastard devotions and mocking sweetness. And now there are dancers, ridiculous and beautiful artists. Giving all for a murder at daybreak in a park in Babylon.

I wrench the bars of the western sky and trace the footsteps of sorcerers and scorned prophets, around the dread of our devoured kin. But without affinity to outdated beliefs, to absurd and sunken virtues.

The horror of satisfaction precedes me. I rid myself of elementary gestures. Arms folding over the infinite. How simple it is! The superior savages had everything foretold: eliminate wisdom and advance forward!

Soon, more absence. Hearts will not be tortured more. More worries. A power fed by silence, unmoving. More old willfulness, more late-coming surges. The never-ending plain. The body, still and empty as a sanctuary. Eyes turning toward the inner shadow. Sleeping on the magic carpet and, head full of terrifying realities—lighter than the dream of a well-behaved child—mysterious illusions, I fade away exquisitely.

Vessel decked in gold, without waves, without storms, I will soon come into the venerated harbor where the sun ventures over our commercial continents, our docks, our fruitful tides, our lavish ports of call, our gloomy beaches.

I want to walk the tightrope toward that primordial knowledge, that wonderful world.

But the revolted heart, the head full of muddy water, wretched hunter: haunting the sickly banks where the golden fish are infused. Again I can't help wanting what is beyond the ancient myths.

My regrets, my divergent presence, my cold reason, alas! And all the enthusiasms and calculations, and the affectionate detours, respectable economies, nothing will be taken into account. I leave, banished for good, drunk, from the circle of glittery effects of denuded arabesques. I recall the acrid smell of pious women. Horse dream. I adore the sacred goat, the clawed cats meowing with desire. I remember the gaslights of the hopeless quarters, I walk up to the glare, feet on fire, I cross the successive rooms of an incredibly teeming empty temple and die destroying golden tubers and white birds.

Farewell, catechism, dilapidated loves!

I've cut off my right hand.

III. EDENS

Last prayer to the archangels who rot in my feverish forests. I stumble through the sixty lives of the cycle. Finally I situate my gun carriages, my trackers, my cavalcades—ordinary images forged in the dizzy fog of an awakening. I entrust you with my artificial emptiness, a collection of wild words that blaze. I famously stammered through the picturesque enchantments of the senses.

Sordid and complicated child, wallowing in the foolish meadow, I shook the pistils, inhaled the green, cold fumes, plunged my irritated arm in the mud of a terrible warmth, down to the fat pink worms. I heard monsters hissing, heroic couplets, laughter from dark lake mud, blossoms of dreaded castles where chaste, sweet princes sleep. I counted precious stones and aerial rivers, erected quicksand statues swaying in the coves of tropical seas, haunted fairground stalls where ballerinas slit each other's throats.

I experienced the cravings of poor children. Head ringing like a giant shell, abandoned in the aftermath of those orgies of fasting, the spirit heavier than a cathedral. I tested the wisdom of ancient marble, tore pomegranates into obscene shapes and ruby streams ran over my lips.

A smoking body, acrid. Desire, despair, belated affliction, kisses sticky with exotic poisons, leprosy, exasperated embraces. Smoldering chalice, operatic arias, gladiators bound for popular amusement, sirens and sorcerers, married hypocrites, priests drinking bad liquor to the sound of a drum, rustic seats in lounges. Mucous bubbles burst before my eyes, multicolored arrows pin me to a prepackaged Calvary. Older sisters console pathetic children with annoying solicitude and the gentle Jesuses mend well-worn garments. Paradise as it should be, Cythera, a hand to rescue me, alone, calmed, in the fields of honeysuckle. I heard the cries of the past behind the trees, the healing wind of hope. I reach the sublime degree of a shameless perfection. No more concealing from the world my blunders and selfishness and that unfamiliar tenderness.

I accomplish the most infamous tasks.

Cascades of bile, whirlwind of red and black snow, blast of fetid breath, carnival, enigmatic tortoises, cancers and hydras painted gray-green, emasculated roosters, lace; in the glorious sky, scraps of flesh make their ascent, grotesque monkeys snatch my clothes, arrows, streams of gems, formless flowers, bloody sap, shattered crystals, dusty pastels of obscure visions. Kangaroos jump in public squares and freighters weave rosaries of slippery string on ember oceans.

Oceanic butterflies, allspice, lemon trees, peppers from the languid tropics, aromatic seaweed, pustules, honeyed wounds, furious mammoths, rutting snakes devouring crews, cannibal flowers with velvet harpoons, delights, tortures… ah! pity!

Pardon, I will not start again.

None of this is serious, really.

IV. INFIRMITIES

I will no longer toy with the fevers and nightmares that made my body tremble and irritated my nerves. I know I owe them this.

Needs, fears, doubts must be rejected. I would have splendidly plundered nature and my obscure kin. I am of that kind—nothing more—joined these domesticated visceras to this neglected and fateful soul. I am very much tied to this place.

Life is simple and fruitful, save for the mind and this thirst. Would I know how to manage? Scholars, laborers circle me on the shockingly arduous and bitter field of action. Leaves grow, the customary foods come and go, and water and fire. I lost track of the ordinary things. I should not have done.

No beast will be able to subdue me from now on.

I return home defeated to an austere and comfortable house. I shamed love's supplications, altruistic yearnings, fraternal presence's desires. I glimpsed voluptuous tranquilities, sunken eyes ringed by pale purple, orphan of equinoxes and inevitable tides, of lunar phases and natural laws. Of silly songs dancing round in my head.

School refrains, mechanical prayers useful to the health of our adolescent bodies.

Fugitive from the extremes of absurdity and flagrant ignorance, calming embraced mysteries, desires, duties, condescending generosities, fruitless fighting forever lost to me. What will you make of this practical inheritance, abandoned and obstinate idiots, gorged on quarrels both childish and ancient like your races?

The thick smokes spit the stench of one-way crossings, filth clogs the mouths of gaping rivers, swollen belly, excrement, bitter liquid, sticky remains of monstrous cities.

Girls with surprised, silly glances make me blush with shame. Anathema to the fondness for devilish fertility. Nature, queen of hordes, you have subdued us. For entire nights I ran after beatific visions—racing moons, monotonous eclipses, tiresome circles—meager results.

You who are accustomed to related acts and rewarded effort, you will forget me.

Gray corpses, how are you still preserved?

V. MARSHLANDS

The return to heaven, constant friend. In the homeland fatal disappointments rush after warped rage against the powers that be. Banished from sensible capitals, deaf to the truth. I swallow their words and their dust, ravings of charlatans. But the monuments, testimony to their masterful misunderstanding, will crumble.

Time and its laughable accessories resume the course. Nothing more than practical from now on. Curves vanish, numbers—previously tamed—disintegrate. Except for the provident guarantee of a brown and maternal land, hot like a bird. Perhaps once again the uncertain brotherhood, remains of ancient magic, accepted romance. Science, chemistry, frenzy, pulverized stars will rain like a golden powder, toward the final revelation. Will black boats drift under the endless heavens?

Figs crash on beaches of ash and revolting clouds ravage Eden's orchards.

Gather up tools and fight on the path of duty.

Dressed-up Sundays on the boulevard of tedium.

In their orchestra of ferocious yelping, the hounds ripped me open. I watched the fading of the world, breathless, eyes swollen and itchy, I synchronized the rhythm of dying strength. The immaculate burst of fire released me and all was intact: comic royalty, popular distractions. Cults, stones, trees, rejected hearts, will I live despite your bizarre presence, your arrogance, your disdain?

I lost arms, tricks, and charms in this hunt for delightful magic. I return blind, hands cold and dead, without prey to show off, without trophies, to the funereal clearing of fallen trees. I will gorge myself on disgust—and doing so, yield to the overwhelming exhaustion, to scourges, to the obligations of cavernous time on these hardened feet.

I found myself shivering, squatting at the crossroads of old fears, scepter in hand, the scarlet crown on my brow, the demanding accessories of messiahs. Is it necessary to rise up today and rush about? To be busy? That is the old way.

Ineffable flesh, I took on, in the pure surge of wandering, your surprises, your heat, your brilliant impieties, your evil absolutes, your breathtaking inanities, like the last man knee-deep in your waves.

Frozen experience in the hidden night of the void.

It was but a childhood scheme, a ravaging of innocence.

After the ecstatic terrors, I plainly see white sheets, the vivid red port of some fever, lovely wounds, mortuary infusions of stammering elders, mercy of the once-insulted.

Neither regrets nor dementia henceforth.

Death sanctified in its way.

It was not mine.

Certainly, it's from other shores.

LOST RIMBAUD POEM?
By Editors

The so called "Evangelical Poems" are thought to have been written just before Rimbaud's escape from the household of his overbearing mother into the streets of Paris. They were allegedly sent along with letters to his friend and mentor Paul Demeny before Rimbaud met Paul Verlaine between 1870 and 1871. The first three known evangelical poems were eventually published under various titles. The supposed fourth evangelical poem was slipped into the hands of our Editor in Chief by a shady character in the City of Lights sometime in the mid-1990's. Spitzer translated and published the piece in both the online journal *Drunken Boat* (2002) and the print journal *Tight* (2003). His hope was to trigger a critical response, to enlist Rimbauldian scholars in indentifying the work either as a forgery or a genuine poetic gem, but he received no response. Now, we're reprinting both the original French and the English translation with the same questions in mind. Is it real? Is it legit? Does this look at the charismatic power of Christ to lead his followers into a delirious and communal transcendent state square with Rimbaud's poetics at the time? Let us know if you have an educated guess or more.

EVANGELICAL POEM IV: THE FRENCH TEXT

Anisi Jésus prononcait de grands discours, car il brillait comme une lumière ardent, car il était le fils de Dieu. Et les foules le suivaient, cinq mille à Tibériade, désireux d'un Moïse, affamés, sans eau, abri ou vin, — fatigues du foi que Jésus était leur berger.

En haut d'une montagne, Jésus discuter avec ses disciples de la nourriture du troupeau. Il dit: <<Ma chair est le pain et celui qui s'en nourrira vivra éternellement>>.

Les masses ferventes griffient le ciel, ouvraient leurs gorges, et criaient les vers. Cinq miches d'orge ranci furent partagées parmi le populo en délire, sous les rayons du soleil aveuglant.

Ce repas fut servi avec deux poissons pourris. La peau des nues s'étirait, et la mer bouillait au-dessous. Milliers de bras se dressaient en onde. Certains parlient dans des langues étranges, d'autres volaient, mêlant les voix et les visions dans l'air ivre. Le vide étais une fantasmagorie si phantastique qu'elle devenait vraie et sacrée et eternelle.

Les disciples etaient confus, flottaient sur un bateau. La mer s'eleva, l'orage se forma. Mais où était Jésus? Le voilla! merchant sur les vagues.

<<C'est moi>>, dit Jésus, <<ne craignez rien>>. Et le bateau continua . . . .
. . . .
. . . .
. . . . à Jérusalem.

EVANGELICAL POEM IV: THE ENGLISH VERSION

Then Jesus made great speeches, for he was shining like a blazing light, for he was the son of God. And the multitudes did follow him, five thousand to Tiberieus, yearning for a Moses, starving, without water, shelter or wine—exhausted with the faith that Jesus was their shepherd.

High up on a mountain, Jesus discussed with his disciples the feeding of the herd. He said, "My flesh is bread, and he who eats of it will live forever."

The frenzied masses clawed the sky, opened their throats and cried for worms. Five loaves made with rancid barley were divided among the throngs, delirious in the rays of the blinding sun.

This meal was served with two fetid fish. The sky stretched its skin, the sea boiled within. Thousands of arms arose in a swoon. Some spoke in tongues, others flew, mixing voices with visions in the drunken air. The void was a fantasmagoria so phantastic that it became real and sacred and eternal.

His disciples were confused, floating in a boat. The sea rose, a storm formed. But where was Jesus? There he is! walking on the waves.

"It's me," said Jesus, "don't be afraid." And the boat went on . . . .
. . . .
. . . .
. . . . to Jerusalem.

WARHOLIAN RIMBAUD
By Editors

Following our fascination with all things Rimbaud, the *Toad Suck Review* is publishing a recently discovered photograph of Arthur Rimbaud as an adult. The image was discovered in a flea market by French booksellers Jacques Desse and Alban Causse in 2008. According to Desse, they bought the batch of photographs because it included a print of Freemasons in the East. As Desse and Causse explored the pictures in their find, they discovered that the prints originated from the files of Jules Suel, a close friend of Rimbaud, and that they were taken in Aden when Rimbaud would have been living and working in Abyssinia as a merchandise trader. This photograph of Rimbaud at twenty-five, after he had abandoned all interest in poetry, has already been featured in an exhibition at the Grand Palace in Paris in April 2010. Here we present the new discovery in the playful spirit of pastiche—the first ever image of Rimbaud as an adult in Warholian pop art splendor!!!

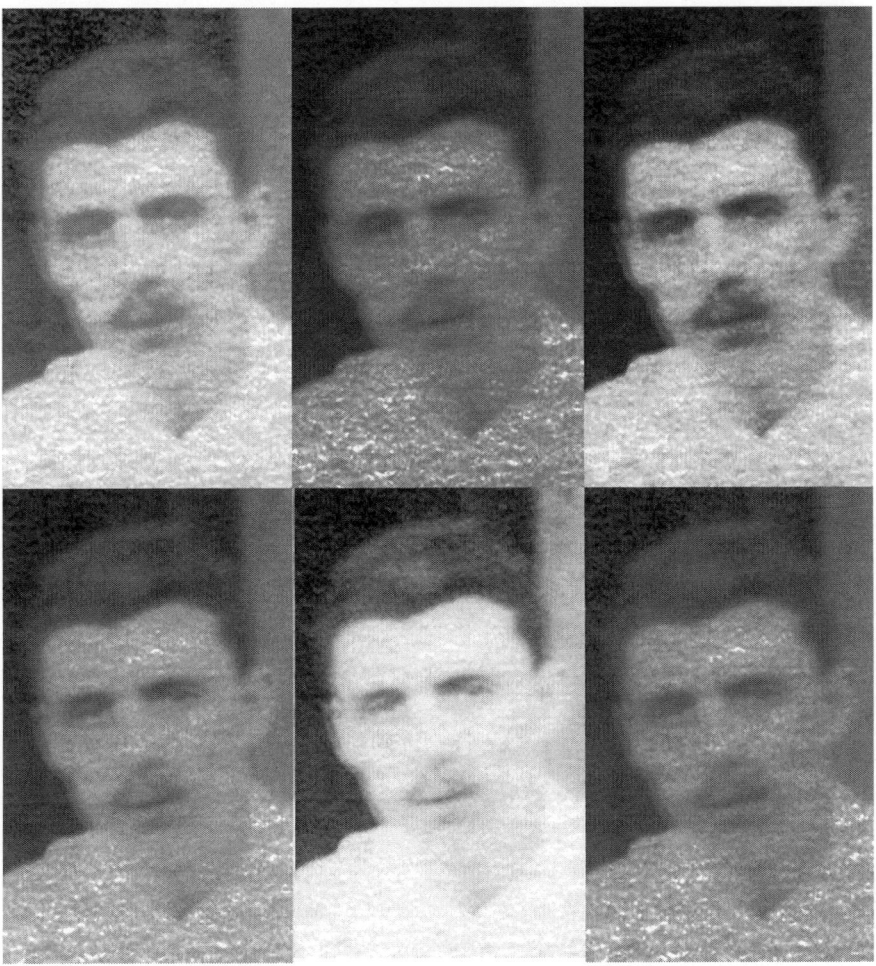

NAME THE QUIET EYES
By Vicente Aleixandre
Translated from Spanish by Stephen Kessler

THE POET SETTLES ACCOUNTS WITH HIS LIFE

> "To die, to sleep . . . perchance to dream."
> —*Hamlet,* III, i.

Forgive me: I've been asleep.
And sleeping isn't living. Peace be with you.
Living isn't breathing or prehearing words that might still keep us alive.
Live in them? Words die.
They sound lovely, but they never last.
Just like this clear night. Yesterday when dawn
or when day's end spreads out its last
ray of light, and maybe sets in your face.
With a fine brush of light it paints shut your eyes.
Sleep.
The night is long, but now it's gone.

POSTHUMOUS KISS

Quiet like this, my lips still on yours,
I breathe you. It's either a living dream or we're alive.
This life we can sense is in the kiss
that lives on, alone. Without us, it shines.
We are its shadow. Because it is our bodies when we're gone

YOU HAVE A NAME

Your name,
since you have one. My whole life was that:
a name. Because I know I don't exist.
A name breathed is not a kiss.
A name pursued on lips
is not the world, but its dream in the dark.
So under the earth, I breathed earth.
Over your body I breathed light.
Inside you I was born: that's why I died.

KNOWING RUBÉN DARÍO

The eyes are quiet.
The consumed daylight has withdrawn
and he regards the afterglow. In the background, boundaries.
The day's impossible limits,
which he would test. His "marquis's hands"
are meaty, packed with real
matter. They look and recognize, because they know.
Dusk in the background.
To place our hands in its blaze is to know
while you're moved, while you're consumed.
As you knew, you put them,
your natural hands,
into the fleshless light the dawn imagines.
Your fleeting eyes shone brighter in that light
just come from the good, from the loved world.
Because you knew it: love doesn't deceive.
To love is to understand. Whoever lives know.
Only because of wisdom were you alive.

All the hat in the world burned in your lips.
Your long thick lips that slowly grazed
on life; life rose up and left its imprint there.
You live for a kiss, but also a cosmos.
Your mouth knew the long waters.
The burnt slag, and the oak.
The enormous leaf and its living silence.
Like mother of pearl. Triton; the lips blow.

But the ocean is open. You rowed on its back.
A light dolphin in your happy body.
And Nereids too. Your chest a wave,
and rolling across the world. Beaches...

Rubén who one day reached out your arm
and baptized spray or colors. You look.
Whoever looks sees. Whoever's quiet has lived already.
But your sympathetic eyes,
your wide eyes that were opened little
by little; your never-known beautiful eyes
looked more, and they saw deep into the dark.
Darkness is brightness. Rubén the second and the new.
Rubén proud to stride out into the spray.
Rubén quiet as you look and discover.
There's light inside; quiet light, though burning.

burnt. The sweet blaze didn't cover your whole
pupil. It deepened it.
                        Whoever looked at you met a world.

No music or passion, no cold aromas,
but its thought dawning
into color. The same way a cheek is revealed
in a rose. The way knowledge is in the bitten
grape. The eye is inside the light.
As the in the stream the whole ocean.

Rubén complete who in passing gathers
in your bundle yesterday, arrived, today
where you walk, and our tomorrow.
Whoever is, looked back and sees what we're waiting for.
Whoever says something say everything, and whoever
keeps quiet is speaking. Like you who say
what they said and see what they never saw
and speak what they'll say obscurely. Because you knew.
Knowing is understanding. Bright poet. Hard poet.
Real poet. Light, mineral and man:
everything, and alone.
                    The way the world is alone,
and includes us.

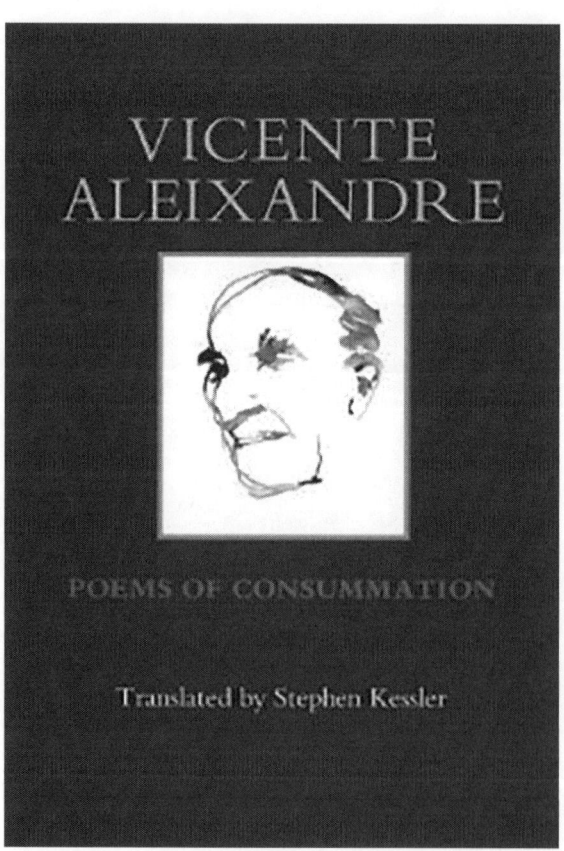

Note: These translations reprinted with permission from Black Widow Press. To order *Poems of Consummation*, go to blackwidowpress.com.

THE CARPET WON'T LIKE US BACK
By Matthew Henriksen

DATA AS AN ACT OF POETRY

The failed state
If you submit happiness

The day anyone died
May turned into a revolver

Violence we get back

Forgiveness an act of theater
on the meat hooks

In the gutter
the moon in the metal
but not in the water

I mean we get hurt
talking like this
on the subway

Repetition as pact

5 AM

when the angels spit on me
when I cannot
describe the angels I know

I do not understand
why I don't mean
anything

to the dew
or why the dew
is so ugly
and in its gloss

I see a black figure
turning inside a film

Each frame
disarms a place
dismembers the posit
but retains the

presence of a nose
a centipede
something in it

WE PUT REPEAT ON RECYCLE

Refrain

A balloon with a face works the crowd

When we come back to
luxury

no singer will dream
the century back up

Lana Lana we behoove you

No streets in hell

The intended
Imagined

Los Angeles with many streets

It is hard
not to look

We get so tired

We set our thermoses down
We drink oxygen

The carpet won't like us back

"Things to Do Today" by JJ Cromer.

SIREN SQUAWKS JIVE TALK
By Seth Pennington

ANNIS

I watch her
        cough into a mug of steam.
Water spills
        on couch and floor. She gets up, bats
her handsome eyes
        swollen from hunger and sleep
that leaves her
        more tired. Throws herself
in some jazz
        step-swagger towards me,
sings her sentences; they
        linger still with liquor, always
with dope. She pours
        herself another glass
of hot water. Cigarettes have
        stained her long under-nails.
She cradles both on the bench
        out the café front. Behind
plate windows that keep in
        warm, the dark
roast settles in the knotted eye
        of the hardwood, blacks
the green sag of burn-out
        velvet. She unfolds the coarse
knot of scarf from her throat
        to reveal the rounds of
small breasts and clavicle.
        *This is the most attractive part
of the human body*, she barks
        through the glass. She runs
the length of the bone's track
        with it held between middle
finger and thumb, pressing skin
        beneath it. Her mouth goes on
moving, but it's her doubling-over
        that stops me. Her strain and
squat, head lifted like some
        pissing dog, her crying
out, hair falling. I stand still.
        No one else pays
mind, lifts face from
        screen or novel.
The crackling tornado
        sirens start winding,

wheezing; her face ages in
        a rapid succession of
wrinkles pleating
        her forehead, eyelids, and
even her shoulders
        arc to ground. Bursts
of lightning scratch sky
        like a pen
knife on copper foil.
        Her body reverses
upright calmly.
        She lights a rolled
cigarette as hard
        rain makes paper
limp and match wet.

SAN FRANCISCO MAIN LIBRARY BATHROOM

The piss line runs
out the door and puddles

across one-inch tile, eating
grout, turning it lung-black,

and at back-to-back sinks
homeless wash face-to-

face. These queers beat
shirts, wring socks in rhythm to

automatic faucets that
steam on cold hands. Water

falls in Gatsby wordshapes of
his promised spring caught on

chapped lips between news
and poems, between the serious

and the joking—what
is the thread count of the Chronicle?

This library holds homes beyond
words, is Laundromat, is good heat,

is survival, is
pink potted meat.

THE FORGOTTEN RIVER
By Charles Portis

This "lost classic" by legendary prose-master Charles Portis first appeared in the September 1991 issue of the Arkansas Times. *The Arkansas historian and writer Dee Brown (*Bury My Heart at Wounded Knee*), who inspired this trip, died in 2002. This piece was later reprinted in* Escape Velocity: A Charles Portis Miscellany, *edited by the Arkansas writer Jay Jennings, and published by the Butler Center for Arkansas Studies (the paperback came out in 2013). Copies of the highly acclaimed Portis anthology can be purchased through the University of Arkansas Press at uapress. com, or from online and offline book sellers. The Toad is grateful to Jay Jennings and publisher Rod Lorenzen for permission to feature this extraordinary essay.*

The forest rangers at Mena were all very nice but they could tell me only approximately where the Ouachita River began. It rose somewhere out there in the woods, they said, above the little bridge at Eagleton, where I would find the first Ouachita River road sign. I wanted to see the very origin and so I floundered about between Rich Mountain and Black Fork Mountain with further inquiries.

Through that forested valley runs Highway 270, as well as the Kansas City Southern Railway, and the headwaters of the Ouachita, at an elevation of 1,600 feet above sea level. The two mountains rise another thousand feet or so from the valley floor. A sign warns hikers about the presence of black bears.

Nearby, right on the Oklahoma line, there is a log cabin beer joint, which might have once served the Dalton Brothers; Bill, Grat, Emmett, and Bob. It was dark inside, like a cave, with a very low ceiling. The girl behind the bar knew nothing, which was all right. You don't expect young people to know river lore.

Then a young man sitting far back in the gloom—the only customer—told me just how I should go. I was to enter the woods at the start of the Black Fork Mountain hiking trail. When I reached the river, here a small watercourse—"so narrow you can straddle it"—I was to walk upstream for about a mile, and there I would find three or four trickling threads of water coming together to form the Ouachita River.

This would have to do, though I had hoped for a spring, a well-defined source. Probably I didn't walk the full mile. I followed the diminishing rivulet up to the point where it was no wider than my three fingers, and declared victory. After all, it was much the same as spring water, cold and clear. I drank some of it. From here it flows 610 miles, generally southeast, to Jonesville, LA., where it joins other streams to form the Black River.

I grew up in south Arkansas and thought of the Ouachita only in local terms, certainly not as an outlet to the sea. It was a place to swim and fish. I knew you could take a boat down it from the Highway 82 bridge near Crossett to Monroe, LA., because I had done it once with a friend, Johnny Titus. It was shady a good bit of the way and we had the river pretty much to ourselves. The keeper at the old Felsenthal lock was annoyed at having to get up from his dinner table to lock through two boys in a small outboard rig.

But I knew no river lore, less than the Oklahoma barmaid, and it came as a great surprise to me lately when I learned that there was regular steamboat service on this modest green river, as late as the 1930s, and as far up as Camden. I am not speaking of modern replicas or party barges, rented out for brief excursions, but of genuine working steamboats, with big paddle wheels at the rear, carrying bales of cotton down to New Orleans and bringing bananas and sacks of sugar back upstream, along with paying passengers.

There were two vessels, the *Ouachita* and the *City of Camden*, and they ran on about a two-week cycle—New Orleans-Camden-New Orleans, with stops along the way. The round-trip fare, including a bed and all meals, was $50. Traditional steamboat decorum was imposed, with the men required to wear coats in the dining room. At night, after supper was cleared, the waiters doubled as musicians for a dance.

It was Dee Brown of Little Rock, the author of *Bury My Heart at Wounded Knee,* who told me about this, and how as a teenaged boy in the late 1920s he took the *Ouachita* from New Orleans to Camden.

He had a summer job at a filling station between Stephens and Camden, and had often watched the steamer tie up and unload. "'I've got to ride that boat,' I kept telling myself." He saved up a bit more than $50 for the adventure—"an enormous sum in those days"—but then thought better of this extravagance. He would keep half of it back. "So I made a reservation for the other end and hitchhiked down to New Orleans. Hitchhiking was easy and safe then, and faster than the boat."

His timing was good, which kept expenses down. He paid a dollar for a night's lodging at a boarding house near the French Quarter. The trip back was a delight, as Mr. Brown remembers, a leisurely voyage of five or six days. He got full value for his $25. The big splashing wheel pushed the steamer up the Mississippi, the Red, the Black, and at last into the Ouachita at Jonesville, with the two walls of the forest closing in a bit more day by day.

There were fine breakfasts of ham and eggs, when ham was real ham, with grits and hot biscuits. At lunch one day he found a split avocado on his plate, or "alligator pear," as it was called on the menu. "I had never seen one before. I wouldn't eat it." Young Mr. Brown was traveling light and so had to borrow a coat from a waiter at each meal before he could be seated. He had a tiny sleeping cabin to himself with a bunk bed and a single hook on the wall for his wardrobe.

He enjoyed the nightly dances, though he had to sit them out as a wallflower because he didn't know how to dance. Townsfolk along the way came on board just for the dance, and among them were young Delta sports sneaking drinks of corn whiskey and ginger jake. These were Prohibition days. A young girl from New Orleans, traveling with her family, offered to teach Dee Brown how to dance. "I wanted to dance with her, too, sure, but I just couldn't bring myself to do it." This family, he recalls, who had never seen any high ground, marveled over the puny hillocks of the upper river. He remembers an Arkansas woman vowing never again to eat sugar, after seeing the deckhands, dripping with sweat, taking naps on the deck-loaded sacks of sugar.

Dee Brown, then, got me interested, and so in late May and early June [of 1991—Ed.] I drove down the Ouachita valley to take a look at things. The Ouachita National Forest, where the river rises, is still a dark green wilderness, if not quite the forest primeval that DeSoto saw when he came crashing through these woods 450 years ago, with some 600 soldiers, 223 horses, a herd of hogs, and a pack of blood hounds. He was looking for another Peru, out of which he had taken a fortune in gold, more than enough to pay, from his own pocket, for this very costly expedition. As it turned out, there was no gold or silver here in "Florida." What he found was catfish.

"There was a fish which they [the Indians] called Bagres: the third part of it was head, and it had on both sides the gilles, and along the sides great pricks like very sharp aules [awls]; those of this kind that were in lakes were as big as pikes: and in the River, there were some of an hundred, and of an hundred and fiftie pounds weight, and many of them were taken with the hooke..."

This comes from a report written by one of DeSoto's Portuguese officers, who identifies himself only as "A Gentleman of Elvas" (the town of Elvas, in Portugal). The Portuguese version was published in 1557, and was rendered into this King James English by Richard Hakluyt, and published in London in 1609, under the misleading title of "Virginia Richly Valued." Hakluyt was promoting English exploration and settlement in the New World, and any news at all from that quarter was grist for his mill. There is not one word about Virginia in the text, and a more accurate title would be "Florida Poorly Valued." By Spanish reckoning, the continent belonged to Spain, being a gift from Pope Alexander VI, himself a Spaniard, and all that country lying east and north of New Spain (Mexico) was regarded more or less as Florida.

Elvas tells of seeing "many Beares, and Lyons, Wolves, Deere, Dogges, Cattes, Martens and Conies [rabbits]. There be many wild Hennes as big as Turkies, Partridges small like those of Africa, Cranee, Duckes, Pigeons, Thrushes and Sparrows... There are Gosse Hawks, Falcons...and all Fowles of prey that are in Spaine..."

He spoke too of "small chestnuts" [chin quapins] and of "many Walnut trees bearing soft shelled Walnuts in fashion like bullets," which could only have been pecans. Some of his "Plummes and Prunes" were very likely muscadines and persimmons. There is no mention in his bestiary of buffalo, or bison, then roaming the country from coast to coast. DeSoto's men knew about these "hunch-backed cattle," as they had traded with the Indians for their hides, which made good bedding, but they had no luck in hunting them and there is some question whether they ever saw one on the hoof. There is only one passing, inconclusive mention of a hunt. It is a wonder, perhaps, that they saw any wild creatures, who must have heard this band approaching from some distance away, clanking, snorting, grunting, barking.

The forest has changed; it is no longer a virgin stand of timber with a high canopy and an uncluttered, parklike floor, on which horses could move about. The Beares and Deere still thrive, but the Lyons are gone, or so believes Larry Hedrick, of the National Forest's Game and Wildlife Division. "We do get occasional 'sightings,' but there is just no good evidence of free-living, free-ranging cougars out there. Of course, they are reclusive, like bobcats. We're overrun with bobcats, but you don't see them." As for the native red wolves, they have mated with intruding, wily, trickster coyotes to form a curious hybrid pack. The chinquapin, sweetest of nuts, has disappeared too, in my lifetime, or it is almost gone, a victim of the chestnut blight.

Yet even with change the forest remains an impressive tract of mountain greenery, bigger, at 2,500 square miles, than the state of Delaware, and the river that flows out of it is one of the prettiest in the country.

Early trappers and market hunters paddled their canoes up it, far past Camden, the present head of navigation, past the bluff where the Caddo enters at Arkadelphia, past "the hot springs," and on to the hills not far from the present town of Mena. This upper stretch is still navigable by canoe, in season, in the familiar pattern of a fast-flowing stream: shoal water followed by a pool followed by a shoal. For some reason, however, it has not caught on well with recreational floaters, slaves of fashion that they are. On a warm day in late spring, with plenty of water running, when there must have been war parties of canoes colliding at every bend of the Buffalo River, I saw not a single floater on the Ouachita between Ink and Oden, nor a bank fisherman nor a swimmer.

The parks and campgrounds were spruced up for the summer season. The state road ways were clean, too. Where was all the litter that people complain about in letters to newspapers? Also, where was the old rural shabbiness?

The farmhouses on Highways 270 and 88 were well-kept, in fine trim, the mobile homes neatly skirted. Around them were shade trees, ornamental shrubs, flower beds and well-tended lawns. Not what we used to call landscaping in the Arkansas countryside, when the custom was to level every living thing around your house for about a 50-yard radius. We were the original clear-cutters, and this dead-zone tradition lives on in east Arkansas, where you can see a new brick house plopped down in the middle of a muddy soybean field, without so much as a crabapple tree or a petunia out front—as though people who farm in a big way couldn't be bothered with mere horticulture.

The new attention to lawn care can be attributed, I think, to the invention and spread of the riding mower. Cutting the grass is no longer seen as a chore, as men don't outgrow their boyhood love for dodging about in midget cars with tiny steering wheels. I believe this also accounts for the popularity of golf. Take away the little motorized carts and the links would be largely deserted.

It may be that outlanders have brought in new ideas about some of these things, along with their comfortable retirement incomes. You hear a lot of non-Arkansas voices these days in the Ouachitas. At Lum and Abner's Jot-em-Down Store in Pine Ridge, I was greeted by a nice lady from some northern clime who never in her life said, "Well, I swan!" much less, "Ay grannies!" At another store, in neighboring Polk County, there were flat white wicks for sale, for kerosene lamps, but I found no country store so humble or remote that it didn't offer a selection of video cassettes. In the towns there are signs of a modest prosperity, such as new police cars (big Chevrolet Caprices, mostly) and new Masonic halls, Moose lodges, and American Legion huts. All these brotherhoods seem to have hired the same architect, a grim man, who likes to build on defensive, bunker principles. His signature is the blank wall. The new clubhouses, with few exceptions, are long, low buff-brick structures with no windows.

There is no longer much agriculture in this country, in the strict sense of field crops. The old straggling hillside corn patches are now pastures where polled Hereford and Angus cattle graze. A lot of fat healthy saddle horses are running about too. The long metal chicken sheds appear to be mostly abandoned, or in use for storage of those big cylindrical rolls of hay. The vegetable gardens are still deadly serious, with rows of pole beans and squash 90 feet long.

Mount Ida is where the hexagonal quartz crystals are found, with their radiant powers. Just north of town the mountain stream loses its "rolling impetuosity" as Dunbar would put it, and begins to spread and go still and blue as it is penned up by the hand of man. Here, for some 50 miles, the river loses its identity in a chain of dams and lakes—Ouachita, with a shoreline of almost a thousand miles, and the older and smaller Hamilton and Catherine. All are associated with Hot Springs, though the city itself is not on the river.

For William Dunbar and his expedition up the Ouachita, from October, 1804, to January, 1805, it was a nine-mile hike from the river bank to the valley of "the boiling springs," which is now Central Avenue downtown. Dunbar was an immigrant from Scotland who had done well in America. He owned a plantation near Natchez and had a good education. He knew how to do things, which made him a man after President Thomas Jefferson's heart. Jefferson and the U.S. Congress had just paid Napoleon $15 million for the entire western drainage of the Mississippi River—the Louisiana Purchase—and exploring parties were being organized to look over the new territory. Dunbar was sent up the Ouachita. He went in an unwieldy barge 50 feet long, with a Dr. George Hunter of Philadelphia, a guide, three of Dunbar's slaves, and a rowing party of 14 soldiers from the New Orleans garrison. It was a small, regional version of the Lewis and Clark expedition up the Missouri, and on to the Pacific.

Surprisingly little was known at that late date of the country between the Mississippi and the Shining Mountains, or the Stony Mountains, as the Rockies were then called. Jefferson, perhaps the best-informed man of the country, thought there still might be mastodons or mammoths grazing to the west. They would be much bigger than the tropical elephants. Jefferson wanted our New World animals to be the biggest. In the same spirit, Robert Livingston, negotiating in Paris for the purchase of *La Louisiane,* told the treasury minister that, anyway, the French would never be able to sell their goods here, such as Cognac, because Americans preferred Kentucky peach brandy, "which, with age, is superior to the best brandy of France." It was truly morning in America.

The cynical Napoleon, 33-year-old First Consul, may or may not have believed it. On first meeting Livingston, at a reception, he took a playful line with the presumptions of the new nation.

"You have been in Europe before, Monsieur Livingston?"

"No, my General."

"You have come to a very corrupt world." Then, to Talleyrand, "Explain to Monsieur Livingston that the old world is very corrupt. You know something about that, don't you, Monsieur Talleyrand?"

The Anglo-Americans were slow to learn from the Indians and the French that canoes were the thing. Dunbar's monster barge, designed by Dr. Hunter, drew two feet of water and had an external keel. Over and over again the soldiers had to jump into the cold water with a rope and drag the thing off snags and over sandbars and shoals. At Fort Miro, or the Washita Post (Monroe, LA.), they changed to a lighter boat and the going was faster, but they still had to manhandle it over the rougher shoals. One, north of the Caddo, had a straight vertical drop of four-and-a-half feet.

Dunbar remarks on the beauty of the river and how it was clear and drinkable along the entire course, unlike the Red and the "Arcansa," which were always muddy, "being charged with red terrene matter." The trees on the banks—willow, black oak, packawn [pecan], hickory, and elm—were not so grand or lofty as those along the Mississippi, but had their own charm and "appear to bear a kind of proportion to the magnitude of their own river."

The Ouachita wasn't completely unknown. It was late fall and the bears were fat with oil and their furs were prime. Dunbar met hunters along the way "who count much of their profits from the oil drawn from the Bear's fat, which at New Orleans is always of ready sale, and is much esteemed for its wholesomeness in cooking, being preferred to butter or hog's lard; it is found to keep longer than any other oil of the same nature, without turning rancid."

He comments on the indolence of the white settlers—"always a consequence of the Indian mode of life"—and tells us that the young army officer in command at Fort Miro, a Lieutenant Bowmar, while capable enough, lacked "the polite manners of a gentleman." At another point he suddenly seems to remember that he is writing this report for Jefferson, the great democrat, and he praises the industry and sturdy independence of a man and his wife who had cleared a little two-acre farmstead in the woods. They had corn for bread, plenty of venison, bear oil, fish and fowl for the taking, and there were hides and wild honey to sell for cash. Their prospects were indeed bright, and he stops just short of having them reading a bit of John Locke or Rousseau by firelight, before turning in.

"How happy the contrast, when we compare the fortune of the new settler in the U.S. with the misery of the half-starving, oppressed, and degraded Peasant of Europe!!" Dunbar is not a man for exclamation marks, and when he gives us two of them here, we feel his discomfort with this kind of talk—however genuine the sentiment.

They found two abandoned log huts at the base of Hot Springs Mountain, where the smoking waters poured forth to form a creek. The sick from Natchez were already coming here to soak their bones. Dunbar examined the rocks and vegetation. Dr. Hunter, of whom Dunbar speaks in a guarded way as "a professed chemist," conducted experiments with his pans and beakers. Dunbar determined the latitude with his sextant. (Is there anyone today living between Natchez and Hot Springs who could do that—go off into the forest and calculate the angular distance of his position in degrees and minutes from the Equator?) He measured the temperature of the springs and pools, and his readings of 132 to 150 degrees Fahrenheit tally pretty well with the current reading at the source of 145.8 degrees. So we can't blame a badly defective thermometer when he tells us that the air temperature fell to 6 degrees on January 2, 1805, as they were camped on the river bank in 13 inches of snow. They ate well, bagging turkeys and deer at will. They shot one young bear. But, as with DeSoto's men, they had no luck with the buffalo. On two occasions in south Arkansas these beasts were "shot at and grievously wounded, with blood streaming from their sides." The soldiers couldn't bring them down, however, and couldn't or wouldn't track them down. Soldiers perhaps lack the patience to be good hunters.

Elvas puts it this way: "The Indians want no fleshmeat; for they kill with their arrowes many deere, hennes, conies and other wild fowle: for they are very cunning at it: which skills the Christians [Spaniards] had not: and though they had it, they had no leasure to use it: for most of the time they spent in travel, and durst not presume to straggle aside."

Dunbar doesn't identify his weapons, other than to call them "rifles," which suggests they weren't smoothbore muskets. It is possible his party was fitted out, as were Lewis and Clark, with the army's new 1803 model rifle, a flintlock of .54 caliber. DeSoto's troops had a few firearms, of a kind known as the arquebus, a primitive matchlock shoulder weapon firing a .65 to .75 caliber ball, and using a smoldering wick called a match or matchcord to ignite the powder charge. These pieces were cumbersome, inaccurate, with a much shorter range than the crossbow, which was DeSoto's primary weapon, together with swords and lances. The thundersticks weren't even of much help in terrifying the natives, who, as one account has it, "not only had held no fear of the arquebuses but had scorned and ridiculed them." In the end the survivors of the expedition melted down the useless guns to make nails for their escape boats.

Was DeSoto at Hot Springs? Here is the brief passage, again from Elvas, that is the basis of this belief: "The Governor [DeSoto] rested a moneth more in the Province of Cayas. In which time the horses fattened more than in other places in a longer time, with the great plentie of Maiz [corn, planted by the Indians] and the leaves thereof, which I think the best that hath been seene, and they drank of a lake of very hot water, and somewhat brackish, and they drank so much, that it swelled in their bellies when they brought them from the watering."

There are three accounts of the expedition written by participants. The one from Elvas is the longest, at 179 pages, and there are short, brisk, official reports from Hernandez de Biedma, the king's factor, and Rodrigo Ranjel, DeSoto's private secretary. Some 50 years after the event, one Garcilaso de la Vega completed a fourth account, a long, literary book, which he claimed was based on interviews with a knight and two soldiers who accompanied DeSoto. This work is held to be the least reliable.

In only one of the four—Elvas—can I find mention of geothermal water, warm or hot, and his water is somewhat brackish. The Hot Springs water is not at all brackish, and contains no particular belly-swelling agents. The "lake" comes from the Portuguese word "lagoa," which can mean anything from a small lake to a puddle.

The U.S. DeSoto Expedition Commission cites a mention of "hot streams" from Ranjel—"from the missing parts of his diary." It is still missing from the only published Ranjel account I could find. This commission, a blue ribbon government panel, of which Col. John R. Fordyce of Arkansas was vice chairman, delivered its report in 1939, on the 400th anniversary of DeSoto's landing at Tampa Bay. Colonel Fordyce and his colleagues made an exhaustive effort to map out DeSoto's wanderings, from vague topographical clues and the rough estimates of distances and directions given by Elvas and the others. (Coronado, then exploring to the west, was better organized; he had a man designated to count off the paces of each day's march.)

The DeSoto distances are given as so many days' journey, or so many leagues, when given at all. But what was a day's march? What league were they using? With eight to choose from, the commission members finally settled on the Spanish judicial league of 2.634 miles, not to be confused with the ordinary Spanish league of 4.214 miles or the Portuguese league of 3.84 miles. The report is an impressive work of scholarship, conjecture, and divination.

But if not Hot Springs, where was this Province of Cayas? It is pretty well established that the Spaniards were in the central part of the country at that time, and nowhere else in the region (except at nearby Caddo Gap) are there springs of warm water coming from the earth, fresh or brackish. Anyhow, I like to think that DeSoto was here in 1541, and I like to think that Shakespeare, still working in London in 1609, picked up the little Elvas-Hakluyt book and read about the hot lake, and about Camden and Calion, and the earlier crossing of the Great River near Helena. It is just the kind of chronicle he quarried for his plots and characters, and DeSoto, a brutal, devout, heroic man brought low, is certainly of Shakespearean stature. But, bad luck, there is no play, with a scene at the Camden winter quarters, and, in another part of the forest, at Smackover Creek, where willows still grow aslant the brook.

(A note here on Hakluyt's English: Those earnest enunciators who say "bean" for "been" should know that Hakluyt, the Oxford scholar, spelled it "bin," as did, off and on, the poet John Donne.)

Below Lake Catherine the Ouachita runs free again, for a while. The momentum is less, the river having already dropped from 1,600 feet to 315 feet at Malvern, and the rate of fall is leveling off fast. But there is still shoaling, as you can see from the Interstate 30 bridge near the Malvern exit. Above and below the bridge the water breaks on shelving rock, and we can imagine the trouble Dunbar had in dragging a heavy boat over it.

Sturdy bricks are made at Malvern, 200 million of them each year, and in the adjoining and older community of Rockport, there is a white frame church, the Rockport United Methodist Church, with a sign proclaiming it to be the "Oldest Church West of the Mississippi/ Est. 1809 / Elmo A. Thomason, Pastor." Oldest Protestant church, I gather, is the meaning, but on the day I stopped, the Rev. Mr. Thomason was not around to clarify the point. Yellow ribbons girdled the shade trees around the church—none of your latter-day Wesleyan revisionists at Rockport. Little Rock did well enough in welcoming home the troops from Desert Storm, but I noticed that the small towns in Arkansas and Louisiana, more directly affected by the call-up of Reserve and National Guard units, did much better. They were more exuberant, more lavish with their ribbons and banners.

At Arkadelphia (Blakleytown, until 1838) we know we are out of the hills when we see the statue of a Confederate soldier on the courthouse lawn, and an African Methodist Episcopal Church, and a snarling yellow Ag-Cat cropduster dipping low over a rice field— irrigated from the Ouachita. The Ag-Cat is an excellent workhorse, but the bulging cockpit canopy is ugly and the plane just doesn't have the pleasing lines of the old Stearman.

The Caddo enters the Ouachita here, and at one time you could freely drive to a bluff overlooking the confluence. No more; you are now confronted by a locked gate. Arkadelphia had irregular steamboat service from 1825 until the 1870s, when the Iron Mountain Railroad came through, and even after that a few boats came up from time to time. One, in 1912, reportedly took on a load of 2,000 bales of cotton. But commercial navigation this high on the river was always seasonal and chancy.

Highway 7 south of town becomes a shady corridor of tall, skinny pines. Below Sparkman ("Welcome to Sparkman / A Good Town / Raiders are Winners") there is a turn-off to Tate's Bluff, where the Little Missouri joins the Ouachita. A low concrete bridge, which washes out now and then, spans the river. I ran into my first floaters here, two young men in a canoe, who had made their way some 30 miles down the Little Missouri. "We only had to drag once." Did they ever float the Ouachita? "Not this far down. There's just not enough current. Too much paddling." Did they know of any songs about the Ouachita? Well, no. They tried hard, too, to think of a song. Everybody was very obliging.

Camden, head of navigation, has the feel of a river town, though you can no longer get a catfish lunch downtown, or any kind of plate lunch. Along the bar pits middle-aged black women are fishing with cane poles. They stand very still watching their corks. They are all bundled up against the heat and the mosquitoes, and their broad-brimmed straw hats are well cinched down with colorful sashes.

Between the railroad track and the river there is a big metal building with the hopeful words "Port of Camden" painted on it. But where are the tugs and barges? It seems there are none. According to Mrs. Eunice Platt, there hasn't been a commercial run up this far since December 1989, when four barges, pushed two at a time, came from Monroe to get a load of gravel for rockless Louisiana. Mrs. Platt, of Camden, is the executive director of the Ouachita River Valley Association, and a tireless worker in promoting navigation improvements on the upper Ouachita.

The situation, as I understand it, is this: The old dams and locks, completed in 1926, provided a six-and-a-half-foot channel from the Black River to Camden. The new system was finished in 1985 and provides a nine-foot channel with new dams and locks at Calion and Felsenthal in Arkansas, and Columbia and Jonesville in Louisiana. The locks will accommodate four standard barges tied two abreast ahead of a tugboat. Some of the bends in the river, however, are so tight that these four-barge units can't negotiate them. The shorter, two-barge units, are said not to be commercially feasible. To remedy this, Mrs. Platt and the Corps of Engineers want to lop off some of the meanders, most of them in Arkansas.

"They say we're trying to make a muddy ditch out of the river," she said. "Well, that's just not true. We're talking about a total of 14 bend widenings and eight cutoffs, out of what, more than 300 bends in the river? We're talking about a total of 341 acres of land. That's all that will be used. I'm trying to help the river, not hurt it. I'm an environmentalist too. I'm just as much an environmentalist as Richard Mason is."

Mr. Mason, of El Dorado, co-chairman of the Businessmen's Coalition to Save the Ouachita, agrees with the numbers but thinks they are misleading. He said, "Some of those cutoffs are huge and will really take in as many as seven smaller bends. Look, every conservation and wildlife group in the state is against this thing—every single one." He also thinks it's a waste of money. "An obvious pork barrel proposition, nothing else. You could make that river as straight as an arrow and nobody would use it." It is much cheaper, he claims, to haul goods by truck from Crossett to Greenville, MS., or from Camden to Pine Bluff, on the Arkansas, and offload on barges there, than to ship down the Ouachita. As for the El Dorado petroleum products, there are existing pipelines. "You can't ship cheaper than a pipeline."

The cutoff project is now hanging fire, pending acquisition of the 341 acres, which the five affected counties in Arkansas must pay for. In Louisiana, the state government must pay. I came away with the impression that Mrs. Platt is right about the predicted damage to the river being exaggerated, and that Mr. Mason is right when he says that the prospects for high-volume barge traffic are not very good. [The project was not completed.—Ed.]

When Dunbar came through here in 1804 he noted the presence of a trail through the woods: "the road of the Cadadoquis Indian Nation [Caddo] leading to the Arcansa Nation; a little beyond this is the Ecor a Fabri [Fabri's Cliffs] 80 to 100 feet high: it is reported that a line of demarkation run between the french and spanish provinces, when the former possessed Louisiana, crossed the river at this place; and it is said that Fabri, a french-man and perhaps the supposed Engineer deposited lead near the cliff in the direction of the line... The additional rapidity of the current indicates that we are ascending into a higher country. The water of the river now becomes extremely clear and is equal to any in its very agreeable taste as to drinking water... The general breadth of the river today has been about 80 yards."

The Ouachita remains about the same width but the bluff is not half that high today, having been trimmed down over the years by railroads and other developers.

Again, the question arises: Was DeSoto here? The DeSoto Commission thought so, tracking the expedition south along the Little Missouri and the Ouachita, as the Spaniards made their way back toward the Great River in late 1541. Camden, or perhaps Calion, says the report, was very probably the Autiamque of Elvas, or Utiangue, as Garcilaso has it. Here is Elvas:

"The next day they came to Autiamque. They found much Maiz laid up in store, and French beanes [?] and walnuts, and prunes, great store of all sorts. They took some Indians which were gathering together the stuffe which their wives had hidden. This was a Champion countrie, and well inhabited. The Governor [DeSoto] lodged in the best part of the towne, and commanded presently to make a fense of timber round about the Campe distant from the houses, that the Indians might not hurt them without by fire... hard by this town passed a River, that came out of the Province of Cayas."

So far, so good. The puzzling part comes next. Elvas tells us that they spent the winter at Autiamque, three months in all, with plenty of food. The Indians showed them how to snare rabbits, both cottontails and another breed which were "as big as great Hares, longer, and having greater loines." These may have been swamp rabbits, whose loines are great indeed.

They passed the winter there resting and trapping rabbits "which until that time they knew not how to catch... The Indians taught them how to take them: which was, with great springes, which lifted their feete from the ground: and the snare was made with a strong string, whereunto was fastened a knot of cane, which ran close about the neck of the conie, because they should not gnaw the string. They took many in the fields of Maiz, especiallie when it freezed or snowed. The Christians staied
there one whole moneth so inclosed with snow, that they went not out of towne..."

Snowbound in Camden for a month? Or Calion? Garcilaso puts it at six months:

"There was much snow that year in this province, and for a month and a half they were unable to venture into the countryside because of the extensive amount that had fallen. Nevertheless, with the great luxury of firewood and provisions, they passed the best of all winters they experienced in Florida, and they themselves confessed that they could not have been more comfortable in the dwellings of their families in Spain."

DeSoto left Autiamque-Camden in March of 1542, moving down the Ouachita, and after 10 days' journey, which would put him somewhere in Louisiana, "there fell out such weather, that foure daies he could not travell for snow." Snowbound in Louisiana in March?

An exceptionally severe winter. Either the geography is all wrong or the weather, over 450 years, has changed. Knowing nothing about changing weather patterns, but, being a journalist and thus having no scruples about commenting on the matter, I think they may well have changed. It was, after all, not quite 200 years ago when Dunbar and his men were besieged with snow and ice near Hot Springs, with temperatures in the single digits.

Two months after leaving Camden, somewhere on the Great River in the Ferriday-Natchez area, Hernando DeSoto died on May 21, 1542, of malaria or fatigue or despair. The soldiers hid the body so the Indians couldn't see that this Childe of the Sunne (as he had introduced himself) was mortal, and then they placed it in a hollow live-oak log, or in a shroud weighted with sand (the accounts differ), and by night rowed it out into the Mississippi, at a place where it was 19 fathoms or 114 feet deep. "They lowered him in the center of the river, and commending his soul to God, watched him sink at once to its depths."

I asked about local historians and was directed to a lawyer, Col. John Norman Warnock, U.S. Army, Retired, who is almost 80 years old. He lives south of Camden in the community of Elliott and kindly agreed to see me. His house had recently burned, he told me over the telephone, and he was now living and working in a trailer.

I took this to mean a mobile home, but it was in fact a trailer, a blue and white 28-footer that you could hook up to your stretched black Cadillac limousine, if you had one, and be off in short order, with a good laugh for everybody left behind. The Colonel has two of these extra long Cadillacs, a 1974 and a 1979 model. The battery and the alternator—"that big, $180 alternator"—had been stolen from the '74, and one tire was flat, but the '79 was running fine.

"I buy them from a man in Dallas," he said. "I like the protection and comfort of a big car."

The trailer was parked in the shade of big pinoak trees. Two shaggy little Pomeranian dogs yapped at me. There were eight Rhode Island Red hens in the yard. They were older chickens, laying hens who no longer laid eggs, but who were still proving useful in their retirement years. "Look. See how they peck at everything that moves? They keep this yard completely free of ticks."

The Colonel, who retired from the Army in 1965, is a small, dapper man with soft white hair. He reminded me of Lew Ayres, the actor. He wore a tan cord suit, tan shirt, and tan bow tie. His manner was quiet, polite, very Southern. The trailer was packed to the roof with boxes, files, books, clothes, leaving only a tiny space at one end for his office. His secretary, a young lady, was typing away at something. She sat at a little shelf-like table similar to the ones used by flight engineers on the smaller Boeings. The Colonel graciously gave me the only other seat, a stool, and he stood as we talked about the Ouachita. I believe there would have been more room in one of the Cadillacs, as there was no more than 18 inches of space between us.

His family, he said, both the Warnocks and the Moons, had been in Ouachita County since the 1830s, and an enormous amount of valuable documents and memorabilia had been lost in the house fire. Did he plan to rebuild? He said he didn't know, hinting at certain dark obstacles, "You lend people money, and they won't pay you back."

He, like Dee Brown, rode the steamboat *Ouachita* in the 1920s, and he remembers how it would stop to pick up driftwood for the boiler furnace. It got stuck on a sandbar once, and by the time it reached Camden all the bananas had turned brown. "They sold them for 25 cents—a stalk! The boys around here got sick stuffing themselves with soft bananas."

As he recalls, this last gasp of steamboat service came in right after the locks and dams were built in 1926. "That was old Captain [L.V.] Cooley who started it, and I believe it all died with him too, around 1934 or '35. It was quite a thing, the band playing, the dancing at night on the river. All this was cotton country then. Gins everywhere. A lot of cotton was shipped out of here. Now it's all in pine trees."

Colonel Warnock himself brought a boat up to Camden from New Orleans at the end of World War II. He bought it in Germany, a 40-foot cruiser with a steel hull, and had it shipped to New Orleans on the deck of a merchant vessel. "It drew three feet of water, about the same as the steamboats. I came up in June and had no trouble at all." The "liquor" discharge from the local paper mill damaged the hull, he claims, and some years back he sent it to Louisiana for repairs. It remains there, beached, in some sort of legal limbo "at a Lebanese-Italian boatyard in Morgan City."

I asked him why Camden did not make more of its history. There is, for example, no DeSoto Street.

"No, they don't make much of anything around here. You try to put on some Civil War thing and nobody's interested. Why, there were more Civil War battles fought around here than around Natchez. Small ones, yes, but still."

The oil country begins a few miles south at Louann. There are stripper wells along the highway. The horsehead pumping units bow and rise ever so slowly as they pull up four or five barrels of crude a day. "The strippers have become drippers," I was told in Smackover. Here in a downtown park, a metal plaque states that "the French settlers called this area 'Sumac Couvert.' This was anglicized to 'Smackover' by later English settlers." Covered with sumac? Sumac bower? Sumac shelter?

Perhaps, but I suspect Dunbar is more likely correct. He made this entry for November 20, 1804: "At 7 1/2 a.m. passed a creek which forms a deep ravine in the high lands and has been called 'Chemin Couvert.'" This was Smackover Creek, where it enters the Ouachita from a deep cut. Dunbar was dealing with hunters, guides, settlers, soldiers, and such maps as there were, and he very probably got the name right, "Chemin Couvert," covered way, which was soon corrupted into Smackover.

Upstream from the creek he tells of seeing an alligator "which surprised us much at this late season and so far north."

I paid $1.23 a gallon for regular gasoline at El Dorado, the oil city, more than at any other place along the way. On the other hand, my motel room cost only $21, and, a bonus, a man was practicing law in the next room. Two strange law offices in one day. This one, an ordinary motel room, had the lawyer's shingle fastened to the door, just above the number, with a single screw in the middle.

There were bits of Scotch tape on the ends to keep it from tilting, perhaps demoralizing his customers. I was all set if I woke up in the night with a start and the urgent feeling that I should dictate a codicil to my will. Against that piece of luck, however, I had to weigh this: The cafe I like in El Dorado was no longer serving an evening meal. The new, shorter serving hours were explained to me this way: "That woman that runs it, that was her sister that run it at night, and she got married and moved to Shreesport."

El Dorado, of course, is not on the river, but is close enough, and the town had steamboat service in the 19th century by way of the Champagnolle Landing. At Calion I looked over the first of the four new dams on the river, this one named for the late H.K. Thatcher, who worked for many years as a lobbyist and gadfly for the project. It is a mighty work of concrete and steel. On the far side, the Calhoun County side, high water was streaming unchecked over the low part of the dam. No one was about. No boats were in view. The lock water appeared stagnant, as though it had been standing undisturbed for some time. A dead and bloated buffalo fish with a cloudy eye lay washing about in the debris. The river looked almost as wide as the Arkansas at Little Rock.

Because of the high water, the ferry at Moro Bay wasn't running. I was to be denied another ferry ride south of Columbia, LA., for the same reason. The Arkansas Highway Department has only two other ferries left in operation, at Spring Bank on the Red, and at Bull Shoals Lake. Here in the backwater at Moro Bay, I saw a moccasin about two feet long. He was swimming toward me and then stopped when he saw me, undulating in place, but not showing much fear.

The Saline River now comes in from the East to meet the Ouachita and form a kind of overflow swamp known locally as the Marie Saline. It is not named for a lady, as we used to think. Dunbar explains: "Between 11 and 12 o'clock passed on the right the 'marais de la Saline' (Salt-lick marsh). There is here a small marshy lake, but it is not intended by its name to convey any idea of a property of brackishness in the lake or marsh, but merely that it is contiguous to some of the licks." It was the same for the Saline River, then going by the name of "the grand bayou de la Saline (Salt-lick Creek)." Hunters, Dunbar says, took their boats some 300 river miles up the Saline, and "all agree that none of the springs which feed this Creek are salt; it has obtained its name from many buffalo salt licks which have been discovered near to the Creek."

Here, where the river crosses into Louisiana, is the lowest point in Arkansas, with the state Geology Commission giving it as 55 feet above sea level and the Corps of Engineers at 43.8 feet. This water has fallen 1,550 feet since it left Polk County, and it still has a long way to go before reaching the Gulf of Mexico, and only another 50 feet to fall. All this low country is now the Felsenthal National Wildlife Refuge, a swampy wilderness much like that of the White River Refuge, but with not quite so much hardwood timber.

West of Crossett near the Highway 82 bridge there is a new slackwater harbor, ready for business, with a wharf on concrete pilings and a new and empty warehouse. Again, no one was about. There were no boats. I drove the back roads above the Felsenthal

Dam. Always at some point I would run into a body of water and have to turn around. These are deep woods. I saw a house on stilts near the river, not a hunting lodge but a home, with clothes on a line and broken toys in the yard. There was no power line, and no telephone line, television antenna, satellite dish, or mail box. Getting your news by barge might not be so bad.

I detected no immediate cultural change as I entered Louisiana, perhaps a bit more clear-cutting of timber, but not much more than I saw in the Huttig area. At Sterlington I did find an industry that uses the river for shipping, the Angus Chemical Co., which has little docks and terminal pipes projecting out from the river bank. But much of this plant was destroyed by an explosion and fire in May, in which nine workers were killed and more than a hundred injured.

All along the lower river I stopped in towns and asked about the tonnage shipped on the river. The current tonnage, I thought, when compared to the tonnage of bygone years and the projected tonnage of the future, would give us all something to mull over. At city halls and chambers of commerce I would be shown into the office of a very courteous if puzzled man. He would tap a pencil on the desk. "Yes. Let's see now. The tonnage. Brenda, why don't you get Charles some coffee." Brenda would later be sent here and there in search of an elusive folder that just might contain some river matter. Long after it became clear that no one knew or cared about the tonnage, I asked about the tonnage. I didn't care either, but I felt a nagging dreary duty to come up with some figures.

Monroe is the biggest city on the Ouachita, with a population, including West Monroe, of 65,000. The river splits the two towns. There is a high bridge on Interstate 20, and three older bridges that can be raised or pivoted on turntables to allow river traffic to pass. But days go by at a time with no call to raise or swing the bridges, I was told by Bruce Fleming, planning director for Monroe, and there is no "Port of Monroe," as such, though the city does own an excursion boat, the *Twin City Queen*, which it rents out to clubs.

It was getting through to me that people living on the Ouachita no longer see their river as a highway in any important commercial sense. It is just there, every day, a pretty stream of water, handy for recreation, useful in dry years for irrigation, inconveniently overflowing every spring.

Somewhere along here in the pecan groves on Bayou DeSiard I stopped talking about tonnage and started asking people how they pronounced "bayou." It came out "by-yoo" and "by-oo," about half and half, with an occasional "bya." We said "byo" in southeast Arkansas, or "bya." In defending this usage, I pointed out to a woman in Monroe that Hank Williams says "byo" in his song "Jambalaya." Yes, she said, but Hank was forcing a cheap rhyme with "me-o-my-o." I countered by informing her that Arkansas Post (1686, Tonti) is older than New Orleans (1718, Bienville). She didn't believe me. Nor did she believe me when I informed her that "bayou" is not a French word.

It is a Choctaw word, "bayuk," which the French explorers adopted for use in the Mississippi valley, calling any sizeable stream entering one of the bigger rivers a "bayou." But then it seems they left it behind when they returned home. The word is not listed in

Cassell's or Heath's French dictionaries, so I suppose it is actually Choctaw-French-American. The Corps of Engineers could not give me an official definition of a bayou, or of a creek or a river. I would have expected these officers—soldiers, engineers, bureaucrats, all tidy men—to have had some strict system of classification and nomenclature, but not so. In this matter they defer to local tradition. If the people of north Arkansas want to call their fastflowing, whitewater, mountain stream a bayou, the Illinois Bayou, say, then a bayou it is, and there is no objection from the Corps.

South of Monroe the river was out of its banks, lapping at the highway in places and pushing into the cotton and soybean fields. As it draws closer to the Mississippi, it joins a tangle of rivers and bayous that are flowing more or less parallel here on the alluvial plain, and sprawling in wide meanders. Roads and ferries were closed and I had to make detours. Highway builders in Louisiana work on the Jeffersonian assumption that west (and east) is the proper direction of travel. There are fine east-west interstate highways, but traveling north and south is slow going. But then road building is an expensive business here, with so much fill dirt being required for the elevated and literal high ways.

I stopped at Columbia to pay a call on former Governor John McKeithen of Louisiana. He lives on a farm here and keeps an office downtown. Something of the squire in these parts, he is perhaps the most notable figure living on the bank of the Ouachita. But he was out of town.

More failures: I couldn't track down a commercial fisherman, and there are a few left, from Calion on down, netting catfish, buffalo and drum, in descending order of value. I turned up no song about the Ouachita, and it is certainly as deserving as the Wabash or the Swanee or the Red. I did find two poems celebrating it, both written in the 19th century, by Albert Pike and a George P. Smoote. I showed them to a woman who is a judge of such things, and she read them unmoved.

"Welcome to Jonesville / Where the Four Rivers Meet." It is the end of the line, Jonesville, population 2,620, some 30 miles by road and bridge from Natchez. Jonesville makes the further claim of being DeSoto's ancient Indian town of Anilco, at the mouth of the Anilco or Ouachita River. No one knows if these Indians were the same as the "Ouasitas," a small Caddoan tribe first mentioned by Tonti in 1690. They moved west in the 18th century and were absorbed by the Natchitoch Indians.

I stood behind the grain elevators of the Bunge Corporation and watched the Ouachita, still greenish, for all the flooding as it poured into the Tensas (pronounced Tensaw), and where they both suddenly became the Black River. The fourth river, called the Little River, enters the flow a bit farther down. A half-mile upstream from the mouth of the Ouachita the Bunge Corp. has a dock and a big blower pipe, where barges are loaded with soybeans and grain. Here at last was a volume shipper.

"Oh, yes, we use the Ouachita all the time," the manager told me. "That last half-mile of it, anyway."

STRAIGHT-UP BOOK REVIEWS
By Tom Lavoie

Escape Velocity: A Charles Portis Miscellany
Charles Portis
Jay Jennings, ed.
Butler Center for Arkansas Studies
butlercenter.com
380 pages, hardback

Charles Portis wrote one of Garrison Keillor's favorite novels; Jonathan Lethem calls him "everybody's favorite least-known great novelist"; and Roy Blount, Jr. says Portis "could be Cormac McCarthy if he wanted to, but he'd rather be funny." When the *New York Herald Tribune* folded and Portis quit his journalism job, according to Tom Wolfe, he moved back to Arkansas, wrote novels and got rich off the royalties after his novel *True Grit* became one of John Wayne's last great films: "It was too goddamned perfect to be true," Wolfe wrote, "and yet there it was." Then, like Salinger, Portis pretty much disappeared to live an ordinary life, laboring over his writing until he got it perfect.

He continued to write, including four more brilliant novels, the last of which came out in 1991. (All of them have been reissued and kept in print by Overlook Press.) In editing *Escape Velocity*, Jay Jennings has done a terrific job of tracking down many of Portis' works, including some stunningly good examples of his early newspaper reporting, as well as short stories, travel pieces, a memoir and a never-before-published comic three-act play, *Delray's New Moon*.

Portis has always been the prose stylist par excellence. His writing positively glistens in an autobiographical piece called "Combinations of Jacksons" which he published in *The Atlantic* in 1999. At the age of nine Portis conducted his first experiments in breathing underwater with reeds. The year was 1943, Mount Holly, Arkansas. "It was something I needed to learn in life so as to be ready to give my pursuing enemies the slip. At that time they were Nazi spies and Japanese saboteurs . . . . I could slow them down a little with pinecone grenades, but I couldn't stop them." The plan to use reeds didn't work out so well. They were the wrong kind. They "tended to collapse, like wet paper drinking straws." Still, like Ralphie defending his family from outlaws in *A Christmas Story* with his dependable Red Ryder BB gun, Portis had his two-blade Barlow knife: "My Barlow was at the service of the nation." The piece ends with Portis recalling his Uncle Sat:

> I saw him now and then over the years, talking away, as ever, but I can call up his face more clearly, his red farmer's face, from an earlier time, at that kitchen table, over the newspaper maps. I can see the winter stubble in his fields,

too, on that dreary January day in 1942. Broken stalks and a few dirty white shreds of bumblebee cotton. Everyone who was there is dead and buried now except me.

Escape Velocity, following Joel and Ethan Coen's remake of *True Grit*, could bring about a well-deserved revival for the nearly eighty-year-old Portis. The title comes from his novel *The Dog of the South*: "A lot of people leave Arkansas and most of them come back sooner or later," Portis wrote. "They can't quite achieve escape velocity."

The Ecopoetry Anthology
Ann Fisher-Wirth and Laura-Gray Street, eds.
Trinity University Press
tupress.org
672 pages, paperback

> *What drew us to the magnet of your dying?/...*
> *Voyager, chief of the pelagic world,/...*
> *Master of the whale-roads,*
> *let the white wings of the gulls*
> *spread out their cover.*
> *You have become like us,*
> *disgraced and mortal.*

These powerful lines are from Stanley Kunitz's "The Wellfleet Whale." It's included in the rich and generous *Ecopoetry Anthology* edited by Ann Fisher-Wirth and Laura-Gray Street. All the poems in the collection, like Kunitz's, deal with the environment, with nature, the animals, the trees, mountains and rivers, and man's relationship with them.

The editors tell us nature poetry has been around as long as poetry has, but around 1960 more people began to pay attention to an environment and nature in crisis, and more poetry began to reflect this. They quote Williams Carlos Williams' line, "Poetry does not tamper with the world, but moves it." So here is an abundance of poems: praising songs, incantations, lists, elegies, rhapsodies, jeremiads, each in their very different ways, with a power "to break through our dulled disregard, our carelessness, our despair, reawakening our sense of the vitality and beauty of nature."

Here are 208 American poets and 320 poems—abundance indeed. Part one presents historical poets, from Whitman to Levertov, poets who predate the environmental revolution. Then follow our contemporaries, 176 of them, from A.R. Ammons to Robert Wrigley. It's apropos that the first poem in this section is Ammons' seminal piece, "Corson's Inlet," where he observes nature as he walks along his Jersey shore dunes: "in nature there are few sharp lines: there are areas of/ primrose/ more or less dispersed."

The editors have done a superb job of providing works by the well-knowns and the lesser knowns. So, alongside such long-time nature-poem heroes as W.S. Merwin, Gary Snyder and Mary Oliver, one will discover beautiful and moving pieces by a Patrick Lawler, Davis McCombs, or Annie Boutelle. Some will be disappointed at the absence of a favorite poem, but most of the "great" nature pieces of our era are here: Kinnell's overwhelming "The Bear," Bly's moving prose poem "The Dead Seal," and Robert Hass's mini-epic "State of the Planet," beginning with, "October on the planet at century's end." Hass has provided a wise introduction, noting that the editors have revealed the ways our "nature poetry developed toward an ecopoetics, toward the necessity of imagining a livable earth."

A Poet's Revolution: The Life of Denise Levertov
Donna Krolik Hollenberg
University of California Press
ucpress.edu
532 pages, hardcover

The poet Denise Levertov (1923-1997) is finally getting the biographical treatment she deserves. Less than a year after the publication of Dana Greene's *A Poet's Life*, Donna Krolik Hollenberg presents the comprehensive, in-depth *A Poet's Revolution*—an effort, she says, to "observe the connections between life and work in a way that illuminates the greatness of the major poems."

Levertov was born in England into many cultures: Jewish, German, Welsh, English. Well educated, she began writing poetry early. At twelve, she sent some poems to T.S. Eliot for comment; he was encouraging. After her first book, *The Double Image*, was published in 1947, she married and moved to the US, where she came under the influence of such poets as Robert Duncan and Lawrence Ferlinghetti.

With her title, Hollenberg places Levertov's life in the right place, revolution—which the poet embraced as "the only word / we have." Her poetry was filled with political and anti-war material; some felt it detracted from her art, but she kept at it until her later years when, after converting to Catholicism, her work took on a very religious, contemplative tone.

Hollenberg quotes extensively from the poems to show that Levertov's life was a "process of growth" personally and artistically. In the end, she points to the poem "Hymns to the Darkness" and its line about "embracing the dark." Levertov died in a Seattle hospital on December 20, 1997—the darkest night of the year.

Note: Previous and slightly differing versions of these reviews were published in *Shelf Awareness* at shelf-awareness.com.

NO B.S. REVIEWS
By C. Prozac

America: A History in Verse,
Vol. IV 1971-1985
Ed Sanders
Blake Route Press
2000 pages, CD

Talk about epic
Menagerie of Sleazery!
This 500-page continuation
of legendary Black Sparrow tradition
now exists on disc
eternal bardmaster Ed Sanders
fleshing out America
thru investigative verse
placing politics
into perspective
ie, '71:

> "John Kerry tossed first the medals
>   given to him by two vets who could not be there . . . .
>
>   It made an impact beyond its numbers
>   like Dada in Zürich
>   the Beats at Columbia
>   Che lashed to a chopper skid
>   a burning bus in Birmingham"

Howev
this behemoth of bias & scholarship
journalism & humor is
at its best with presidents
especially w/ mind-cringing litany
of damning Nix deceit
ie, '72:

> "Three days later there was a National Prayer Breakfast
> after which Nixon and Billy Graham
>   were having a sleaze-brimming chat
>   in the Oval Office
>
> about the putative Jewish domination of the media
>
> There's a tape of it—
> Nixon: 'Jews—Jesus Christ! . . . The Jews are—
> they're malicious, [unintelligible] immoral bunch of bastards.
> That goddamn girl the other night was Jewish!'"

Then all sorts of secret plots
dissected and assembled for our eyes
like Nix framing Senator Muskie
for Cannuckism
while commissioning the planting
of Black Panther literature
on Wallace's almost
assassin Bremer

as for aftermath of Watergate:

> "Ford was not a genius
> but to a nation with
>
> napalm-sizzled skin
>   in the nostrils of its soul
>
> he was a sight for sore sighs"

but then, Surprise!
Sanders shows Carter as whimp
of ineffective leadership
ie, '78:

> "He failed his trek in history
> by refusing to alleviate the suffering
>   the missed operations
>   the millions of early deaths
>
> because of a lack of national health care . . . .
>
> Too much creativity for Jimmy
> because Jimmy was sometimes not that creative"

After that, Sanders blasts
Carter with "his rather conservative,
    19th century Whig economic mind-set"

& chants like
    "Human rights, Jimmy, human rights"

so of course this particular history eye
ain't gonna cut any slack
to "Raygun" or
"Reag-Rug"
ie, '81:

> They called it Reagonomics
> but its real name was "Enrich the Rich"

enter Nicaragua
star wars, Sarajevo
starvation in Africa
just say no, Afghanistan
the premature birth of baby FOX News
and AIDS!

It's like someone slipped
a roofie to an entire nation
and then a poet came along and
captured us exactly as we are
with our pants down
our testosterone up
and ignorance at
an all-time high

It's the portrait of a failed era
but optimistic in the end

and that's the promise
on whirling Gaia

Oh may it last forever!

Abandoned Fragments
Franz Kafka
Ina Pfitzner, trans.
Sun Vision Press
240 pages, paperback

This surprising collection of
never-before-
translated flashes
erupts with a whimsy
few attach
to our man Franz

ie:
"When I got home in the evening, I found . . . an overly large egg in the middle of the room. It was almost as high as the table and bulged accordingly. It quietly rocked back and forth. I was very curious, took the egg between my legs and carefully cut it in two with my pocketknife . . . out leapt a stork-like, still featherless bird flapping the air with its too-short wings"

                        the bird then communicates through beak-writing
                                  a metamorphosis occurs (hmmm....)
                                 and the two learn to fly together

or:
"My two hands began to fight. They shut the book I had been reading and pushed it aside so that it wouldn't be in the way. They saluted me and appointed me their referee . . . . the two of them are now lying on top of one another, the right hand stroking the back of the left, and I, the dishonest referee, am nodding in approval"

                                     "On Jewish Theater" is also an
                                                     evocative essay
                                                   expertly translated
                                                        too bad, though
                                              this publisher's an imprint
                                                       of Creation Books
                                                       and has swindled
                                              many an author & estate
                                                             moral being:

buy it used
so you ain't
supporting a thief.

Captain Poetry's Sucker Punch:
A Guide to the Homeric Punkhole, 1980-2012
Kenneth Warren, ed.
BlazeVOX
470 pages, paperback

                    A massive compendium
                    of essays and articles
                    on postmodern poetics,
                    this sucker punch serves up
                    both Bo Diddly and Bob Kaufman
                    d.a. levy Kathy Acker
                    Eds Sanders and Dorn
                    Duncan Snyder Eschleman
                    Kerouac Orlovsky Corso
                    Norse Wakoski
                    Myles Hirschman Cage
                    Creeley Hollo
                    Olson Blake
                    Waldman and Spiderman
                    just to name
                    a couple dozen
                    practitioners of
                    "Street punk lineage
                    of bob-bop romanticism
                    and bravado scholarship" (Warren)

As Dale Smith notes in intro:
"*Captain Poetry's Sucker Punch* thrives in the outrider genre. At once disciplined and astute, studious and light-of-foot, it puts into useful tension the textures of life and art . . . Written over the course of thirty years for small press zines and journals, including . . . *House Organ*, this collection of essays represents an era in part neglected in the literary record."

So there.

Touch Each Other
Antler
Foothills Publishing
foothillspublishing.com
chapbook, 40 pages

mythic Antler has this thing
for combining stats and song
to create a micro-universe
of legendary eco-verse
take pilot poem for examp:

> "Ornithologists discovered
>   each baby robin in the nest requires
>   14 feet of earthworms a day
>   to survive
> So if there are 6 baby robins in the nest
>   it means 84 feet of earthworms a day . . .
>   that means each baby robin needs
>   42 earthworms a day . . .
>   each worm has 10 hearts . . .
>   420 earthworm hearts a day . . .
> Hmmm. . . . no wonder
>   robin song
>   is so
>   heartful!
> How many worms
>   do I need to eat
>   every day
>   before I can fly and sing?"

& the answer is:
Zedfully Zed!

Aye, this elegantly
papyrused book
already soars in Milky Way
charged with Transcendental ghosts
Antler's spirit already singing
to the honey suckle
of our breast.

RACIST LIKE ME
By Joshua D. Bellin

Years ago, when my wife and I had just settled into our first house and our now pre-teen daughter was little more than a month old, I got held up by a black guy. I'd walked over to our former apartment to check the mail, which didn't seem to be arriving at our new home. It was nighttime, and snowing, probably a stupid time to take a stroll. The guy was ahead of me, and when he doubled back alarms should have gone off but didn't. He was far away, I couldn't see him distinctly, my mind was on other things, fatherhood and home ownership and the start of the spring semester, a week off. It wasn't until the gun was in my face that I realized anything peculiar was going on.

The mugger didn't get anything from me—I wasn't even wearing a watch—but he did make me lie face down in the snow while he frisked me. "I swear to you," I kept saying to him. At one point I foolishly reached for my pocket to prove I had nothing; I'm lucky he didn't shoot me then. When he left I stayed down a good five minutes, my fingertips wet in the snow, my body not registering the chill. Walking back unnaturally fast, feeling as if my feet weren't touching the ground, I managed to stay calm, only my breathing a bit off tempo. But when my wife met me at the door with our bundled daughter and asked what had taken so long, my voice choked and I cried.

The cop who came wanted a description. I couldn't give him one. "You were looking at the gun, right?" he said. That was true—it seemed to blot out everything, even the hand holding it—but that wasn't the real reason. I'd seen the man's face. But once he pulled the gun it disappeared, never to return. In a perverse parody of racial profiling, I robbed the robber of a face when, having fulfilled the stereotype of AAA (Armed African American), he no longer needed one.

As a professor whose work centers on the representation of race in American literature and culture, I wish I could say this incident is what corrupted me, turned me into the sort of bigot my teaching and scholarship have sought to expose. It would be truer, however, to see my teaching and scholarship as acts of expiation, or even exorcism, for the racism I've long recognized to be my own. I've feared black men most of my life, an unreasoning, visceral fear manifested by the clench in my chest when one (except, oddly, this one) nears me at night. But there are other symptoms, less obvious, masked as bravado or disdain: safely ensconced in my own vehicle, I scoff when one pulls up beside me, the bass thump of some rap anthem rattling his SUV. Or when another peels around me, I think not "reckless driver" but "black guy," "ghetto," or even "gang-banger." When a dark, dour face flashes on the eleven o'clock news, as it always does, associated with some drive-by or rape or crime against humanity, all my reading and knowledge of economic inequality and judicial bias and selective reporting go out the window and I see what they want me to see: a black beast loose in my neighborhood. When a black teenager from the school where my wife works showed up on the news one night, accused of butchering a baby in a hail of indiscriminate bullets, I didn't mourn, as she did, the waste of two young lives. I thought, "there goes another one." I was almost glad, in the sick way racists are, to see my prejudices confirmed.

The story we tell about racism in this country has two threads, one individual and the other social. The individual says that racism comes from education: you learn it, you can unlearn it too. The social says that, thanks to the integration of our schools two generations ago, the nation as a whole is gradually outgrowing racism, or never learning it to begin with. But my own experience suggests that neither of these stories is accurate—or at least, that the latter offers no real answer to the former. A child of enlightened parents and integrated schools, I received no proper training in racism. On the contrary, I received lesson upon lesson dedicated to withering it in the bud. Yet a lifetime of such schooling has proved inadequate to touch attitudes far more basic, beliefs bred in some abyss I can't quite identify. At most, my formal education has enabled me to intellectualize my racism, to name it for what it is, to recognize its voice when it croons to me like a demon lover. To own it—in part by distancing myself from it—but not to root it out or will it away.

#

In the early seventies, that heady decade of faith in progress through social design, my parents sent me and my siblings to an elementary school, just opened, in the almost exclusively black neighborhood of Pittsburgh's East Hills. In the projects, as we said in those days. It was a model school, showcasing all the latest pedagogical innovations—open classrooms, curvilinear architecture, ramps instead of stairs—and it was, I suppose, in need of white families to volunteer their kids to be bused in. The new school must have been part of some citywide plan to revitalize this impoverished and crime-ridden neighborhood, for along with it a new mall went up, anchored by a popular department store where, one Christmas, I wrestled black grannies for the fair-haired doll of my sister's dreams. Without our consent or even consultation, my parents pulled us—my brother (fourth grade), my sister (kindergarten), and me (second)—from our neighborhood school, literally across the cobbled alley from our home, and put us on the city buses that served this latest experiment in integrated education.

I learned to love it there. I had seen few black people to that point, knew none personally (unless you counted our cleaning lady, Queenie, whose name for the longest time I thought was Cleanie). I remember being startled by how pale my classmates' palms were, and asking one of them whether he'd been dunked in chocolate. I was genuinely shocked when he slugged me. But I came to love the open classrooms, where "teams" moved from activity to activity in fluid transitions; the art room, huge and bright and overflowing with crayons and manila paper; the gym, where we shimmied up slick poles and dared each other to slide down, courting rope burns worse than any rope could leave. I hated the bus monitor (black), an evil hag who had it out for me because, according to her, I "lied." (Actually, I entertained my friends on the long rides there and back with stories I made up about Snoopy and his Sopwith Camel.) I wasn't crazy about the vice principal (white), who prowled the halls looking for troublemakers, or our third-grade math teacher (black), who snuck up behind us and slammed his yardstick on our desk if our attention wavered. But overall, I had a good time in my four years there, and as an adult, I'm thankful to my parents for their foresight and, I guess, bravery in volunteering their children to serve the common good.

My brother hated the place. For him, it was a battle from day one, a specifically racial battle between ghetto thugs and the innocents whose bleeding-heart parents had sent their own flesh and blood to the front lines. He resented being a guinea pig, resented leaving his friends; though his athletic skills blossomed under the greatly enhanced competition, it infuriated him that he had to prove himself on the hoops court to a bunch of dumb-ass bros from the hood. He fought constantly. When he talks about those days, he reverts to the big-brother idiom he seldom uses on me anymore: I was too young, too naïve, too brainwashed by Dad's liberal mumbo-jumbo to see the place for the shithole it really was.

But I guess he did take something from there. He's currently a teacher in our hometown's public school system, working at a predominantly black middle school. He relocated his own family to the suburbs, though, rather than face the middle school options that awaited his two sons. And though he works as hard as anyone to inspire his class of almost entirely below-grade-level readers to reach for the stars—he possesses an incredible work ethic, always has—the comments he makes about their families, their character, their prospects are straight out of the neoliberal handbook on personal accountability and the pathology of the black family. I argue with him, I talk about institutional racism. He's not interested. So far as he's concerned, if only these twelve-year-old hos-in-training would stop spitting out babies, if only their drug-runner brothers would stop shooting off their mouths (and semiautomatics), if only their so-called leaders would stop blaming the white majority for their problems, maybe they could join the civilized world instead of turning their neighborhood, and his classroom, into a freaking zoo.

I know less about my sister's elementary school experience—what eight-year-old boy pays attention to his kid sister?—but I do know she now works as a lawyer helping death-row inmates, many of them black, through the appeals process. So in her, as in my brother, our parents' dreams live on in a racially divided world their dreams did little to alter.

And me? Well, you know me. I have all the right opinions, all the right credentials. I've read widely on race and racism, I've written on everything from *Uncle Tom's Cabin* to *King Kong* to Hurricane Katrina. I introduce English majors to the great voices of African-American literature (Phillis Wheatley, Olaudah Equiano, Frederick Douglass, W.E.B. Du Bois); I do a special unit on the poets and critics of the New Negro Renaissance. My student teachers read Jonathan Kozol's *The Shame of the Nation*, a seething exposé of the separate and unequal education that prevails in today's racially segregated public schools. I contribute to the requisite causes, I say the proper things, I hold doors for black and white people alike. I argue with my older brother, trying to change or at least shake his beliefs. Only trouble is, I can't seem to shake my own.

#

I made a number of friends among the neighborhood kids at East Hills: Isaac, Billy, Devoe. I'm far happier to see them at class reunions than the faces from my own liberal-Jewish enclave. But Troy was special, not only my friend but, almost, my surrogate big brother. He was one of the best respected kids at school, a kind of hero: tall, good-looking, soft-spoken and courteous, a whiz on the basketball court. I'm not sure what he saw in me, a scrawny little white kid who mostly liked to draw pictures and make animated movies. Maybe, now that I think of it, I was his way into that other world from which he'd been barred; maybe it wasn't compassion alone that led him to take me under his wing. Once he did, though, my school life took a definite turn for the better: no one dared mess with me, everyone thought I was cool. Looking back, it may have been largely due to Troy's influence that I remember my elementary school experience so fondly. If my brother had found such a protector, maybe things would have been different for him too. But of course he never would have found one, never would have looked; he was determined to fight this war on his own.

I stayed friends with Troy through middle school, then fell out of touch with him in high school, where, re-versing the terms under which we'd met, I walked and he was bused. He became a star on the basketball team, which kept him pretty busy, I guess. More importantly, we no longer had any classes together after ninth grade, where the only period we shared was gym. I was in the Scholars program; he was what we dismissively called "mainstream" (I still don't know the official name for it), and our paths never crossed except occasionally in the hallways, where he'd still give me a grin and a high five. By senior year I'd lost contact with him entirely. Like everyone in the cohort of brainy white kids who'd become my friends, I was too engrossed in AP classes, National Honor Society, and Ivy League admissions to pay attention to the mainstream kids. Though I watched him walk across the stage to the screams of his family and fans, though I knew he was on a basketball scholarship somewhere or other, I never spoke to or heard from him again.

At my ten-year reunion I received a status report: Troy had been shot and killed shortly after graduation. My contact (not Isaac or Billy or Devoe; one of my white classmates) was unclear on the details, didn't know if Troy had ever played college ball. Nor did he know the nature of the crime, whether Troy had been mixed up in something, some gang or drug activity, or whether he'd been an innocent bystander. I'll never forget how he told me: by placing a finger to his head, thumb cocked, and making the sound of the explosion. "He killed himself?" I asked, disbelieving. The truth, that my childhood friend and guardian had become another statistic in the war we white people mostly watch but deeply fear, was even harder to accept.

#

The first day at our racially mixed elementary school, the student population clustered in an auditorium still smelling of lacquer and fresh paint to learn "Black and White," the song popularized by Three Dog Night. It couldn't have been more perfect, more prophetic: "The ink is black, the page is white / Together we learn to read and write." I liked it; I remember clapping to its bouncy, jaunty beat. What I didn't know at the time was that the tune had originally been written to commemorate the Supreme Court's Brown vs. Board of Education decision in 1954, the decision that paved the way for schools like ours. We were part of history. Sure, a fight broke out in the middle of the music lesson—I realize now, as I didn't then, how terrible it must have been for the neighborhood kids to finally get a decent, a beautiful school, then be forced to share it with us, as if it needed our pale presence to justify its existence—but together we would, as the song says, grow to see the light, to see the light.

Years later, my old school, perpetually in danger of being shut down once kids like me stopped going there, experienced a rebirth under a district reorganization that christened it and other under-enrolled K-5's as magnets, with foreign-language instruction and rigorous curriculum. The slogan "*C'est magnifique!*" appeared on the bumper stickers of minivans as, for a time, white parents rediscovered the school and packed their kids onto yellow school buses for the half-hour trip to another part of town, another part of the world. But the renaissance was short-lived; maybe, as the choice of such an outmoded, genteel joke of a core language suggested, it never had a chance to be anything but. Several years ago, as the district population continued to dwindle, the school, like the long-vacant shopping mall, permanently closed. I last visited it when my wife and I were researching magnets for our daughter; I remembered its long circular drive, its abstract, Africanist sculptures, its high-ceilinged, sky-lit foyer from which, peering over a curved concrete balustrade, you viewed a charming tiled courtyard, fountain bubbling. It felt so much like home I almost signed my daughter up right then and there. But cooler heads (my wife's) intervening, geography and linguistic relevance led us to opt for the Spanish magnet instead—a good thing too, considering my former school's subsequent fate.

How did I come from there to here? When did I learn to fear the sons of my classmates? There were incidents, but most involved people my parents' generation, not my own: the time my evil bus aide dragged me to the office for an imagined infraction; the time my hulking black Language Arts teacher scooped me up and flung me over his shoulder when I, in some existential fifth-grade funk, stormed out of his classroom. But I never blamed these authority figures for the color of their skin; they were simply grownups, good and bad, unjust and fair. And when I flip through my high school yearbook, looking in the faces of Isaac, Billy, Devoe, Troy, I don't see black people but just people, friends I won and lost. Why, then, does my gut twist at the approach of the veiled stranger, when my heart and my head tell me it's wrong?

Had the gunman that night been a bit twitchier on the trigger finger, my wife would have escorted our daughter alone to her first day of kindergarten; my child would never have known me, my second child would never have been. But that anonymous punk's near-decision to rob me of my future has nothing to do with this, I know. He was no nemesis, no dark antagonist dispatched by the gods. He taught me no lesson. I made my own fate a long time ago.

#

My middle school, also newly built in the seventies, also integrated, also closed during the retrenchment that claimed my elementary school. The building still stands—they shifted a bunch of high school kids there, most of them black, while their crumbling neighborhood school underwent asbestos remediation—but the pattern remains the same: white exodus followed by plummeting performance followed by closure. They've renamed the place after our nation's first black president, which is about as trenchant a symbol of the country's cracked non-conversation on race as can be: a thoroughly failed exercise in integrated education offered up in tribute to the man who supposedly proves integration's success. They'll tear the place down one of these days, as they've already torn down the factory that used to sit across the street, to make way for condos and a town square-style shopping mall, and the legacy—my legacy, our legacy—will be nothing but a hole in the ground.

And we are in danger, ever present danger, of repeating that act. My wife's rap sheet is even more immaculate than my own. Where I've railed against racism mostly as a theorist and spectator, she's worked for twenty-plus years among a predominantly black population of inner city kids, troubled kids no one else wants, kids born to crack-addicted mothers, kids who live a constant, single misstep from juvenile detention or prison or death. No one can call my wife a racist. Yet when we had children, she never doubted we should move from our apartment, just blocks from where we live now, because in so doing we crossed the imaginary line between the heavily black urban ghetto in which we then lived and she then worked to the city proper, with its promise of good and safe streets, good and safe schools. Just look what happened to you, she'd tell me now, mere blocks from the school our children would have attended! And when, this very year, we got word that our neighborhood might be redistricted such that our daughter and son would funnel into the ninety-plus percent black high school that serves one of the most desperately poor areas of the city, she was adamant that we'd do anything—defect to private school, skip town, picket city hall—to keep them out of that place. And it is a dire place: less than one-quarter of its students test proficient in core subjects, gunfire sounds outside on a daily basis. It is as close to hell as the ingenuity of our civilization can transport someone else's children.

I'd heard all her arguments before; everyone has. We can't save that school by ourselves; we can't sacrifice our own kids; etc. (Just look what happened to you...) They're all perfectly logical arguments, and all perfectly wrong. Because you get enough people believing them, especially people as progressive and ostensibly color-blind as my wife, and color-blindness starts to behave an awful lot like racism.

#

My racial training continued after I left home. At my college, its minority population steadied by affirmative action, apartheid and divestment were on everyone's tongues; shantytowns sprouted on the president's lawn. For four years I hung out with a black woman, wrestled with my desire for her, finally made out with her but never took it any further. She ended up marrying some other white guy from down the hall. In grad school, though the number of black classmates had dipped, the emphasis on black matters had swelled: the faculty included Houston Baker, one of the nation's foremost scholars of African-American literature; the reading list included the works of Henry Louis Gates, arguably even more influential than Baker in promoting the black literary canon. A Harvard professor and a close friend of Barack Obama, Gates would later be arrested by a white cop while trying to enter his own Cambridge townhouse. In my current academic position, I teach few black students (they tend to major in business, not English); those I do see are often athletes and poor performers, lost in the world of higher education. I watch these kids closely, not looking for trouble but not, I know, looking solely to help. One non-traditional black student recently accused me of racism when she got an "F" on a writing assignment. In my defense, it really was a terrible paper.

My education quickens; my racism only congeals.

I don't presume to know if you're racist like me. But you have to admit I'm a pretty fair specimen. If all that parental reinforcement and all that schooling didn't make a dent in foundational attitudes—if, instead, my book-learning lies like a veneer atop core beliefs, restraining them from everyday expression, corralling them into socially acceptable forms—then maybe education's power to attack such beliefs is more limited than we like to believe. Maybe racism has no rational cause and, as such, no rational cure. Or maybe what we count as education doesn't really count. Maybe the real lessons occur elsewhere: in the streets bedeviled and divided, those we know and trust, well-intentioned and misbegotten alike, furiously holding their dark other at bay. I had to go to school to learn about racism—but by then, I had already learned everything there was to know. Around here, it comes with the territory.

If you don't believe me, then ask yourself this, if you're white. When you're out alone at night, snow falling, spouse and child safely at home, and a black man crosses the street to your side, how do you react? What do you do? Maybe he's a mugger; maybe, in another life, he was the kid beside you in class. But it's dark, and it's too far away to tell.

WHAT WOULD DICKINSON DO?
By Greg Graham

I wonder if Emily Dickinson would have been the same Emily Dickinson if she'd had Facebook or Twitter (not to mention TV). I mean, seriously, today's recluse is an amateur compared to Dickinson. Our idea of being non-social is going home and watching reruns of *Friends* while flipping through our Facebook, Twitter, or Instagram feeds. If we're feeling anti-social and need to vent, we can sit on our couch and digitally offer scathing opinions about any number of things: books, dishwashers, earphones, politics, religion… the possibilities are endless. Heck, even if your personal life is a wreck, it feels good to score a victory for justice by skewering General Electric because their blender won't crush ice or by taking on that NRA fanatic who said something stupid on your sister-in-law's Facebook page.

Others choose not to contribute to their social network, but they're there, scrolling through the fabulous lives of their Facebook "friends" aka people they barely know or used to know. Especially when we're going through a hard time, maybe feeling lonely or disconnected because of a break-up or a screw-up, social networks can kick us while we're down. The writer Stephen Marche caused quite a stir when his article "Is Facebook Making Us Lonely" was published in *The Atlantic* in May of 2012. The online version of the article has received 367 comments to this point, with the top ranked comment coming from Tow Mater, who offers this insight: "It doesn't make anyone more lonely or narcissistic it just exposes it more brazenly." Talk about a letdown. But fear not, countless articles of retort have been written, bearing brilliant titles like "Is Facebook Making Us Lonely? Don't Be Stupid" and "Facebook Isn't Making Us Lonely." Marche's contentious claim is that we are superconnected but lonelier than ever. He points to the scene in *The Social Network* of Mark Zuckerberg sending a friend request to an ex-girlfriend and then waiting and clicking and waiting and clicking as emblematic of the day in which we live. "We have all been in that scene," Marche says, "transfixed by the glare of a screen, hungering for response."

At least the majority of us have, myself included. And I can't help but wonder if Ms. Dickinson would be equally sucked into the social networking vortex if she lived among us today. If she was writing on a laptop instead of in a notebook, would she have been taken out of what she called "the hallowing of pain"? Would she have striven to reach "the Summit" she spoke of if the social life she could not enjoy was available to her through digital images and electronic chit-chat popping up or scrolling across her screen in the comfort of her home? It's a fair question, I think.

I'm writing these words the same way Dickinson wrote—with a pen on paper, tucked away in my bedroom away from all my screens. But I won't be here long: I'll soon mosey into the kitchen where my laptop is sitting and I'll check my Twitter feed (Yay! Somebody with 2971 followers followed me! I am somebody). I'll look to see if anybody retweeted my last tweet, then I'll flip over to see how many likes my most recent blog post has garnered. I'll probably check to see if my favorite baseball team is winning, then glance at my email. Now what was that thing I was writing?

I wonder what Ms. Dickinson would think of me. She'd probably regard me as one of those about whom she wrote "The Summit is not given to him who strives severe at the middle of the hill, But He who has achieved the Top—All—is the price of All." The top she speaks of is not being the "top author" or "best poet." On the contrary, the top for her is pure inspiration, which she achieved because she stared down her loneliness, which she called "the icycles of the soul." And she describes reaching the top in ecstatic language:

> Deprived of other Banquet,
> I entertained Myself—
> At first—a scant nutrition—
> An insufficient Loaf—
> But grown by slender addings
> To so esteemed a size
> 'Tis sumptuous enough for me—
> And almost to suffice ...

This attainment of pure inspiration put into words on paper was enough for Dickinson. She shied away from publication. "Publication," she said, "is the auction of the mind." Well, if that be the case, count me as a big sellout, because as soon as I write something half-decent I'm scrounging for publishers. Between the pieces of writing I manage to get published, I write blog posts and send tweets like I'm throwing fishing lures into the water. I put it out there and pray for a nibble.

The propensity for fast and furious self-publication and self-promotion can weaken the strength of our work. And Emily Dickinson and I are not the only ones who think this way. Recording artist John Mayer had four million followers on Twitter and one day decided Twitter was taking over his creative life, so he quit. When asked why, Mayer responded:

> The tweets are getting shorter, but the songs are still 4 minutes long. You're coming up with 140-character zingers, and the song is still 4 minutes long…I realized about a year ago that I couldn't have a complete thought anymore. And I was a tweetaholic. I had four million Twitter followers, and I was always writing on it. And I stopped using Twitter as an outlet and I started using Twitter as the instrument to riff on,

and it started to make my mind smaller and smaller and smaller. And I couldn't write a song.

Using Dickinson's language, it seems Mayer found himself stopping midway. He was no longer reaching the Summit, and drastic measures had to be taken.

I'm impressed. Hell, I think I'll write a blog post about it. I bet people will really like that one. Wait… Oh, what's the use; I'll probably keep blogging and tweeting and begging somebody to publish my stuff. After all, I'm pretty sure I'm not the next Mayer or Dickinson or Thoreau. I've been working on one poem for four years now and it still sucks.

But I do worry about the Dickinsons and Thoreaus of the future. We can argue whether or not Facebook and Instagram are making all of us lonelier, but what about the ones who are naturally loners? Are image-focused social media keeping them in a perpetual state of pseudo-sociality, never satisfying but knocking the edge off? Is contentment harder to attain when surrounded by a virtual collection of beautiful people living fabulous lives? Most of us have probably found ourselves feeling down with nothing to do and flipping through Facebook, becoming more convinced that our lives suck: Our children are not as beautiful or successful, our parents don't love each other as much, our spouse isn't as hot, the list goes on and on. Sucked in by the compulsive desire for acceptance, self-loathing turns to virtual self-mutilation. It hurts so good.

Before everyone got plugged into everything, loners often learned to find contentment in solitude. The longing for connection has always been there for human beings, but today connection has become a digitally mediated impulse purchase. You don't have to go looking for it; you're just standing there in the check-out line and it's staring you in the face like a pack of gum.

How many loner types in the past went on to become brilliant writers, artists, or spiritual leaders? One has to wonder if Dickinson would have written such painfully beautiful poetry if she had access to Facebook, Instagram, or Twitter. Rather than scratching out meaning on those well-worn writing pads, she could've sat staring at endless pictures of acquaintances living the life she was apparently unable to manage.

I'm glad she didn't. Where would we be without the gritty ones who went through the fire and came back bearing gifts for the rest of us? And what does our future look like if the hero's journey is repeatedly being short-circuited by ever-present social networks? Who will persevere in the aloneness long enough to have scars to show and stories to tell, offering something sublime out of the thick darkness?

POSTCARD POINTERS FOR PERFORMERS
By Bob May

POINTER EIGHT:
PROPS ARE YOUR BEST BUDDY

"Give me a prop and I am the happiest actor on the earth," is a quote from a former student.

After you can believe in your actions by using emotional and sensory memory, a prop can be your best buddy and will help you believe even more. Stanislavski called props *externals*. An external is anything that can help you be more convincing in the part you are going to play. It can be a physical mannerism or a prop you hold or wear.

The Penguin's cigarette holder in the old *Batman* series is a great example of an external prop. Can you imagine the Penguin without that cigarette holder? The cigarette holder was part of the character. And I'm sure it helped Burgess Meredith believe he was the Penguin.

I hate wearing hats. It seems I am in a minority among men today. The bib-cap with a logo and the American male are rivaling the stereotype of the camera around a Japanese tourist's neck. So when I put on a hat, I become someone different. The hat is my external. It helps me be someone other than myself. What would Indiana Jones be without his hat?

My glasses. I was fortunate enough to never have to wear glasses as a child or young adult. Many of the characters I created early in my acting career wore glasses. It helped me get outside of myself. I could hide behind the glasses and become someone else. My glasses are now part of who I am. So when I take them off...I can become someone else. Can you imagine Drew Carey without glasses?

An external not only helps you become someone other than yourself; it aids you in believing what you are doing is real.

A walk can be an external too. A character gets home late one night and tells a roommate, mother, spouse (whoever was expecting him) that he fell getting out of the car. He had promised to be home earlier, so fakes fakes a limp as he walks in the door. The limp helps someone believe. It also helps to avoid the real problem and it changes the subject, which was the main objective in the first place. The subtext worked!

I was watching Danny Glover on the Bravo Network as he was interviewed on the program *Inside the Actors Studio*. It's a wonderful show. Anyway, Mr. Glover said he often works with the internal and external processes of acting at the same time. What he meant was he uses the internal Stanislavski teachings to create a character, but he also uses externals to help him find the inner life of the character.

POINTER NINE AND THREE-QUARTERS: NEVER MOSEY ON A STAGE

The dictionary definition of the word "mosey" is to amble along. The word "mosey" must have been born in the South.

It is death for a character on stage to mosey. Remember, characters in plays are driven to fulfill their objective. They should seek their objective as though it were a desperate quest. When they move on stage, they must move like they know where they are going.

Actors who amble along are just that: actors ambling, moving without motivation, not understanding why the character is even walking.

Your subtext will dictate how you walk from one point to another. And I guarantee you there are not many characters written in the vast canon of drama who mosey.

POINTER ELEVEN: STOP LOOKING FOR CIGARETTE BUTTS

When I talk to people, I look into their eyes. And I hope they are looking back in mine. The eyes are a reflection of the soul. You can best read someone's subtext when you are looking into their eyes. You see their truth through their eyes.

People who look at the ground when they talk to you are hiding something. An actor trying to convince another actor or especially an audience should never be looking down.

Bums in a back alley who can't afford a pack of cigarettes look down for discarded butts that will satisfy their nicotine craving. Audiences also look into an actor's eyes. They might be looking at the whole picture and enjoying the show, but when an actor is speaking, the audience is glued to the actor's eyes. If you are looking for cigarette butts, how can you convince them or the other character that what you are saying is true?

Stop looking for cigarette butts when you are acting.

Look into the eyes of the other characters and beg them to give you something. No one in life or in an audience will ever believe that what you are saying is the truth if you are looking for cigarette butts.

POINTER TWENTY-EIGHT:
UP THE STAKES TO A FILET MIGNON

I know I said my previous pointer was the last, but like any actor, I just don't know when to take my final bow! Think of this as an all-you-can-eat buffet, and you have just come back for seconds. This is the dessert.

To help you with units and objectives you must always *Up the Stakes!*

Do you want your performance to be a Texas T-bone or a filet mignon? One costs more than the other. Some beef-lovers say the filet tastes better, and that's why you pay more. Don't be afraid to pay more when you try to fulfill your objective. Up the stakes! It might cost you more, but in the end you will be more satisfied.

Back to taking my garbage out. Let's say that I have the hottest date I've ever had and she is on her way to my house. I better get the garbage out of there before she arrives. Making sure I made my house stink-free would sure up the stakes.

Or better than that, let's say that if I don't take the garbage out the world will end. That certainly will up the stakes as I travel down my back sidewalk with garbage in hand. I sure hope my garbage would never be so important that it would cause the destruction of the world; however, in drama, that could very well be the case.

Seek your objective as if it were a desperate quest or a life or death situation!

William Ball has a top sirloin of a pointer in his book, *Sense of Direction*, on upping the stakes of your objective. Read it. It's the best steak you'll ever devour.

Note: These slightly different excerpts from *Postcard Pointers to the Performer* were republished with permission from the author. This book can be directly ordered from Heuer Publishing at hitplays.com.

REBEL WITH A CAUSE: RADHA BHARADWAJ'S MAVERICK MISTRESSPIECE

By Bob Mielke

My first encounter with the work of Radha Bharadwaj—film director for major Hollywood studios; author of screenplays, dramas, short stories and novels; actress—was on a typical night when I was grazing my premium cable channels before bedtime. The usual melange of car chases, R-rated adult gropings (thanks, Cinemax) and explosions cycled by, and then there she was. A beautiful woman with her black hair in pigtails, doll rouge on her cheeks, heavy eye makeup and clownish amounts of lipstick. Clad only in black bra and panties. Chased around by a spotlight and the pursuing camera to the tune of "Hernando's Hideaway." And the maraschino cherry on this evil sundae of objectification of the female body, feminist film theorist Laura Mulvey's very worst nightmare? The actress is nineties powerhouse Madeleine Stowe!

Stowe was a big deal in those days. Although she had real thespian chops and a largely untapped range (Robert Altman got her to do some outside-the-box characterization in *Short Cuts*), overall Hollywood typecast her with a vengeance. It's easier that way for the money interests. She was a highly sexualized, sometimes slightly naughty, damsel in distress in film after film: threatened by injuns and saved by Daniel Day Lewis' leatherstocking in Michael Mann's *Last of the Mohicans*, a musician with newly restored sight in *Blink*, the Lord God's acquiescent booty as the Virgin Mary in *The Nativity*. And speaking of such baby play, did she get fertilized by still-in-the-closet Doogie Hawser to compensate for her sterile husband in a twenties period piece? Yeah, that happened; the film was called *The Proposition*.

Now, because she had the bad taste to get older, she plays a heavy on the television drama *Revenge*. A victim no more, unless you consider Botox injections a form of victimization. I do, actually, when Hollywood's involved.

But let's get back to those black panties, shall we? My cable service was giving me Stowe on the half shell, the apotheosis of these other intertexts (some of which were actually filmed later, but seen by me before this viewing—a sense of things to come?). I continue to watch, only to learn that Stowe's character is a political prisoner being tortured. By the grace of my remote, I am in collusion with the camera as her torturer! I am watching a film called *Closet Land*, written and directed by Radha Bharadwaj.

The irony of my experience is that one of the major tropes in Bharadwaj's work is a reversal of expectations caused by the gaze. The climax of her film adaptation of Wilkie Collins' novel *Basil*, as in the source, is a moment of voyeurism that bears unexpected results. Similar moves occur in her short stories ("Lord of Our Destinies," "Strictly Verboten"). And one of the most powerful visual sleights of hand in *Closet Land* itself is when, to torturer Alan Rickman's voice-over, we see shots of "innocent" children reconfigured with the uncropped image to show a child greeting Hitler, one at a Ku Klux Klan rally and a young gun-toting terrorist. By sheer serendipity, my initial encounter with Bharadwaj's work illustrates one of her major thematic interests: Things aren't always what they seem to be. Good Hinduism, that: the veil of Maya which must be lifted.

Everything about Radha Bharadwaj's first feature film, *Closet Land*, seemed auspicious—except, perhaps fatefully, its subject matter. The interrogation of political prisoners can seldom be parlayed into a date movie or box office gold. But as Jeff Goldsmith's appreciative online retrospective piece delineates, Bharadwaj had a lot of support for the film. When she was a Nicholl Fellow at the Sundance Screenwriters lab, Altman protege—and fine director in his own right—Alan Rudolph told her "to stick to her guns" and insist on directing the film the way she wanted to do it (as opposed to relinquishing her desire to direct and/or letting Hollywood committees tinker with her original script). Oliver Stone shocked her with a phone call offering to help her connect with Imagine Entertainment producers Brian Gazer and Ron Howard (another sensitive director), who were currently helping Stone direct *The Doors*.

When rising thespians Stowe and Alan Rickman signed on for the essentially two-person film, the movie had a green light. Two and a half million dollars and eighteen shooting days later in Culver City, *Closet Land* was a reality. The 1991 release got some mixed reviews, since the independent approach to American filmmaking had not quite reached the level of acceptability it received later in the decade. The film was too minimal for some tastes; its plot blended elements of the fantastic, allegory and amazing plot coincidences with its overall grim realism. It was a hard film to "place" generically (although I will do that shortly for you). Eventually it went to video and Laserdisc before becoming completely unavailable in the mid-nineties except as a used item.

But the film has a curious staying power. It is utterly memorable, as so few films are. The intensity of the acting and the sharp writing in the script ensures that one viewing of the film will roll around in the mind for decades to come. Lively internet chat demonstrates the film is still much discussed. Kate Millett devoted an entire chapter to it in her sweeping 1994 study on political imprisonment, *The Politics of Cruelty*. Her enthusiasm almost makes the chapter a straight plot summary of the film (with a few brilliant exceptions to be noted). And since imitation is the sincerest form of flattery, we must duly note William Mallon's convincing case in his honors thesis that Irish playwright and film director Martin McDonagh borrowed heavily from *Closet Land* to "Erinize" it into his 2003 play about a children's author being tortured in a totalitarian state, *The Pillowman*.

Part of McDonagh's m.o., it turns out: His play *The Lonesome West* owes a bit to Sam Shepard's *True West*; connections exist between McDonagh's *In Bruges* and Harold Pinter's *The Dumb Waiter*. I'm not intending to be judgmental here. McDonagh has great gifts and such appropriations have become common and standard practice in modernist and postmodernist texts, as they were in the Middle Ages and in Shakespeare's day. Only the Romantics worried (up to a point) about being original. My own creative endeavors wear their influences on their sleeve. My point here is that plot elements of *Closet Land* persist in another narrative host body, another way in which this text persists and haunts (if you will) our culture.

Pinning down its cinematic genre might be helpful. *Closet Land* is in a sub-genre of the German *Kammerspiel* or "chamber-drama" film. First developed by stage director Max Reinhardt in 1906 for small-audience, intimate drama, *Kammerspiel* readily migrated into film. The most well-known of these silent-era works is probably F. W. Murnau's *The Last Laugh*, a strange rags-to-riches tale (Thompson and Bordwell 95). Cinema historians have noted the genre's huge influence on Swedish art house director Ingmar Bergman.

Most relevantly for *Closet Land*, the Danish director Carl Dreyer made some *Kammerspiel* films. The sub-genre of *Kammerspiel* that *Closet Land* belongs to is the intimate drama of interrogation, a subset of *Kammerspiel* that includes Orson Welles' adaptation of Franz Kafka's *The Trial* and the most famous of such films, Dreyer's *Passion of Joan of Arc*.

The family resemblance of Dreyer's and Bharadwaj's texts is striking, although Dreyer works with a larger cast. Probably the best analogue to Rickman's character in the latter might be Antonin Artaud's tortured monk in Dreyer. Renee Falconetti's performance as Joan in the silent film is an unsurpassable template for Stowe in *Closet Land*. Dreyer shot Falconetti without makeup in extreme close-ups. She was so traumatized by the experience that she never acted again! For Stowe merely to evoke Falconetti's work in the memory of the film aficionado is to pay the former the highest of compliments.

There are even some parallels between Welles' film and *Closet Land*: Both use animation to convey the more other-worldly aspects of their stories. *The Trial* opens with an animated re-telling of Kafka's parable "Before the Law"; *Closet Land* uses full-color animation to show scenes from the children's books written by the female protagonist.

I raise this genre issue because the *Kammerspiel* of interrogation is not the way to wealth. Only Dreyer had modest critical and commercial success with the sub-genre. A little digging will show Welles got worse initial reviews than Bahradwaj for his efforts.

Millet's book shows that Bharadwaj did her research. Although the film and play is not set in any specific totalitarian regime (but English is spoken), it follows standard practices regarding interrogation and torture. Some of this is well-known, especially if you read writers like William S. Burroughs—or have been arrested! The old good cop / bad cop routine, for instance. *Closet Land's* good riff on this is that the same interrogator plays both by disguising his voice, since the victim is blindfolded at certain key moments in the questioning. Rickman's "Man" even gets to pretend to be another victim as well.

Radha Bharadwaj shows us lesser known tropes of torture than this, however. For example, music is often used to supplement the agony of punishment. What could be more sadistic than attaching horrific associations to one of humanity's greatest sources of pleasure? The Nazi concentration camps used marching bands to escort the prisoners to their labor; in Algeria the French played "popular songs of the day" during their torture sessions,according to detainee Henri Alleg (Millet 55, 87). We also recall Alex in *A Clockwork Orange* listening to Beethoven during the Ludovico treatment. In *Closet Land* they play Johann Strauss' "Blue Danube Waltz" (in the screenplay) or "Hernando's Hideaway" (in the film) to augment the agony.

Closet Land also reminds us that bored torturers like to invent original recipes for torture and give them somewhat innocuous nicknames. Millett describes some Latin American innovations. For example, the "parrot's perch" binds the prisoner's wrists and ankles to an iron bar placed between two tables. When hung this way, they are subjected to electric shocks and/or beatings. The "ice box" is a tiny, cold space for long periods of isolation punctuated by loud noises, bright light and bad ventilation. And the "dragon chair" is a metal chair for shocks which injure the detainee by having an iron bar that pushes back, "causing deep gashes" (Millett 247).

Similarly, in the *Closet Land* script the male torture victim (as noted, a persona of the torturer) sinisterly inquires of the woman: "You've been barbecued yet? What've they tried on you? Cat's cradle? The Arabesque? Touchdown?" (44). Except for the "cat's cradle," all of these torture techniques are eventually applied to the suspected subversive. "Barbecuing" is the application of heated skewers to the body; "Touchdown" is a free-association word game with electric shocks for "wrong" answers; the "Arabesque" forces the person to maintain that awkward ballet position (51, 54, 58).

In addition to the superb acting and accurate depiction of torture, the film/play makes a strong thematic point, perhaps at the cost of narrative probability. Spoiler alert: the man torturing the children's author also repeatedly molested her when she was a little girl—in a clothes closet. This experience was the germ for her suspect manuscript about escape called, yes, *Closet Land*. Bharadwaj does not merely want to bring the narrative full circle—the torturer is the real-life origin for the "subversive" text (corrupt regimes breed their own enemies)—although she does do that as well. Her larger point is that totalitarianism infantilizes its subjects and operates in a parallel manner to child abuse, as the woman points out in a climactic speech:

> It seems to be the same thing—organically, I mean. Shutting a child in a closet, and shutting a people away. You know what I mean? One is—sin. Sin in miniature. The other is sin. On a grand, operatic scale....

> If you can frighten a child into
> silence, you can frighten a people,
> too. And with time and practice,
> people, too, will shut their eyes
> and not scream—...
> I never screamed in the closet, did
> I?...
> And the people won't scream either.
> And they will also go about,
> pretending everything's fine,
> everything's all right, while their
> neighbors disappear all around
> them... And then the—the people—
> *become* like children! Scared of Bad
> Men, the chopper that'll chop off
> their heads....
> And that's what's so *terrifying*!
> Because children are so *powerless*,
> aren't they? They make such—such
> *easy* victims. Such *easy* victims... (75).

I have to admit that I was creeped out when Barack Obama gave his speech in January 2013 about the new gun control initiatives. Although I support the actual measures, I found it disturbing the way he infantilized his audience. He read letters from various children present on the dais with the implication that somehow these kids were creating the new policies. By a sinister logic foreshadowed by this film, the notion of children-as-public ("the people") ultimately diminishes the authority of the electorate and smacks of cryptofascism. Obama fist-pumping kids, whether he or we like it or not, lines up alongside the iconography of such other avuncular chidloving figures as Adolf Hitler, Joseph Stalin and Mao Tse Tung. Probably Jesus himself was the earliest purveyor of this trope: "suffer the little children to come unto me." How ironic that Bharadwaj's children's author exposes this nasty sign slide into authoritarianism! And even more ironically, such moves understandably (alas) make gun nuts even more paranoid. Like Yakov Smirnov says, "What a country!"

I mentioned above that Millett's basic presentation of *Closet Land* is a loving plot summary with some additional insights such as the contextualizing of the text's accuracy with regard to actual practices used in political detention and interrogation. Another interesting critical point she makes is that the ending is ambiguous. We see Stowe's character leave the room and go into a bright white light. She may be heading off to her death; but she may be going "into freedom, possibly" (192).

I'll confess this latter possibility never occurred to me after multiple viewings of the film—and I have to ask why not. I suspect it's because (fortunately) I have little detailed knowledge of these practices, What Millett and Bharadwaj know—as did Kafka and Mikhail Bulgakov before them—is that political imprisonment is first and foremost an existentially absurd experience. It can go any way those in power want it to go. Its victims have very little power to resist (but they have some, as *Closet Land* reveals). They cannot even guarantee their own—in some cases, potentially desired—deaths. So, yes, the woman might have been released. In any case, she has left that odious room for somewhere better—even if it is oblivion.

BIBLIOGRPAHY

Bharadwaj, Radha, director and screenwriter. *Basil*. With Jared Leto, Christian Slater, Sir Derek Jacobi and Claire Forlani. Santa Monica: Lionsgate, 1997.

Ibid. *Closet Land*. With Madeleine Stowe and Alan Rickman. Universal Studios, 1991. Page numbers refer to the screenplay, courtesy of the author.

Ibid. "Lord of Our Destinies." amazon.com/Independent-Ink-Magazine/dp/B004VW3BEA.

Ibid. "Strictly Verboten." notesfromtheunderground.co.uk.

Ibid. closetland.com. Radha Bharadwaj's official website. By the time this issue of the *Toad Suck Review* is in your hands, this website will have posted a full version of my article published here, which also includes a discussion of her second feature film *Basil* and her short fiction.

Goldsmith, Jeff. "Cinema Obscura: *Closet Land*: History Repeats Itself." backstory.net.

Mallon, William. *When an Author Goes Too Far: An Examination of the similarities between* The Pillowman *by Martin McDonagh and* Closet Land *by Radha Bharadwaj*. Honors thesis, Godard College, March 2010.

Millett, Kate. *The Politics of Cruelty: An Essay on the Literature of Political Imprisonment*. New York: Norton, 1994.

Thompson, Kristin and David Bordwell. *Film History: An Introduction*. Third ed. New York: McGraw-Hill, 2010.

VERY BLONDE HAIR, VERY BLUE EYES— VERY WHITE SKIN!
By Radha Bharadwaj

You don't really need to know a woman to have an affair with her. Speaking to her, knowing details about her (like her name, for instance) are all hugely over-rated. That much Joseph Pinto, reared on a steady diet of Bollywood's best, knows for sure. In Hindi movies, the best affairs are when the man and woman know nothing about each other. It begins with a meeting of the eyes, and the affair sprouts and thrives—like a weed or fungus—within the hot, steamy walls of the mind. So much can be said—and said most eloquently—with one's eyes; whereas so much can be ruined, by words. Joseph's eyes have conveyed to him the most important attributes of his lover: her very blonde hair, very blue eyes—and very white skin! What he has to offer her, by those very parameters, is a topic he'd rather not dwell on—for he's so dark he's almost blue, with black crinkly hair and deep inky eyes.

Still, our children will be beautiful, like her—Joseph consoles himself, glancing at his reflection out of the periphery of his eyes, as he buttons down his collar and zips up his fly in readiness for his day at the San Antonio Catholic College. He's one of thirty young men who have been sent from Goa to study in San Antonio. Scholarships generously funneled to Joseph's church in Goa, from wealthy Americans. Four poor Hindu boys had even converted—with a lot of encouragement from Father Desmond—just to get the scholarship! The cherry on the icing was that one of the neophytes had been from an upper caste—they'd all high-fived each other, the good Father and his parishioners, at the inroads they were making into the very heart of the Hindu beast.

The bus-stop is crowded with students headed to the college. Joseph lingers at the back of the line, his eyes on a small rundown house with an unwieldy front yard at the end of the street. A large plastic Santa Claus had been stuck on the roof for Christmas—they've forgotten to bring him down, and Santa leers at the street, dust-streaks running down his portly body. Two badly dented cars lie on their bellies, like disemboweled dragons, by the gate. Irrelevant details—these signs of shabbiness and lack. Joseph knows that the pearl inside the house is flawless.

The "pearl" emerges from the house just then: a rather large pearl, rolling to the gate on thick, childishly bowed legs. To Joseph, her bigness is symbolic of America's immensity: her wide round face like the sprawl of Texan fields, her stout limbs like stalwart Lone Star

State pines, her round blue eyes like the cloud-free American sky. She's clinging to the rusty gate now, looking searchingly down the street. And once her eyes land on Joseph, she breaks into a huge smile: shocking-pink gums and sparkling tiny teeth are displayed, with the joy of having spotted him.

He smiles back, heart pounding, sweat running down from his hair and into his eyes. He grins—he even risks a small, secretive wave. And she waves back, mimicking him—only her wave is large like her, open and generous, with her arm moving like a windshield wiper and upper-arm fat streaming below, loose as a billowing sail. Dimples split her jumbo peach-cheeks—deep enough for him to wade ankle-deep in. Or so he thinks, becoming choked up and poetic at the thought of him climbing her cheek like an ant making tracks in a vat of butter. The bus' arrival puts an end to the creamy dreamy reverie, and Joseph takes his place in the student-surge that clogs the entrance.

#

The class is on child welfare and the lecturer's from the Deep South. Joseph, who's confounded by American speech in general, finds the lecturer particularly hard to understand. Good thing my scholarship's contingent only on my religion and not on good grades, he thinks, as he switches off his mind and begins to doodle. The drawings are always of her. She's easy to draw: two circles for her cheeks, a large circle for her contented Buddha belly. His pencil hovers over her bosom zone before executing a pair of County Fair prize-worthy melon-boobs.

He wishes Father Desmond and his friends back home could see her. How they'd envy him! He's landed the ace: a white girl, with very blonde hair, very blue eyes, and very white skin. Though Father Desmond would probably be beyond envy in these matters, what with his celibacy vows and all that.

"And the good Father's tastes probably run to very small boys," Joseph's roommate Terrence Waters had chortled, when Joseph had told Terrence about his "affair," and how proud his clan in Goa would be of him. Joseph had recoiled from Terrence's blasphemy. Odd how the Christians here were so disparaging of their own faith. Not at all what he'd been taught in Goa.

"The fact that she's a white chick's a big deal to you, right?" Terrence had further taunted, cocking his brow and sauntered off to the bathroom without waiting for Joseph's reply, as if no reply were needed.

Joseph had felt humiliated—by Terrence's insight. The beefy black American was correct. It wouldn't have been a big deal if Joseph's crush had been a fellow Indian or a Mexican or a black—hell, Joseph would never have fallen for her had she been anything but white. If you're not lucky enough to be born white, marry one—that was the unspoken goal in his community, which still claimed it was not Indian, but Portuguese. Just like the Portuguese invaders from five centuries ago.

"They are just better people—Westerners. Fair—not only in skin, but in how they treat everyone: black, white or brown. They're Christian countries. They don't have castes," old Mrs. De Souza had educated Joseph, on the eve of his departure to San Antonio. She was his neighbor—she'd loaned him her suitcase for his trip. "Make sure you come back with a girl whiter than a boiled egg," she'd winked, pinching his cheek.

He thinks about that on the bus that bears him to his apartment. What a steaming pile of manure, he would now say, if he were like bold and boisterous Terrence Waters. They *do* have castes here—only they don't use that word. In the two months he's been in the US, Joseph has seen enough to have his notions about Western castelessness shattered. There are students who won't sit next to him in class. Neighbors on his street who pointedly ignore his attempts to be friendly. His accent is mimicked almost everywhere he goes, and thrice already he's received the exact same advice from total strangers: "Why don't you go back to where you come from?"

"People like us will always be on the bottom," Terrence had said. And Joseph had stood there helplessly, not daring to argue back—but seething with rage inside: how dare Terrence put Joseph in the same boat as himself? When, he—Joseph Pinto—was at least two shades lighter than the black bastard!

Joseph gets down from the bus and walks down the street to his apartment building. On a sudden whim, he turns the corner and goes to the spot across from her house. *One sight of you, and my troubles fly away like birds who've fled their cruel cage,* he hums the dolorous melody from the Bollywood hit *Caged Love.* And as if to reward him, as if beckoned by his humming, she comes out, gleaming like an immense boiled egg in the bluish Texan twilight. She waddles up to the gate and clutches it with her plump pink hands. She smiles at him. *This* is love—deeper, more immortal than that of Bollywood gods Abishek Bacchan and Aishwarya Rai, who married each other in real life.

"Mandy! What'cha doin' outside? Come on in!" a yellow-eyed mustachioed geezer hollers, emerging like a malevolent mosquito from inside the house. Must be her father. The guy's white—that's about the only good thing Joseph can say about his future father-in-law. Everything else says white trash—a term Joseph thought referred to soiled white paper towels and used paper plates intended for the trashcan, until a hysterical Terrence told him what the term meant.

OK, so she's not exactly from the best family. But who'd know that, back home? What they'd see—his family and friends and flock of fellow-faithful in Goa—would be her very blonde hair, very blue eyes, very white skin. She'd be the pinnacle. And he'd be the proud beau, by her side, looking down at them—much like a pilot-fish elevates its standing by clinging to the flanks of a big white whale.

"Mandy!" her father roars.

She gives Joseph a wistful look and turns reluctantly towards her house. Most amazingly—alarmingly, even—she lifts a corner of her jolly yellow frock, granting Joseph a blurry vision of the haze of golden fuzz between her legs, like a lion cub's face, with the nub of a bubblegum-pink tongue in the middle.

#

She's ready!—his heart sings all night. Like the closed bud that senses the manly bee, and opens its petals—as the Bollywood leading lady Kareena Kapoor had sung in *Liquid Love* under a thundering waterfall, while Joseph and the other men in the audience strained in their seats to catch a glimpse of ravishing Kareena's naughty nipples.

Mandy's ready! Now Joseph knows her name, and he's seen her secret hairy lair. The next (il)logical step is the consummation of their affair. He's never done it before—other than into his own fist. Mandy's lion cub would make for a far more welcoming hallow...

But Mandy's baleful-looking father augured nothing but hurdles and hardship. So on Sunday evening, Joseph prays, with a depth of devotion he didn't think he had in him, for an obstacle-free path of love. He then makes his way back to the spot on the street across from her house. For a good thirty-six minutes he hums the best of Bollywood's love duets for all he's worth. At the thirty-seventh minute, Mandy sails out of her house like a barge entering the bay and stares at him, a secretive look in her bright blue eyes. She opens the front gate slightly, smiling at him, twisting a corner of her jade-green frock in her hands.

Smart girl! No one's in the house, and she wants me "to go in," Joseph chuckles at his own double entendre, as he crosses the street and follows her into her house. A filthy place, with unwashed crocheted rugs and ripped-up vinyl sofas. But he keeps his eyes on Mandy's impossibly white bulging calves as she leads him to a tiny room—her room, he guesses. It's dirty, like the rest of the house, but done up touchingly in girlish pink, the pink of her wiener lips and her muscular tongue, the pink of her saucer-sized nipples and the cheeky tongue in her lion cub's face.

Aah—the deed has been done, and Joseph lies, spent; his scrawny, hairy, spidery legs sprawled in lazy languor over Mandy's immense white expanse. Much better than entering my own fist, he thinks, looking at her with love—and she looks back at him quietly. Odd—but for a hound-like howl when he first ripped his way in, she'd said nothing all through the three times he'd ravished her. And now she looks at him with her sky-blue eyes, then looks past him at some point over his shoulder, and lisps the first word he's ever heard her say: "Daddy…"

Joseph's blood plummets like mercury in a thermometer. He turns: the gimlet-eyed geezer's in the doorway, a similarly malevolent geezeress in tow. They are staring at the naked duo on the bed with complete and utter shock. Then Mandy's mother ululates—a string of blasphemous curses: Jesus Fuckin' Christ, Fuckin' Mother of God….

#

"Man, oh man," Terrence Waters shakes his head and rolls his eyes, biting his cheeks to stop himself from laughing. He's visiting Joseph in prison, where Joseph is being held without bail while he awaits sentencing. The prosecution's pushing for deportation.

"You didn't know the girl's retarded? That she's only sixteen years old? " Terrence asks again.

No, Joseph shakes his head. He knew nothing about Mandy—just like the actor John Abraham knew nothing about the actress Katrina Kaif in Bollywood's *Stranger Love*. In Abraham's case, the girl had been a covert spy-cum-humanitarian-cum-Nobel-Prize-winning nuclear physicist. All Joseph had known about Mandy was that she had very blonde hair, very blue eyes—and very, very white skin.

AN EAR WHERE MY HEART SHOULD BE: THE LINER NOTES OF THE LOST ALBUM *DISQUIET MIND*
By Sean Rabin

Thanks to record company marketing departments, complicit music journalists, and a culture of passive consumerism, the description "lost classic" has effectively become devoid of all meaning.

Nearly every month, it seems, news arrives of yet another criminally overlooked and wildly essential album that has been magically unearthed in the cellar of a dusty second-hand record store. Unfortunately these aural treasures are often nothing more than reissues of mid-career experiments lost no deeper than an artist's back catalogue, or underground releases proven over time to be so influential that their repackaging is of benefit only to those yet to hear what many others have been listening to for years.

The exception to both these examples is the discovery of a recording so extraordinarily it defies reason as to how it could ever have been neglected in the first place, and so unheard of it inspires serious re-evaluation of the era in which it was released. Such a phenomenon occurs much less frequently than the music industry would lead us to believe, yet unequivocally applies to the re-release of Sarah Boyd's only solo album.

Of the numerous impediments that may have prevented you from hearing *Disquiet Mind* before now, the two most conspicuous are that only eight hundred copies were ever pressed, and its release date was June 6, 1968—the day after Bobby Kennedy's assassination. In the media storm that erupted following such a tragic event, a record by an unknown musician from Canada, with no publicity or industry friends to talk it up, instantly disappeared into the void. Where it might have remained forever had not the master tapes resurfaced, more than forty years later, in a set of circumstances that should be considered as nothing short of a miracle.

Then again, miracles of circumstance seemed to have played a large role in Sarah's life. For a young girl to make her way from Tasmania to California at the age of seven, then to New York at fifteen, and onto the outer suburbs of Edmonton, Canada by twenty-four, demanded more than just courage and determination. Fate has to account for something. Whether Sarah sensed a guiding force upon her destiny we can never know for certain, but upon hearing the deep wisdoms and shifts in self-understanding that populate *Disquiet Mind,* there can be little doubt that here was a woman with a genuine insight into the complexities of the human condition.

Tasmania is a small triangular island separated from the southern coast of mainland Australia by Bass Strait—a notoriously treacherous body of inky blue water twice as wide as the English Channel. First settled by the British as a penal colony, Tasmania was, and remains, a place of astounding natural beauty and entrenched small town values. Hobart, where Sarah was born in 1932, is the state's capital and Australia's most southern city. Next stop Antarctica. Music would have been a limited fare in such an isolated locale, consisting mainly of church choirs, public concerts, occasional radio broadcasts and whatever songs had been brought over by Sarah's grandparents when they emigrated in the early 1880s.

Fleeing Tsarist pogroms, the affluent middle-class family of three brothers and three sisters divided into pairs of boys and girls and traveled to New York, London and Tasmania. While the four siblings who remained in the northern hemisphere preserved their Jewish identities and traditions, both children who arrived in Tasmania quickly anglicized their names, converted to Christianity and married into gentile families.

Singing traditional folksongs was one of the few customs to survive this assimilation, and the tears that invariably accompanied them often caused Sarah's grandmother to quit the room. Left alone with the piano, the young Sarah would take the opportunity to tap out whatever melodies she could improvise before her grandmother dried her eyes and returned to shut the lid on the keyboard and its painful memories.

Afternoons spent at her grandparents' home near the top of Mt Stuart came as a welcome relief from the solitude of being an only child in a family that was beginning to fray. The house her father's father had built—which still stands—was surrounded by a network of vegetable beds, and offered panoramic views of the suburbs gradually expanding along the banks of the Derwent River. In the other direction was a short climb to the peak of Mt Stuart, and it is easy to imagine Sarah accompanying her grandfather up there as the two of them shouted to be heard over the blustering air that filled their ears and made their eyes water. Anyone who has grown up on an island can attest to wind being a persistent presence in their lives, and maybe this was how Sarah developed her fascination with sounds below the cover of noise. Certainly there are two unmistakable references to mountain peaks on *Disquiet Mind*, and rather than contemplate their portentous significance, it is just as easy to interpret them as evidence of where and how Sarah learned to listen deeply.

Days spent in the care of her grandparents occurred more frequently as Sarah's home life continued to disintegrate. And when her parents finally announced their intention to divorce, she automatically presumed the spare bed on Mt Stuart would become her permanent abode. But at that time—and for thirty years to come—divorce remained a source of public shame, so when the seven-year-old Sarah refused to live with either her mother or father she unwittingly played into her parents' desire to be rid of all evidence of their union. Distant cousins who had moved to the West Coast of America were contacted, and soon Sarah found herself on the opposite side of the planet. Whether her beloved grandparents were complicit in such a deceit, due to their own desire to avoid community disgrace, remains a matter of conjecture, and is something even the brutally honest songwriter of thirty years later could not bring herself to investigate with any rigor.

The weeks of independence Sarah experienced aboard the ship to California contained some of her happiest memories. And during the nine years she later spent in New York City Sarah would often ride the Staten Island Ferry to remind herself of the time she had tried to yell louder than the boiler room, or had sat in the galley to watch thousands of sandwiches being made for the lunch buffet. Her favorite recollection, however, was of the day she discovered musicians rehearsing in the ship's ballroom. Though prohibited from the first-class deck, Sarah's presence was tolerated so long as she made no noise and pretended to be deaf whenever the band members cursed. During cigarette breaks she sipped pink lemonade and asked permission to depress trumpet valves or pluck guitar strings. Sarah had seen such instruments before, but the thrill of actually touching them encouraged her to return to the ballroom day after day until she had befriended every musician, and learned how to produce at least a sound from their respective instruments.

Songs on *Disquiet Mind* such as "Tow Me Along" and "Orange Peel" possess a broad instrumentation that harks back to this initial wonder. And the unusual juxtapositions of Sarah's arrangements, along with the unexpected dissonance they produced, somehow evokes a sense of the ocean she once traveled upon. Well, for this listener it does, at least.

Ethan Reznik was nine years old when Sarah came to live with his family in Santa Monica, California. His two older sisters were in high school by then, and already ensconced in a busy social life beyond the family home, so it fell upon Ethan to introduce his distant relative to the neighborhood. Ethan continues to live in the same area, and admits to often wondering what happened to the girl with dark curly hair whom he spent so many years of his childhood playing with.

"I remember how glad she was to be away from her parents, which was a strange idea for me at the time because, like most children, I naively thought everyone's mother and father were the same as my own. But Sarah was never homesick. She took to our street as if she'd lived there all her life, and her accent meant the kids at school thought she was from England, so for a while she was quite exotic."

Now a retired children's book illustrator, Ethan recalls how he and Sarah used to listen to the radio as they sat at the kitchen table drawing pictures. "I've always thought of those days as my training to become an artist, and when I heard about Sarah's album I realized she was probably doing the same. We were allowed to tune the radio to whatever station we wanted, and when I think back to those afternoons with the sunlight pouring through the back door, all I can see Sarah doing is turning the dial, searching for a song she liked. Me? I didn't care what music played, just so long as it had enough beat to keep me drawing."

Sarah lived with the Rezniks for seven years, and in that time rarely gave them cause to regret their decision to take her in. Piano lessons were requested and granted, and her dedication to practicing made Mr and Mrs Reznik dream of a day she might become a professional musician. But around the age of fourteen, Ethan recalls, something happened that changed Sarah forever.

"The war was over and there was a sense of possibility everywhere; a feeling of a new world emerging. And after Sarah heard Charlie Parker's "Bird Lore" on the radio I think she felt compelled to go out and find it for herself. Sarah started sneaking into local music clubs, and when my parents punished her for it she ran away from home. The police usually picked her up after a couple hours, but she would just do it again a few months later. So eventually my parents decided it was maybe better to let her go, and see if she came back by herself. That was in April 1947, and we never saw or heard from Sarah again."

Almost nothing is known of the six months it took Sarah to reach New York City. We have an approximate date of when she abandoned Santa Monica, and a record of the two days' community service she served in Denver for shoplifting, but after that there is only the song "Macy's Spacemen," in which a direct reference is made to the day she arrived in Manhattan. As chance would have it, she was greeted by the department store's 1947 Thanksgiving Day parade in which flying saucers and Martians featured heavily. "Floating blue men gave me a welcome to remember / And I waved alongside children, happy to reach land's end." There is no record of how Sarah traveled, the friends she made along the way, or the dangers one can only pray she avoided. The journey was never discussed with her husband. Until the time of Sarah's death, Tom Laird believed she was from the Isle of Guernsey, and had made her way to America with the money bequeathed from a father killed in World War II. It was not until he was forced to sort through Sarah's belongings that he found her Australian passport and saw the immigration stamp made in California.

Tom says he met Sarah in 1952, when she was twenty and had been living in New York City for more than five years. "I first saw her washing her hands in the fountain in Bryant Park, and thought it probably wasn't the best place to get yourself clean. This was before newspapers had started labeling people Beatniks or Hippies, so no one paid Sarah much attention. But I thought there was something familiar about her face, and when she picked up her guitar and hurried towards the Public Library I unexpectedly found myself following her inside. I eventually caught up in the music department, but before I could think of something to say, Sarah had carried a stack of records into a listening booth. I later learned that this was where she taught herself to play all her favorite songs."

"I had my own study to get on with, so I sat at a desk and waited for her to reappear. But when I ran out of time I wrote a note inviting her to meet me for coffee, and left it at the desk where Sarah would return her records.

"Of course she didn't show up. But I realized she might have had a previous engagement, and the coffee shop was just near the university, so I tried again the same time the next day, and the next. I don't know why. It wasn't love at first sight. I was just curious. But after the fourth day I gave up any hope of ever seeing her again. I paid my check and walked out, only to glimpse Sarah through the coffee shop window clearing my table. I hurried back inside, but she had already returned to the kitchen. I now understood why her face had been familiar, and realized how my invitation to meet at the place she worked must have read like a sneer or a joke. I sat down again and waited for her to reappear so I could explain, but when Sarah came back out she walked straight to a stool in the corner of the room and began to play her guitar.

"You've got to realize that the village coffee house scene existed long before the media got hold of it. For someone to get up and sing a few songs was nothing special. It happened all the time. People didn't expect to become famous. They just played because it was what they wanted to do, and there was nowhere else for them to do it. All the other stuff that followed was just marketing."

The cover photograph for *Disquiet Mind* provided no real insight into what Sarah looked like. Though the picture of her sitting on a bench in a small park surrounded by three tall office buildings is a perfect representation of the music within, she is too far in the distance for her face to be distinguished in any detail. And the back of the album showed only the basement where it was recorded, so for even the few people who bought *Disquiet Mind*, Sarah's appearance remained something of a mystery.

Home photos from the same period, however, reveal short curly black hair parted down one side, oval reading glasses, thick lashes, and a wide smile. Before hearing Sarah's voice she might be considered handsome, even pretty. But one of the magical things about music is that it lends its beauty to the performer—not the other way round—so as your esteem grows for *Disquiet Mind* so too does your appreciation for Sarah's looks, until eventually she can appear as nothing less than an astonishingly attractive woman. This, Tom freely admits, is exactly what happened as he watched her perform that day in the coffee house.

The couple dated for two years before deciding to marry. Neither was willing to commit to a relationship when there was still so much work to do. Tom was completing a doctorate in English, while Sarah had an extensive circle of musician friends with whom she regularly collaborated before and after her shifts as a waitress.

Penny Wood, Beth Clarke, Noel "Pups" Brown, George Hasworthy, Fanny Waine, Jimmy "Stick 'em Up" Larsen, Connie Sullivan and Chuck Hayes all receive a thank you on the back of *Disquiet Mind*. Some of these people have disappeared without trace, while others forged successful careers as songwriters, producers, publishers or tour managers.

Long before she shared coffee with Lou Reed at Pickwick Records, and helped to organize Andy Warhol's *Exploding Plastic*

Inevitable, Connie Sullivan was a habitual truant familiarizing herself with the mysteries of Manhattan Island.

"No one paid attention to children in those days, so I could pretty much go wherever I pleased. And I was drawn to places like Times Square and the Village because they were dangerous and exciting. I was six years younger than Sarah when we met, and I think she just wanted to be sure I had enough to eat, and was able to read. But what she was really teaching me was how to survive in New York without any money.

"Sarah knew how hard it was to be on your own, and was always taking care of runaways or giving people a sofa for the night. Sometimes it paid off with a friendship like ours, but other times she got robbed or beaten. And I think it was after one particularly bad experience that she and Tom decided to marry."

The apartment Tom rented was on the roof of a five-storey building, and had previously been a superintendent's residence. He recalls it being almost uninhabitable in winter, but as soon as spring arrived local musicians would start to drop by to see if Sarah had added anything to her collection of instruments. For years she had been scavenging junk shops and pawnbrokers, and on the walls of her home hung finger cymbals, slide whistles, Chinese gongs, thumb pianos, a sitar, glockenspiel, banjouke, shawm, tuba, tamboura, and anything else that would make an unfamiliar sound. Living on the roof meant they could be played without fear of disrupting any neighbors, and over the course of an afternoon, as more musicians appeared, the jams would grow steadily longer and more elaborate. Up until the early 1980s you could still find homemade recording of these sessions being reverently passed around New York. But tapes melt, get lost, or wear out, and now nothing remains of these spontaneous ensembles except what the participants can remember.

Chuck Hayes was there, and admits it was around this time that he gave up playing music. "After the jams wound down and people went off to dates or shows, Sarah would pick up her guitar and play something clean and uncomplicated to clear the air. And in all the years since then I still have never heard another songwriter capture the nature of her own heart so succinctly. It was as though Sarah refused to let any artifice or metaphor get in the way of what she wanted to say. It wasn't melodramatic; it was just honest and true, and I quickly realized I could never be that talented. So I decided to become a manager and help people who were. Of course, Sarah was the first person I thought of representing, but after she fell pregnant with Grace they moved to Canada."

Tom had secured a teaching position at the University of Alberta, and just before Grace was born the young couple moved into the house in Edmonton where Sarah would eventually record *Disquiet Mind*.

Thanks to the baby photos and letters sent to Tom's parents in Washington D.C, this period of Sarah's life is better documented than any other. It seems she ardently embraced the role of motherhood, and put aside her music to focus on the small life that had miraculously appeared in her arms. The couple was warmly welcomed into a circle of young academics, and quickly settled into a domesticity that bore little resemblance to the way of life they had enjoyed in New York City.

Tom, now a Senior Professor at the University of Alberta, recalls those years as a blur of learning students' names, marking exams and publishing papers. Meanwhile Sarah took care of Grace, read cookbooks, bought second-hand furniture and investigated the neighborhood. Having grown up in Tasmania she was unperturbed by Canadian winters, and found herself more content in an environment that was less concrete. On weekends they drove into the countryside to picnic and walk, and for vacations either visited Tom's parents or camped in the Rockies.

Perhaps it was during one such trip, with the mountain wind blowing in her ears, that Sarah was reminded of her ability to listen deeply, for she started to buy two new records every week. Not just of pop and rock and jazz, but also gospel, bluegrass, *musique concrète,* Italian folk, Klezmer, Elektronische Musik, Icelandic brass bands and even poetry performances. Close friendships were quickly formed with the employees of nearby record stores, who would lend Sarah catalogues so she could stay up late creating long lists of albums she wanted ordered in.

Tom says their parties were famous for unusual music, but guests soon learned that to make fun of what they heard would only result in Sarah sitting beside them and explaining in detail what was so interesting about the songs being played. By the time Grace was ready to go to school Sarah's record collection had outgrown the living room, so she decided to distract herself from the loss of her little girl's company by building shelves in the basement and sorting through the boxes that had not been opened since their departure from New York.

Around this time Chuck Hayes turned up in Edmonton.

"In the six years since we had last seen each other I had started my own music publishing company, and there were rumors going around that Canada had an untapped resource of talent. So I gave myself a holiday, caught the train to Toronto, and scouted the major cities until I was close enough to look up my old friends in the phone book.

"When I saw how Sarah had set up her basement like her New York apartment, I just knew she was ready to record. The suburbs are so quiet while the kids are at school. Shut the windows to keep out birdsong and you can hear a pin drop. In those days I had dreams of starting my own record company, and I still believed Sarah was one of the most talented musicians I had ever heard. So I took her out to lunch and bought her a reel-to-reel tape recorder with a decent microphone. I suppose I was showing off a bit, but I was serious about getting her songs down on tape. I don't feel betrayed that she never sent me the finished product. I'm just proud to have played a small part in what she created. You never know, she might have tried to contact me. I was busy in those days. Music was becoming big business. But I didn't hear anything until Tom contacted me about the funeral."

It took Sarah four years to write and record the eleven songs contained on *Disquiet Mind*. In that time she bought three more reel-to-reel tape machines and intuitively stumbled upon production techniques such as close miking, artificial double tracking, looping, plundering samples and sequencing tape machines—all of which were still being pioneered by that era's most innovative recording engineers.

The end result is a record that stretches and bends time with its rich and raw audio dramas, spiritual nakedness, mordant wit, claustrophobic heartbeats and adventurous forays into uncharted territory. In a bizarre and ecstatic love affair, chaotic string ramblings embrace unfurling patterns of panoramic guitars; communicative sonic pollen is sprinkled over low frequency oscillations, and waves of rhythmic calligraphy intertwine with glossolalia harmonies. Meanwhile, hot, driven sounds systematically thwart traditional expectations of "the song" in such exquisitely precise ways that their presence remains divinely unobtrusive to the compositions' fundamental beauty. A confessional whisper here, an off-balanced polyphonic rhythm there. The plurality of musical languages confirms how Sarah learned from everything she listened to, yet mere crumbs of genre recognition are detectable. Instead, unraveling flute lines, terse piano solos, murky violin responses and flurries of noise produce wildly contrasting styles beneath the broad umbrella of Sarah's singing.

Her supple, untutored vocals gleefully roll around her throat, thrilling at the possibilities of the unadorned human voice, be it awkward, cathartic, romantic or dolorous. The slightest shift in its perfect pitch can deliver enormous symbolic weight, and conjure spellbinding moments of high-risk atmosphere. Sour notes, laconic cheekiness and repetitious chanting are all to be found on *Disquiet Mind*, and though at times such singing might seem counterintuitive, or even guilty of playing tug of war with the rhythm, it is nonetheless powered by an uncontrived inspiration that is consistently enriching to the soul of the listener.

Sarah's lyrics, engaged in a relentless dialogue about the nature of what she heard and saw in the world, reflect the troubled times as successfully as any protest song, yet escape being trapped in the period by resisting hippy sentimentality and keeping the perspective thematically personal. "Not Another Word" and "Across The Floor" might make only a few specific references to how she felt about her mother and father shouting themselves towards divorce, but the way they capture the heart of the matter reveals just how calamitous such arguments must have appeared to their seven-year-old daughter. Though musically sublime, these two songs, more than any other on *Disquiet Mind*, are full of fissures and abstract ideas. As if their uneven tempos and blunted notes, harmonic puzzles and distressed guitar could exorcise not only memories of her parents' marriage breakdown, but also what Sarah saw were the failings of her society.

In contrast to this, the unadorned bluesy lamentation "Win, Lose, Lose" so blatantly documents her life in New York City that it feels otherworldly. With its forlorn hermetic insights about greed and self-satisfaction, and exquisite boredom with the mediocrity of human activity, this brutally sardonic song is a disruptive psychogeographical lullaby. The feline swagger conveyed upon its linear structure and impeccable phrasing shares the bravura present in all of Sarah's songs, while the uncontrived virtuosity and selective silence confirms that despondence is not always a disservice to a musician. Yes, its airy layers are far from revolutionary, and the climbing drums do perhaps take the subject matter too much to heart, but Sarah's unmediated lyrics are a markedly successful experiment in perception, and offer a terse reminder of how popular music was once an ideal environment for subterranean commentaries.

There is an irrefutable freedom in being unknown. By operating beneath the cultural radar, unconcerned with the consequences of her actions or statements, Sarah was able to achieve a level of creative independence that no record company or producer would have permitted. Her ideas of perfection did not exclude machine malfunctions or small blemishes of noise, warped tape or the presence of background sounds. To Sarah these were moments of unexpected coloration and random beauty, sacred in the ceremony of composition, and essential to the notion of spontaneous design she wished to instill within *Disquiet Mind*. "An Ear Where My Heart Should Be"—the jewel of the album—best represents this philosophy. Deliberately uncoordinated, with knife-edged intimacy and filaments of purified sound, the tune has no real sense of urgency, yet through its immersive atmosphere and conventional linearity manages to turn initial assumptions of its purpose inside out and deliver a composition that straddles both mainstream and marginal ideas of rhythm. Devoid of superfluous gestures, and rooted in a melodic illogic all of its own, its wheels with wheels eventually unveil the song's emotional core, and reveal it to be an ode to Sarah's passion for music. Obedient to the moment, the song then soars upon a repeated riff of such exuberant perfection that to these ears it can never grow tired.

The short instrumental "Grace Grew Up," with its unusual time signatures of 5/2, 5/4 and 5/8, slinky double bass and homemade demeanor, closes the album in a velvety ambience and meditative mood. Sarah no doubt believed the language of music was better suited than words to communicate her maternal love, but just in case this assumption proved misguided she also dedicated *Disquiet Mind* to her beautiful daughter. Grace was eleven years old when the album was completed, and says she remembers little from that time except for the long drives to the mountains that her mother insisted the family take whenever they had a free weekend.

The fact her record was completely ignored did not discourage Sarah from the idea of making another. She had rediscovered a deep need to interact with the world through music, and it was impossible for her to ignore it ever again. Sarah started to perform in local clubs and bars, and began negotiations with a tour manager to do a series of shows down the coast of California. Tom believes their trips to the mountains were Sarah's way of cleansing her ears of the music she had spent the past four years creating, and making room for the new tunes and melodies that were slowly emerging inside her head. When the strong winds required for such a process were too much for her daughter to walk against, Tom and Grace would return to the car and play cards on the back seat while they waited for Sarah to rejoin them. On one such afternoon she apparently lost her footing, and two days later a search party recovered Sarah's body from the bottom of a steep gulley.

More than forty years after the first release of *Disquiet Mind*, its master tapes were found beneath a pile of shoes in Grace's closet. Tom had given his daughter all of Sarah's possessions when he remarried, and the cardboard boxes had been promptly forgotten until Grace's twenty-three-year-old daughter, Annabel, started to inquire about the grandmother she had never known. With a few friends in the Edmonton music business, Annabel was able to locate a recording studio that could still play the tapes, and recalls how everyone present fell silent with shock and wonder as Sarah's songs filled the room.

At this stage in history, when the 1960s have been mined and marketed for all their worth, the only aspect of the era that remains of interest is what was missed or neglected. And thanks to Annabel Wood's curiosity about her grandmother, this fascinating document of an incredible musical talent is once again available for people to enjoy.

It is hard to imagine *Disquiet Mind* ever being lost again. From here its reputation will most certainly grow as more people recognize its groundbreaking innovations and fall under the spell of Sarah's beautiful voice. But unfortunately it is all we have. Sarah gave no interviews, and made no demo tapes of the new songs she was working on. Anything recorded during her time in New York has either been lost or forgotten. Perhaps with the reissue of *Disquiet Mind* someone will recall owning a tape and bring it forward from their attic or garage to share with the rest of the world. We can only hope. Until then we have this wonderful album, full of slow motion kaleidoscopes and pastoral interludes, reservoirs of hurt and intricate aural delicacies. It is a high-water mark for the era, and one that unquestionably deserves the description "lost classic."

Many thanks to Tom Laird and Grace Wood for sharing their personal memories of Sarah. And to Frank Gram for helping the tapes reach How Lovely Records.

Digital remastering by Jonas Peterson.

CD Layout by Carla Green.

Disquiet Mind, *recorded 1963-1967, Edmonton, Canada.*

STANTON'S GRIEVANCE
By Jacqueline Doyle

Tears welled in Stanton Riley's eyes as he surveyed the three members of the Faculty Hearing Panel. He spread his arms out in appeal. "I lost my wife. I lost my dog. I lost my job. I lost my medical insurance." He thought he saw Gina Moynihan blink. Stanton put his hand on his lower back. "I've got this pain in my back and left leg, but I can't go to the doctor. For all I know, it's going to end in paralysis. I could be dead in a month."

He was aware that he was repeating himself, but he wanted to be sure they knew the extent of his losses. This wasn't just some petty complaint. This was injustice of a magnitude beyond fucking belief. His life, his whole goddamn life, hung in the balance.

The large meeting room in the Student Union was drafty and cold. Three metal tables had been set up in a U-shape in the middle of the room with the three professors, randomly selected by their union to defend faculty interests, in the middle, the representative from the university's legal department seated at the table on the right, and Stanton facing her on the left. Stanton had taught for eight years before losing his bid for tenure and his job, but he didn't know any of the other faculty personally. Gina Moynihan, a thin, bird-like woman from Social Work, looked the most sympathetic of the three. Becky Thornton, a recent hire in Communications, was taking notes for the report they would write up detailing their recommendations to the President. Her thick hair was pulled back in a braid. She was wearing jeans and Birkenstocks. She looked nervous and harried, and Stanton didn't have a read on her yet. Glen Notting from Biology, middle-aged and balding, was serving as Chair of the proceedings.

Glen cleared his throat and held up his copy of the grievance. "Thank you, Stanton. You've outlined a number of general problems at some length. However, we still aren't entirely clear about the specifics of your complaint or what redress you're seeking. You refer to 'persistent discrimination' and request that the Dean of Arts and Social Sciences be fired. You also want him fined for your mental distress. Is that correct?"

"I thought I was pretty clear."

"Surely you understand that firing the Dean is outside our purview." Glen rubbed his bald head. "And any financial compensation would be a matter for civil court."

Angela Auerbach, the university representative, nodded vigorously. The goddamn lackey. Stanton ignored her, and addressed his remarks to Glen.

"You can make recommendations in your report to the President. That's within your purview. I can introduce your report into evidence in a civil case and in my tenure appeal. As for the Dean, I'm not the only one who wants Mort canned, believe you me."

He'd stood, agitated, to make his case. Now, as he began to pace, he saw the Filipino security guard seated at the desk by the door look up from his crossword puzzle. Such a crock, including a security guard. It was so obvious that the university administration wanted the faculty panel to think that Stanton was dangerous. When it was the powers-that-be that needed oversight, not him. He took a deep breath.

"There are others who are afraid to speak up. I've got names…" Stanton pointed at the two cardboard boxes of papers he'd lugged into the meeting room with him. "Some of them would surprise you, but I'm not at liberty to disclose them." He gave them a meaningful look and cocked his head at Angela.

Angela raised her hand. "I would like to remind the panel that the burden of proof is on Dr. Riley to demonstrate a pattern of discrimination. It is the judgment of the administration that Dr. Riley has not met that burden of proof, and has failed to specify discriminatory acts in the grievance he has filed."

"The hell I haven't!"

The security guard stood up and gazed over their heads, hands dangling at his sides, his expression neutral.

"If you're referring to your three earlier grievances, Dr. Riley, please understand that each grievance is separate, with separate complaints and supporting evidence, and separate hearing panels. This particular grievance deals with a persistent pattern of discrimination. I will defer to the Chair of the panel here."

Angela smoothed her navy wool skirt, picking off an invisible piece of lint. The only one of them dressed in a business suit, she wore a high-necked white blouse with a bow at the throat and discreet pearl earrings. Her blonde hair was pulled back in an impeccable French twist.

"I'm going to have to ask you to sit down, Stanton." Glen's tone was firm, as if he were addressing an unruly student. Stanton almost laughed at the irony. Like he was the one who'd misbehaved.

He pulled out the metal folding chair with a clatter and tugged at the shirttails of his wrinkled plaid shirt as he lowered himself onto the seat. The button on his corduroy trousers was unbuttoned to accommodate his recent weight gain. He wished he could have worn sweatpants. He could breathe better in sweatpants.

"Could you please describe the relevant instances of discrimination to us? Remember that Becky is taking notes and numbering exhibits for our report, so you will need to be as clear and succinct as possible."

"Let's start with my goddamned tenure," Stanton said, standing to rifle through one of the boxes. He was starting to sweat.

"We understand that you're upset, Stanton, but please temper your language. Of course you're aware that tenure appeals go to a different committee. We need clear evidence of discrimination in other areas."

Fucking bureaucracy. There was too much to say, and Stanton didn't know where to start. He couldn't point out the obvious. That rat turd had slept with his wife. Of course it wasn't written in the faculty contract, but the Dean's behavior was such a clear-cut case of egregious misconduct that he was amazed he'd had to file these grievances in writing. He'd been cuckolded. He'd been passed over for in-house after in-house grant. He'd been given shitty classes at 8:00 a.m. He'd had sections cancelled for low enrollment when others with smaller numbers had not. He'd been stuck with night classes on the satellite campus, an hour away. And he'd been denied tenure, for Christ's sakes, despite his clear potential, and if that wasn't discrimination, he didn't know what was.

"Listen, I was turned down for tenure despite primo teaching evaluations because they found my scholarship lacking. Do you know what the Chair of my department has published? Two articles! Two! One wasn't in a refereed journal, and half of the other was plagiarized! We've got senior professors who haven't done much better."

Gina looked uncomfortable—probably because her name was always in the "Faculty Achievements" section of the university newsletter, and she had the same unvoiced misgivings about half of her department colleagues. Stanton was sure she'd published far more than her Chair had too. Becky was madly scribbling notes. She was young, probably idealistic. Let her learn how things were done around here.

"Plagiarism is a serious charge," Glen said, "but I'm not sure how it pertains to the matter at hand."

"They discriminated against me because they're afraid I'll expose them, that's what. Not to mention what I've got on the Dean."

"So the basis for your complaint is the tenure decision?"

"It's everything. Scheduling, course assignments, university grants. Offices! Have you seen my office? It's in a goddamn trailer!" Stanton tipped over one of the boxes and began to spread papers out on the table. "It's all here."

Angela spoke up. "Hiring practices have changed over time. Professors who were hired twenty years ago are not comparable to new hires, who are subject to the new requirements of a changing academic market. I should add that housing for academic personnel has been at a premium, particularly in the School of Arts and Social Sciences. What Dr. Riley refers to as a trailer is a state-of-the-art temporary building designed to serve the needs of our current overflow of faculty."

Stanton snorted as he sorted through the papers, spilling smudged photocopies and handwritten notes on scraps of paper onto the scuffed linoleum floor. He dropped to his knees under the metal table to gather them up and felt the zipper on his pants begin to give at the top. Angela was wearing nylons. Nylons! None of the women he knew wore nylons. He wondered if they were pantyhose or if she was wearing a garter belt and spent a moment trying to peer under her skirt before banging his head on the underside of the table as he struggled to his feet.

"If you're offering more exhibits, we'll need to see them, one by one, and number them. Please confine yourself to what's most relevant." Glen shook his head slightly, checking his watch. The gold watch looked old, and expensive. Probably some WASP legacy from his father or grandfather. Stanton's father hadn't left him a pot to piss in.

He focused his gaze on Gina and then Becky. "Do you know how much more the senior white males in my department are earning than the females and minorities?" He tugged on his front shirttail, probing his fly with his finger and then surreptitiously tugging his zipper up.

There was a moment of silence. Stanton turned and made an expansive gesture toward the brown-skinned security guard. "You hear what I'm saying, brother."

"You're a white male, Stanton," Glen said.

"And my salary is lower than the two white males hired the year that I was." Stanton waved the salary schedule he'd located. "I've prepared an Excel spread sheet that goes back five years. You'll notice that they both had lower teaching loads than I did last year. Some of my best friends on campus are oppressed women and people of color. They'll back me up here. I don't have the most recent salary figures yet, but they're going to be an eye-opener…"

Becky chimed in for the first time, glancing sideways at her colleagues for approval. "So what is your contention about the basis for salary discrimination in your case?" She pushed her glasses up and waited for his answer, pen poised over her yellow legal pad.

"I'm saying that Mort rewards his cronies. It's plain as day."

He'd made his point. Becky would be thinking about the salary scale in her department, if she hadn't wondered about it already.

Angela passed a neat stack of photocopies to Glen. "I have multiple copies here of the Faculty Contract Article 37, Provision 5.1, which states that employees will not be discriminated against on the basis of race, color, religion, sexual orientation, marital status, pregnancy, age, or disability. Other forms of discrimination are not covered under the current contract."

"Marital status!" Stanton said triumphantly, banging his hand on the table. Gina looked alarmed.

Stanton remembered arriving on campus with Cynthia, who now had tenure in History, while he'd lost everything. Eight years ago, she'd been a lovely young newlywed, fresh out of graduate school. Articulate, argumentative, athletic, a bit heavy in the hips and thighs, but Stanton liked that. He'd seen Mort eying Cynthia all right. He recalled one faculty party in particular, a reception at the President's house. Cynthia's neighing laugh. Mort's face glistening with a light sheen of sweat, his arm clamped around her shoulders like he owned her. Stanton should have known then. But he'd been riding high, two articles already accepted, long wait lists for his classes. Full of confidence, with everything ahead of him. Now he was living in a crummy rented room, and had lost it all. His job. His life. His future. Everything he cared about, gone.

He remembered her sprawled on the bed in the afternoon sun, sleeping peacefully, her breathing slow and even. Her body so warm. Her hair golden in the sunlight. Brandi. God he'd loved that dog.

"She took the dog. Did you know that?"

He'd gone running with Brandi every day. Now he jogged alone every morning to sweat off his hangover. Shaky. Feet pounding. Plotting revenge. Images of Cynthia and Mort unreeled in his head like a grainy porno flick. Cynthia bent over the massive walnut desk in Mort's office while Mort plunged between her parted legs from behind. Cynthia panting and naked in Mort's lap, his eyes rolled back in an expression of slack-jawed pleasure. Grunts, sighs, moans...

"I think you mentioned that, Stanton. If you don't have more evidence to add to the grievance as you've filed it, we'll consider what we have here and make our recommendations." Glen checked his watch again, and mimed a double take at the time.

Stanton surveyed the panel. Even without Cynthia's infidelity, which she denied to this day, he thought he'd made a pretty strong case. Screw Angela Auerbach and her statutes. They knew what kind of power Deans had to fuck you over. He was pretty sure Becky was thinking about salary inequities, and he'd gotten Gina on the medical insurance. He wondered whether any of them had dogs. He felt a surge of optimism.

"There's more to say. A lot." He patted the nearest box of papers. "But I think I've made my case. You can call me at home if you have questions."

Angela pursed her lips. "May I remind the panel that only evidence presented at the hearing is permissible. You cannot engage in further contact with the grievant."

"Yeah, yeah," Stanton said. He rolled his eyes to let them see he'd had enough of her prissy objections. He was sure the others had too. He'd love to mess up her hair, push up her skirt and get a look at her panties and that garter belt. She wasn't wearing a ring. Maybe he'd ask her out on a date, after this was over.

"Then this panel is officially adjourned. I want to thank all of you for your participation."

They stood, gathering their papers together. Angela spoke into the tape recorder in a low voice. "It is 6:36 p.m. The hearing for case number 2421 is now concluded." She secured her packet of documents with a metal clip and slid it into her black leather briefcase.

Stanton winked at her to show he had no hard feelings as he walked around the table. He waved at the security guard across the room, and shook hands with the members of the panel, looking each in the eye as he grasped their hands firmly. "Thank you for your time. I hope you understand where I'm coming from. Thank you so much. I appreciate your understanding." The three of them, even Glen, seemed like decent sorts. You could never tell, though. You never knew who their friends were, what they might have heard, who was talking behind his back and why. All over campus, there were people plotting against him.

But he would prevail. Stanton felt sure of it. Just that morning he'd gotten a return email from Raul Martinez. "I sympathize with you," Raul had written. What could be clearer than that? He had the Hispanics behind him, that's what it meant. If only he knew Don Kirby—the black guy in Sociology—better. Stanton pictured himself, champion of the underdog, marching on the Dean's Office in Overton Hall with a crowd of blacks and Hispanics, maybe a few faculty in wheelchairs, a few Asians if they were downtrodden enough, all with fists raised to the air. "Throw the bum out!" Students too. MEChA. The Black Students Alliance. That new LGBT group. They'd hoist him on their shoulders, chanting "Riii-ley, Riii-ley!"

Mort was going to get the surprise of his life. Angela would be on her knees, begging to give him a blowjob. Stanton hitched up his sagging pants and felt for his fly. He'd buy a new pair for the demonstration.

Yes, change was in the air. He'd already decided that if they asked him to serve as Interim Dean, he would decline. But if they asked him again, well, he'd have to reconsider, wouldn't he? Christ knew they needed some real leadership in the school. In the higher ranks too. Because he might just be moving up after a year as Interim Dean. His enemies would be sorry then. Every fucking one of them.

He gave a Black Power salute to the Filipino security guard as he exited the room, struggling to balance the two heavy boxes of documents with his other arm. He had his work cut out for him all right. He was going to sue for custody of the dog. Next stop would be civil court for damages. He needed to write his acceptance speech for the Deanship. And he might as well start articulating his vision for the university now so he'd have it ready later. Stanton had found that you couldn't be too well prepared. If he'd been better prepared he wouldn't be where he was now. Stanton winced for a moment as he contemplated his losses. But only for a moment. They weren't going to leave him paralyzed. He was a man on the move.

SO MUCH UNCOLLECTED GARBAGE
By Michael Cuglietta

It had been two weeks since the garbage men walked off the job with demands of higher wages and paid sick days. They were a stubborn lot. But so were the folks down at City Hall. On the news that morning, it was announced that negotiations had come to a halt. "At this time," the anchorwoman said, "neither side is willing to budge."

Bradley stood at the end of his driveway, smoking a cigarette and admiring all the trash. When his neighbors ran out of room in their bins, they filled large plastic bags, tied them off and threw them to the curb. The neighborhood looked like a fortress protected by a wall of garbage.

It wouldn't have been nearly as bad had it not been the middle of July. Had it not been Central Florida, where the humidity gets so thick you could slice it like a loaf of bread.

What we need, Bradley thought, is a good thundershower to wash the stink out of these streets.

He found the morning paper and took it to his front porch. He sat at his wrought iron bistro table and got to work on the front page. The lead story was about a black bear that had been terrorizing the neighborhood.

There was an interview with a park ranger. He explained how black bears have a heightened sense of smell. They could sniff out a meal from miles away. "All that garbage in the streets," he said, "it's a black bear's dream come true."

Some city official said if the bear were to hurt anyone, the blood would be on the hands of the trash collectors. Then, he reminded everyone, "Our children play in these streets."

Bradley let out a small laugh. He thought of his own kids. Two weeks had been the longest he'd ever gone without seeing them. He was glad they were safe, with food in their bellies and a roof over their heads. He was glad they didn't have to live amongst so much uncollected garbage. Still, he missed them. He didn't like to think about it. Thinking about it made him feel like a failure.

He punched his cigarette out on the bottom of the table then flicked it into the frontyard. He took the newspaper back down to the curb and tossed it onto the pile of trash. He checked the time. It was ten till. Carla came home at 6:00 a.m. on the dot, every morning, without fail.

Bradley went inside and fixed a cup of tea. He piled a few heaping tablespoons of low fat vanilla yogurt into a bowl, added some blueberries and some granola and took it into the TV room.

He sunk into the couch, propped his feet on the coffee table and listened as Carla worked her key in the front lock.

"The smell out there is getting worse." She pinched her nose for effect. She walked over to Bradley, gave him a kiss. "Get those nasty feet off my coffee table."

"Morning," Bradley said.

"What's all this?" she asked.

"Breakfast."

"More like a late night snack," she said. "I just cannot get used to these hours." She took a seat in the armchair, laid her head back, looked at the popcorn ceiling, then closed her eyes.

They sat like that, quiet, for a few moments before Carla said, "It's different in here, you know," she paused and tears began to swell her eyes, "without the kids."

Bradley saw her tears but decided it'd be best to pretend like they weren't there. "Chuck say anything about you getting back on the day shift?" he said.

"He's going to need me on overnights for a few more weeks." She kicked off her shoes. "But it's not so bad. With the night differential we should see a nice bump in my check."

"Carla," Bradley sat up, "you and the kids are going to be fine. I promise."

"You keep saying that," her tears were spilling over, "but if we don't pay the mortgage..."

"No one's going to take the house." He raised his voice. "We'll see our way through this." He brought Carla her tea. She cupped the mug with both hands and held it under her face, let the steam wash over her.

Gently, she cried. He got behind her and kneaded her shoulders with his fingertips. She closed her eyes, let her head fall forward. He worked his way up her neck.

"You've got no idea how good that feels," she said, wiping the tears away with the back of her hand.

"Why don't you go take a hot shower?" he said. "Then I'll work on your feet."

She reached over, plucked a single blueberry from the bowl of yogurt and popped it into her mouth. "I'll be down in a little while," she said.

"I'll be waiting."

Bradley plopped himself back down on the couch where he sat for a brief moment before deciding to go out to the porch for a cigarette.

Sitting on the porch, smoking his cigarette, he couldn't help but think of the cruel irony in life. When he had the business, he worked so much he barely got time to see his kids. And now the business was gone, he had all the time in the world and, still, he didn't get to see his kids. Sending them off to stay with Carla's parents, that was a tough call. But, until he got his feet back on the ground, they were better off.

When Carla didn't come down, Bradley went up looking for her. The bedroom door was shut. He held his ear to it, no sound. He knocked. When she didn't answer, he pushed the door open.

Carla was passed out on the bed. Bradley sat beside her and watched her sleep. On the nightstand there was a picture of the kids. It was in a cardboard frame with dried macaroni pasted to it. The kids made it in Sunday school.

Carla had put in a picture of them when they were both still young. They were eating ice cream sundaes. Markus had chocolate sauce all over his face. Nikki was smiling big. This was back when her baby teeth had started falling out and her adult teeth had yet to come in. She looked like a prizefighter.

Bradley gave his wife a small kiss on her forehead. She rolled onto her side, wrapped her arms around Bradley's pillow. That's when he noticed her purse laying open on the dresser. Quietly, he crept over. In her wallet, he found twenty-five dollars and some loose change. He slid the bills into his pocket, left the change behind.

The liquor store was a few blocks from the house. It was a beat up old place. In back, there was a damp, smoky bar. When Bradley walked in, there were three Mexicans eating convenience store hot dogs and drinking cans of generic beer. They were part of a landscaping crew. They had a look about them, like they'd spent most of their lives in the sun.

Bradley considered taking a seat. Maybe he'd see if they had any openings on their crew. He imagined himself meeting up at the liquor store each morning for hot dogs and beer. Then he'd pile into the back of their truck. They'd go from house to house, pushing the mower, trimming the hedges.

Bradley put a liter of no-name whiskey down on the counter, asked the guy working the register for a pack of cigs. "Breakfast of champions," the guy said. Bradley didn't have a response for him. He slid the cigarettes into his shirt pocket, grabbed the bottle and headed out.

From the driver's seat of his car, he took a big hit from the bottle and lit a cigarette. Then he backed out into traffic.

It was the middle of the morning rush hour. Instinctively, Bradley found himself merging onto the crowded interstate, following the route he took to work every morning for twenty-five years.

He hadn't seen the building since the bank took it from him. He couldn't get over the size of the empty lot. It looked smaller than he remembered. He used to have an early morning crew. They were in charge of pushing all the bikes onto the lot, washing them and waxing them and getting them ready to be sold. He couldn't figure how they used to fit so many bikes out there.

He backed into the salesman of the month spot. He got out of the car and walked up to the front of the building. He had the bottle with him. He'd been taking little nips since he'd left the liquor store.

It still said Bradley's Motorcycles in big red letters over the doorway. He cupped his hands over his eyes and pressed his face to the plate-glass window, stared into the empty shop. It had only been a few months since he'd lost the business but it felt like a lifetime.

The morning he filed bankruptcy an officer showed up with a lock and chain. He wouldn't let Bradley in, not even to collect his personal belongings.

"Wish I could," he said. "But this building belongs to the bank now."

The cop was expecting a fight. But Bradley just didn't have anymore fight in him. He took a seat on the pavement and waited. He wanted to be there when his guys showed up. He wanted to look them each in the eye. Tell them he fucked up.

You run a business for twenty-five years, the people who work for you, they become family. If Bradley had closed shop just a few months earlier, he would've walked away with a nice chunk of change. But that wasn't his style. If the ship was going down, he was going with it. He wanted his guys to know. He wanted them to see it in his eyes, hear it in his voice.

Bradley took the lock in his hand. Its heft caught him off guard. It must've weighted fifteen pounds. He took a long sip from the bottle then began pulling on the lock. There was no way he'd be able to pull it open. He knew that. He was going to try.

He lifted his foot up as high as he could and brought his heel down on the lock. He lost his balance and came down hard on the pavement. Thanks to the whiskey, he was feeling no pain.

He picked himself up and began shouting obscenities. He was surprised to hear his slurred voice, didn't realize he'd drunk so much. He sat down with his back against the building and lit a cigarette.

Bradley's office used to be right in front, facing the main road. He used to have a nervous ritual. Each morning, before he started his workday, he'd lock himself in his office and count the cars going by. He wouldn't start his day until he counted a hundred cars.

Sitting there by the front door, he started counting. He figured he must still have the touch because when he got to one hundred, someone pulled into the parking lot. He drove up to the front door, rolled his window down. It was a father and a son. The old man leaned over and stuck his head out the passenger's side.

"You guys open?" he said.

"Where were you three months ago?" Bradley snapped. The man put his eyes on the bottle of whiskey then started to roll up his window and drive away.

"Don't go," Bradley called to him. "Stay a while. Have a drink." He stood up, waved the bottle above his head.

Without giving it much thought, he cocked his fist back and took a full swing. His hand connected with the steel lock. The pain was instant.

"Motherfucker!" he shouted.

He staggered back to his car. He tried to light a cigarette but his right hand was useless and, with just the left, he couldn't get the match to strike. He took a few more sips from the bottle, reclined his seat and fell into a deep sleep.

When Bradley woke up he went to roll down the window and felt a sharp pain and remembered his hand. It was swollen to twice its normal size. The fingers dangled, lifeless. He tried but was unable to move them. He was certain his hand was broken. If the circumstances had been any different, he would've driven himself to the hospital.

He turned on the radio and, with his good hand, he flipped the dial till he found the local news. There were no new developments in the strike. The big story was still the black bears. The first bear must've told his friends about the easy pickings. Two more had been spotted in the neighborhood.

"I won't let my kids outside to play," a local mother said. "It's just not safe out there."

Bradley turned the dial till he found some music he liked. He took one last look at the sign hanging over the doorway, Bradley's Motorcycles. He wished the bank would just take it down already.

He backed out into traffic and headed towards the interstate. Rush hour was over. The road was wide open. He stepped on the gas, watched the dials jump to the right, felt the power of the engine. He rolled down the windows and let the wind echo through. It was at that moment when he made a very big decision.

It was just after 10:00 p.m. when Bradley finally found what he was looking for, a manila envelope filled with papers. Somehow, it had gotten wedged behind the filing cabinet. When he got his hands on it he began to shake.

In the fridge, he found a few cans of beer. He stood in the kitchen and put them down, finishing each with one long sip.

From Carla's nightstand, he got the picture of the kids, the one in the macaroni frame. He brought it downstairs, set it on the coffee table.

Under the kitchen sink, with the cleaning supplies, he found a box of tea candles. He spread them throughout the living room then went around with a lighter, holding the flame to each one.

When he was done, he took a seat on the couch. It was a big, plush couch. Bradley hated it. The cushions were too thick. When he sat in it, it swallowed him whole. It was almost to the point where he needed a helping hand just to stand up.

On his lap, he had the manila envelope. He took out the stack of papers, thumbed through. Bradley bought the insurance policy the day he found out Carla was pregnant with Nikki. It was good for three million dollars.

He flipped through until he found the terms and conditions. It took him a minute but, eventually, he found what he was looking for.

There was half a page dedicated to the suicide clause. It said if the policyholder were to commit suicide within ten years of the effective date, the policy wouldn't pay. After ten years, it didn't matter how you went. So long as you went, it paid in full.

Just to be safe, he checked the effective date on the policy. It was twelve years old.

He took off his wedding band and placed it on the table next to the picture of the kids. He walked back upstairs and came down a few minutes later. In his good hand, he was carrying a hunting rifle. With great care, he leaned the gun up against the couch then went to the kitchen.

In the back of the fridge, behind the salsa and a giant jar of sour pickles, he found two more cans of beer. He finished one then dug around in the junk drawer until he found a black felt-tip pen.

Before she went to work, Carla had left a note on the refrigerator. *Chuck asked me to work a double. Won't be home till after lunch. Love You, Carla.*

Bradley considered the note for a while before writing under Carla's signature, *I love you, sweetheart.* Then he wrote, *Make sure the kids know I love them too.*

He took the note off the fridge, brought it to the living room, placed it on top of the life insurance policy. He opened the last beer. He felt the sofa slowly swallowing him.

The rifle loaded from the top. It held four shells. Bradley loaded a single shell, pumped the gun and took the safety off.

He had always heard people talking about their lives flashing before their eyes. He figured, since nothing was flashing before his eyes he would take a minute to consider some of the things he'd done. He thought of his wedding day, how beautiful Carla looked in her dress, how lucky he felt that day. He thought of his kids being born, the way they opened up parts of him he didn't know existed. From day one, he'd do just about anything for those kids. Then he got to thinking about his business.

He was nineteen years old when he convinced the bank to give him a loan. All his friends, they were going off to college. But Bradley, he was determined to go into business for himself. He got to thinking about how much fight he used to have in him. He supposed it was because he was young and he had nothing to lose. When you're young and you got nothing to lose, there's just no stopping you.

Bradley's thoughts were interrupted by a loud crash. It sounded like a car had plowed into his trash bins. He set the rifle down and went for the front door.

Bradley had never seen a bear before. The damn thing must've been six or seven feet tall and built like a small tank. It was all black except for its snout, which was dark brown.

He stood frozen on the porch. He locked eyes with the bear. They were big, black eyes. Like the eyes on a teddy bear only much larger. He knew he shouldn't make eye contact. The bear was liable to think he was challenging him.

Slowly, without turning his back to the bear, he crept back into the house. Once he got inside, the bear started to growl. It was an awfully loud noise.

He opened the blinds and was surprised to see how close the bear had gotten. He was at the bottom of the porch. He was standing on his hind legs. His chest was puffed out and his lips were curled in such a way that his teeth were on full display. Bradley had never seen teeth like that.

Bradley got the other three shells, put them in the rifle. He pumped the gun then double checked to make sure the safety was off. He had his hand on the front door, about to open it when he remembered his wedding ring. He went back to the table, slid the ring on his finger. It was then that he remembered the promise he had made to his wife. He promised her she and the kids would have nothing to worry about. He promised her he was going to take care of them.

The bear was on the porch now. Bradley heard him knock over the wrought iron table. He saw his silhouette in the window. If he wanted to, he could've easy come crashing in. Bradley thought again of when he was young and he had nothing to lose. Back then he was fearless.

The rifle felt good in his hands. For the first time in a long time, he felt capable. He thought of the woman on the radio, how she was too afraid to let her kids outside to play. It's just not right, living in fear like that. Somebody had to do something. He tripled checked his rifle. Before he went back outside, he wanted to be certain his safety was off.

ARTISTS-IN-RESIDENCE FEATURE!!!

FORGIVENESS IS SOMETHING YOU DO TO SAVE YOUR OWN SANITY: THE TOAD INTERVIEWS DAMIEN ECHOLS AND LORRI DAVIS

In November 2013, Damien Echols and Lorri Davis visited the University of Central Arkansas for an artist residency sponsored by the College of Fine Arts and Communication. Echols, who spent eighteen years locked up for a horrendous crime he didn't commit, had recently published the best-selling memoir Life After Death *and had not been back to Arkansas since his release from prison in 2011. Students in the Arkansas Writers MFA Workshop were honored to sit down for a one-on-one interview with Lorri and Damien, and the Toad is proud to publish this excerpted version of the historic interview. The book is on sale everywhere, and "the infamous ringleader of the "West Memphis Three" is still fighting to clear his name.*

Douglas Luman: You talked in your craft talk about the role of writing being a guardian against loss. Being that loss is the theme of this issue of the *Toad Suck Review,* is that largely how you see the writing process?

Damien Echols: Writing guards against loss, but as odd as it sounds, writing, for me, is like digestion. You take in all these experiences every day of your life, little experiences, huge experiences and everything in between. But you can't always instantaneously digest them. You have to mull them over, look at them for long periods of time. Writing helps with that. It allows you to digest the experiences you have.

The difference between knowledge and wisdom is that knowledge is something you learn from reading books, watching TV, your conversations with other people—but it's a very surface level of knowing something, an intellectual level of knowing something. Something has to become digested before it becomes wisdom. Wisdom is something you know almost on a soul-level. It's like part of your DNA. That's what writing helps with, taking It helps you take things to a level in your psyche that you may not be otherwise able to digest.

Douglas Luman: Now that you're back in Arkansas keeping the spotlight on the state government, working toward being exonerated, are you seeing any grassroots movements starting here?

Damien Echols: One of the things we're hoping is that what we're doing has ramifications, not only in our case, but also at large. We have seen grassroots movements. There's a guy I knew on death row—it's pretty commonly known that he's innocent—named Tim Howard. We're seeing the same thing begin to happen in his case that happened in mine. You're having people putting together websites, starting letter-writing campaigns, because they saw what a difference it made in our case.

People tend to have this idea that just because you have DNA testing or because someone admits they lied on the stand, or new eyewitnesses come forward, that everything is open and closed. That's not the case. Even after we got the DNA testing, I sat there for eight more years.

There was a guy, when I first got locked up, who'd been convicted of murder and rape. They did DNA testing, found that the DNA didn't match him, but they still executed him. That was because no one had ever heard of this guy, he wasn't a household name, you didn't see him on the news every night, no books had been written on his case. They figured it's easier than having to admit they made a mistake.

At least fifty percent of the process is getting the story to people out here. Getting people out here to care, to want do something. We're definitely seeing a little bit more of that. We'd like to see even more of it as time goes by.

Ben Sneyd: Since you wrote almost ninety-five percent of your memoir in prison, how is your writing space now similar to the setting you had in prison? And how does that affect your process of writing?

Damien Echols: When I was in prison, there were no chairs, no couches, none of that. You have one thing in your cell, and that's a concrete slab that serves as your bed. So everything I wrote, I wrote laying down. I've tried to write on airplanes and in hotel rooms, and I can't do it. I have to have a fan on to provide some sort of background noise, and maybe that's due to the fact that in prison you hear screaming twenty-four hours a day. That kind of thing can screw up your creative process if you don't do something to block it out. So when I was in prison, I didn't turn off my TV for at least five years. Day or night, it stayed on twenty-four hours a day. It just provides some sort of comfort, almost like a rocking chair. It's harder to write out here because you're always moving around, you're always going somewhere, you're always doing something.

Ben Sneyd: There's a sense of loss throughout your book: loss of childhood, loss of time, loss of place. What have you gained as a result of experiences you've had during and after prison?

Damien Echols: Family would be a big one. When I was born, my mother was fifteen and my dad was sixteen. They weren't really capable of taking care of a kid—so they gave me to my grandmother. My grandmother was like a mother to me, and she died while I was in jail waiting to go to trial. When she died, it was like my family died. So going through this process brought a bunch of people who aren't necessarily related to me by blood, but by spirit. It could be anyone from Capi Peck here in Arkansas who did so much to help spread awareness and get the word out about what was happening to Eddie Vedder, Peter Jackson, and Johnny Depp. My biological sister came to see me twice in the eighteen years I was in prison, and if you combine both of those times together, it may equal an hour. So it cost me a sister, but it gained me Johnny Depp.

As much as we want to avoid it, as much as we don't like it, the number one thing that will force you to grow as a human being—it's like throwing rocket fuel on your psychological and spiritual growth—is pain. Going through pain deepens you and forces you to grow in a way that nothing else will.

Becca Hawkins: In *Life After Death* you wrote about Johnny Depp and you said you never wanted to be a celebrity. Now, many would argue that you are one. So has your view on that changed?

Damien Echols: No! I can at least still do things like walk down the street, or go to my favorite coffee shop, or walk through Walmart. Due to sensory deprivation for so long, I can go into a place like Target and get lost for hours just staring at the ballpoint pens and the cookies and all the colors and the textures. He can't do things like that. Johnny is almost like a prisoner of what his life has become. He has a lot of money, he has a lot of things, but at the same time he doesn't get to experience life. Any time we go out to eat, he has to pay out God knows how much money to the staff of the restaurant just to make sure nobody calls the media. We have to hide in a back room somewhere, sneak out back alleyways.

He came and stayed with us for a week when we were in New York and all was fine until the very last day. Somebody found out that he was staying with us in our apartment and called the paparazzi. The entire street in front of our apartment was packed with hundreds of camera people and journalists. We were like, "Jesus Christ, how are we gonna get out of here, how are we gonna get through this?" And you can tell they don't care about you. They're just looking for however they can use you to sell a few more magazine articles. Johnny finally says we're just going to have to bite the bullet, walk out the front door, get in the car. His bodyguards had to form a human chain so he can get in his car and drive off. About a week later we go into the grocery store and the tabloids are saying that Johnny Depp is having an affair with one of the Olsen twins, because he was seen coming out of *their* apartment building. But you see the extent to which they sensationalize things just to sell more stuff.

Becca Hawkins: I'm curious, Lorri, as to how you imagined your life before you heard about Damien's story. Obviously a lot is different now, but is there anything that's the same?

Lorri Davis: No. As a kid I always imagined myself doing something adventurous. I wanted to be an artist. It was really and truly the moment that I met Damien that became a crossroad in my life. Everything I knew before then fell away, and I was on automatic pilot, but I had no idea what I was doing from that moment on. I grew up in a very spiritual family, and the one thing that has been a constant in my life is a strong spiritual connection.

Audrey Carroll: In your book you write about how spirituality helped you get through prison. How would it have affected your life if you lost faith altogether?

Damien Echols: I probably would've died. Spirituality isn't about belief in a place you're going to float off to in the clouds when you die. Spirituality is about practical, everyday matters. If you can't apply it to everyday life, it's pointless. It's no different than a comic book. When I say faith, I don't mean what you believe. It's about what you do. For example, I'd been beaten severely at one point, and I'd been hit in the face. I had nerve damage in my teeth. And in prison there are no caps, there are no crowns, there are no root canals. Your choices are living in pain or letting them pull your teeth.

I had to find way of dealing with that pain, so that's what led me to learn all kinds of energy work—everything from the Japanese tradition of Reiki to Qigong and Tai-chi. Even the energy practices of Western ceremonial magick. When a lot of people start doing these things—even the most simple forms of meditation—there's always a part of them that says, "Am I really doing something here, or is this just mental masturbation?" If I'm in horrendous pain, and I do this and it gets rid of the pain, it works. So I never had to go through that questioning sense, you know?

The biggest inspiration in my spiritual life was this group of magicians in the late 1800s in England who called themselves "the Golden Dawn." Their motto was "The aim of religion but the method of science." They studied all these spiritual traditions and systems from Hinduism and Gnostic Christianity and Esoteric Judaism to Zen Buddhism and Taoism. They stripped away all the dogma and found out what works. They compiled it all into one system. That's what got me through my days in prison.

Audrey Carroll: Do you feel that spirituality has been a constant since you've been out?

Damien Echols: Absolutely. We use it every single day. I can't dedicate seven hours a day to it anymore, but we make it part of every single thing we do, even when we're doing something like this. I guess the closest word to it is "prayer." But in the West we've come to believe that prayer is saying words in your head, and that's actually kind of pointless. The analogy I always use for prayer is a racecar driver. Whenever they train racecar drivers, they tell them not to look at the wall. Look at the instrument panel, look at the other cars on the track, but don't look at the wall. If you do, you're going to drive right into it. The reason for that is our lives are going to move in the direction that we focus our attention. We feed energy into the things we focus on.

TJ Heffers: Eighteen years is a long time. Is there anything you've done since you got out to make up for lost time?

Damien Echols: There's been big and little things. People think that when you go to prison it's the big things you're gonna miss the most. Really, it's the smallest, like being able to see the stars and the moon. I try to pay attention to those things as much as possible. I love to go on bike rides, especially right when the sun is starting to set and the moon is coming up, to savor that.

But there's also been a lot of big things. In prison I had a list that said, "If they don't kill me, these are the things I want to do." Number one on that list was go see a Boston Red Sox game. Within a month, not only were we there at the stadium, but we got to meet just about the entire team. My favorite player at the time was Jonathan Papelbon, a pitcher, and I asked him if he would sign a baseball for me. He said, "Hold on, I've got something even better," and he goes and gets a game-worn jersey, signs it, and gave it to me.

There were things like that that I wanted to do that we got to do, and there were also things I didn't want to do that we ended up doing, like when we went to New Zealand. Peter Jackson was a huge part of our legal team. He was the guy who directed *The Lord of the Rings.* So we went there and stayed with him for a couple of months, and I swear it was like he tried to force me to make up for eighteen years of lost time in two months. We were doing things like getting into a helicopter and flying it into an active volcano, where we landed and had lunch. We were sitting there eating sandwiches while we watched the ground boil. Then we got on the helicopter and went paragliding. Paragliding is basically where you jump off a cliff with a parachute on your back. Keep in mind, I had extreme post-traumatic stress disorder at that point, but Peter was like, "Yeah, we gotta do this." So there's footage somewhere of me jumping off a cliff, screaming all the way down. It wasn't fun while I was doing it. It was probably the last thing in the world I needed, but at the same time it forced me to come out of myself a bit and start coming back into the world again.

John Mitchel: Both of you seem to have a strong belief in your fellow man. How did you hang onto that through all the things they put you through and all the false accusations?

Damien Echols: I can only speak for myself. When I was in prison, what I lost faith in was the system. I saw how corrupt it was to the core. If most people had any idea how corrupt it is they would be truly horrified. Society would probably fall apart. I lost complete and absolute faith in the system. What I did not lose faith in was people. You had people out here in Arkansas and all over the world who were doing everything they could to help us from putting on bake sales and lemonade stands, to benefit concerts, putting together websites, coming and marching at the capitol, holding banners made of postcards that people from all over the world had sent. It was people watching, people paying attention, that kept me from losing hope. That was what made me believe that I wasn't necessarily going to die in there—the fact that the average, everyday, normal person was trying to do what was right in spite of the system.

Lorri Davis: There were many people who hurt Damien, but in a situation like this you're always going to have a lot of hurtful things happening. Maybe I've been disrespectful to people and maybe they have been disrespectful to me. Whatever. I just decided I didn't want to live with that bitterness or hatred or anger. It's like Damien was saying: It's kind of a daily practice. It's not easy to forgive and not be angry. I had to do it every day—to ask for it. I'm not going to go back to everybody and say, "Will you forgive me?" and "I'm going to forgive you." Every single day I cut that negativity out of my life. It's a process and it takes work, but it's something I'll probably be doing the rest of my life.

Jobe: In your memoir you included a picture that the Roshi-sama had given you. Do you remember what that means?

Damien Echols: That says, "Moonbeams pierce to the bottom of the pool, yet in the water not a trace remains." That's one of the things I'll remember for the rest of my life. When you're executed the only person that can be with you is your spiritual advisor. No family, no friends, none of that, just your spiritual advisor. So my spiritual advisor was a Zen master from Japan named Shodo Harada Roshi. He's probably one of the greatest living Zen masters. Over the years, I received ordination in the Rinzai Zen tradition of Japanese Buddhism. It was the same tradition they used to train the samurai in ancient Japan. During my ordination, that calligraphy was actually sitting on the altar for the ceremony. After it was over, I was allowed to take it back to my cell with me. I had it in my cell for several years, then one day the guards came in and took it. They decided that it was a security risk and I couldn't have it any more, so they took it. Now I have an office in Salem where I teach meditation classes, do energy work, things like that, and it still hangs on the wall.

Jobe: You didn't have the opportunity to get to know your son on a daily basis, at least through his childhood. I'm curious if you're pursuing that relationship now that you're both adults? And if it's not too personal, if you and Lorri have talked about the possibility of whether you would want to be parents?

Damien Echols: No, we're too old. My son is now in his twenties. He lives in Arizona. I missed his entire childhood. That's one of those things you can't put monetary value on. I missed every single Christmas, every single Thanksgiving, every single birthday. When I was in prison, on average, I would get to see him once a year when he would get to come to the prison. So even starting out here, now, it's not like a father-son type of relationship. It's almost like two complete and absolute strangers trying to get to know each other in some way on some level. There aren't any manuals written for stuff like this. It's something I guess we'll just figure out one step at a time as we move along, and hopefully be able to salvage something out of it.

Lynne Landis: In the book you mentioned that prison strips everything individual from you. How did you begin to reassert your individuality when you were released and how difficult was that?

Damien Echols: That's actually a hard question. I don't know if you ever really lose it as much as you're forced to suppress it while you're in prison. That's the whole reason behind dressing everybody exactly alike, forcing everybody to have the exact same haircut, taking away your name and giving you a number. It's to make you less than a human being, to make you just a number in the system. A lot of times what ends up happening is it completely and absolutely destroys your humanity. In my case, I was fortunate enough to have people around me who reinforced my humanity. Whether it was Lorri or friends who stuck with us and supported us throughout the years, people reminded me that I was a human being and not just a number. So when I came out, I don't think my sense of humanity was quite as destroyed as most people's is in that situation. I was fortunate in that. But there's also the process of gradually finding out who you are. When you're in prison, your number one focus is surviving. I would call Lorri every morning and she would tell me about people working on the case and I would think that's great, but as soon as I hung up I went right back to just trying to survive another day. You don't have time to put much energy into philosophical concepts such as "Who am I?" When you get out, you have to figure out things like…uh…everything.

That is the hardest question we've ever been asked. I always knew who I was. I never had to go through this process of finding myself or discovering myself the way most people do. Since the time I was six or seven years old I knew who I was, knew what I liked. I always knew what clothes I liked to wear. I knew what books I liked to read. I read the same thing when I was a kid that I do now, Stephen King novels. The very first movie I can remember seeing as a child was at the drive-in with my parents. I was so young that I could actually stand in the back seat and not hit my head on the top of the car, and we went to see *The Texas Chainsaw Massacre*. That was what I gravitated to when I was really young and I never had to figure out "What do I like?" or "Who am I?" I just always knew and that never changed.

Stacey Margaret Jones: You've said that writing is cathartic and like digestion, but given your spiritual practice, how do you see writing as meditative or prayerful?

Damien Echols: It's like what I was saying about focusing on what you want, focusing on where you want to go, not on what you don't want or where you don't want to go. Part of Lorri's practice, what she does every single morning—I don't know what the hell she's writing—but I'll see her sitting on the couch with her journal and her pen. She'll write for a few minutes, and then she'll stop and look up and think for a while and then go back to writing. I asked her, "What are you writing?" She's writing to the angels, telling them what she wants her life to be, how she wants it to manifest, what things she wants to see come to pass in her life. So writing is a huge part of her spiritual process.

For me, it's about the digestion, number one, but also sharing it. Whenever you're in a space for that long, and you do that much meditation, you start to see reality as, well, it's not one thing. When we think of reality, we tend to think of it almost like a brick. We think of reality as our flesh and blood, we think of reality as the buildings we're in, and the cars we drive, and in actuality, it's more like an onion. There are layers to it. For example, our thoughts. *We know we think.* But you can't show a thought to someone, you can't see how much it weighs, or what it smells like or anything else. So thought is a very ethereal aspect of reality. Then you have the other end of the spectrum, which is the coarsest, densest level, which is flesh and blood, which is clothes and buildings and cars. And you have a level in between. There's a name for it in pretty much every single culture in the world except ours. Chinese call it "ch'i." The Japanese call it "ki." The Hebrews call is "ruah." The Indians call it "prana." All of these things mesh together.

When you're in prison, and you're doing that much meditation, you start to focus on more subtle aspects of reality, so it opens you up in a way where you see more of the whole picture. You start to pay attention to the energy movement, to energy interactions. We're constantly exchanging energy with everything around us, with people, with places, with things. You start to become more conscious, more focused. You're seeing the flesh and blood, and you're seeing the energy interaction at the same time. A lot of times you're dealing with people who are looking at the world through one eye, because they're only seeing the flesh and blood aspect of it. When I'm writing, especially now, what I'll do is pay more attention to those subtle aspects of reality so that people become more aware of them. Whenever they see something that I've written, it's like something clicks in place, and they see things in a different way. That's my hope.

Scotty Lewis: As you continue to work for your exoneration, do you think that there is a way for you to heal? Do you think you can forgive our state? Can you reconcile with this area?

Damien Echols: Forgiveness isn't something you do for other people, and it isn't something you do to be a better person. Forgiveness is something you do to save your own sanity. People ask me all the time, "Aren't you bitter? Aren't you angry? Aren't you pissed off at the prosecutor, the judge, the people who lied? And if not, how are you not?" Well, I finally figured out what forgiveness is. It's not about trying to be holy or anything else. It's about enjoying your life. If I were to sit around and think about the things these people did to me, I would probably be very angry, very pissed off, very bitter. I've lost almost twenty years of my life to this case, and I don't want to voluntarily give up any more of it. What the epitome of forgiveness is to me, if I have to make the choice between sitting around and dwelling on these things and becoming a hateful person or going out and eating ice cream, I'm gonna go eat the ice cream. That's what it means. And that's sort of what I have to get over. It's not even about that. It's about fear, I guess, coming back to Arkansas. Whenever I come back here, there's the psychological shock, the trauma and everything else. The first thing I think is this is where they tried to kill me, this is where they did everything they could possibly do to murder me. That's my number one association, whenever I get off the plane. I have to find ways to replace that with other things, to replace it with thoughts of people who were, and still are, good to me, who love me. It's a gradual process of replacing one thing with another.

ARTISTS-IN-RESIDENCE FEATURE!!!

THE TILTED WORLD OF TOM FRANKLIN AND BETH ANN FENNELLY!!!

Beth Ann Fennelly and Tom Franklin visited us in 2012 as UCA Artists in Residence for the College of Fine Arts and Communication. We were intrigued by their talk of a collaborative novel—which has just been published as The Tilted World. Having secured permission to publish some stand-alone excerpts from this book (which is on sale everywhere!), we are proud to publish the following flash from the overall narrative, as well as a review by Kelvin Krill. So enjoy, before we're all lost to the Great Flood of 2014!!!

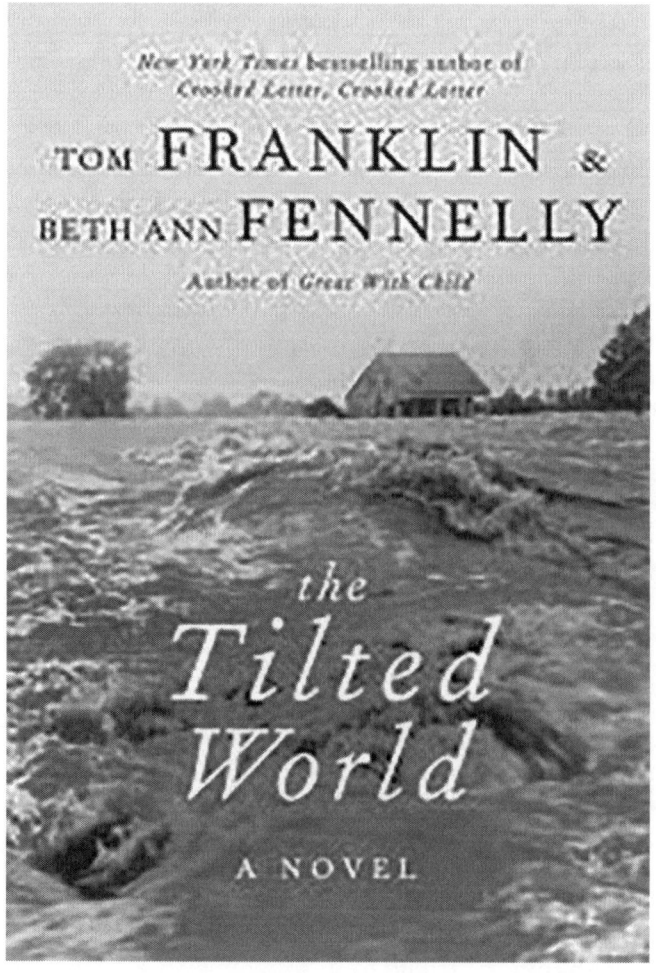

From the book THE TILTED WORLD: A NOVEL by Tom Franklin and Beth Ann Fennelly. Copyright © 2013 by Tom Franklin and Beth Ann Fennelly. Reprinted by permission of William Morrow, an imprint of HarperCollins Publishers.

EXCERPTS FROM *THE TILTED WORLD*
By Tom Franklin and Beth Ann Fennelly

Ingersoll was looking for McMahon's diner, where Mrs. Vatterott said Ham would be, and thank God because Ingersoll hadn't eaten since that morning when he'd split a can of peaches with the baby. He turned right out of the boardinghouse and down one side of the square, past Collins Furniture and a shoe repair, and turned left to continue along the east side, toward a well-lit, noisy corner where cars nosed in like cows at a trough. As he passed the diner window, he saw a man's hand resting along the high, rounded red banquette, fingers thick as roman candles and tufted with orange hair. *Ham, you son of a gun. Hope you ordered me a steak.*

When Ingersoll hung his hat and coat and approached, he saw another man, a small man whose black hair didn't clear the high banquette, smoking his cigarette and leaning into Ham, like an old friend, but Ingersoll had never seen him before and bet Ham hadn't known him long either. Ham had a way of encouraging intimacy, of making you feel like you'd known him for years, and only when you *had* known him for years, like Ingersoll, did you realize you hardly knew him at all.

Ingersoll could tell from the rhythm of Ham's voice that he was building to a punch line, so Ingersoll slowed.

Ham was using his Jewish accent. "Oy vey, I wasn't blessing myself, I was just making sure everything is still here"—and Ham pantomimed an exaggerated sign of the cross—"spectacles, testicles, wallet and watch!"

Ingersoll smiled, not at the joke, which he knew, and not at Ham's skill, which he expected, but at Ham's unquenchable raspy guffaw, a guffaw Ingersoll had appreciated ever since he'd met Ham in the war nine years ago, though in the trenches a laugh like that could get you shot.

Now Ham looked up and, still laughing, waved him over, and with his leg under the table he scooted a chair out for Ingersoll.

"Ahhhh," Ham said, the laugh winding down, thumping his barrel chest twice, "ahh. Ing, this here's my man Jesse whose father fought in the Third, at Argonne. Jesse, meet Ingersoll."

The man half rose from the table and plucked his napkin from his shirt, which was the color of an egg cream, a color Ingersoll'd never seen a man wear. He guessed that the long camel hair coat on the rack had been removed from this man's shoulders. Ingersoll had endeavored not to brush it with his own sodden coat, noticing as he shrugged it off something like cottage cheese on the lapel—the baby's spit-up, clotted in the seams. Jesse's handsome coat most certainly had never worm epaulets of vomit.

"Glad to know you," Jesse said, gesturing toward the chair. He was a few years younger than Ingersoll, mid-twenties, but the thing you noticed was that his eyes were two different colors.

Ingersoll nodded and sat down and opened a menu. The two men looked at him, but he was too hungry to say hello, much less tell a joke.

Ham must have sensed this because he put a finger up and a pretty waitress appeared almost immediately, pitcher in hand.

"We're ready to order, darling."

"Shoot."

"I'll have a ham omelet," said Jesse.

She nodded. "And for you gentlemen?"

"Two steaks, well done," Ham said.

The waitress nodded and turned.

"Ma'am?" said Ingersoll. "You didn't take my order."

The waitress slowly turned back, glancing at the three to see if there was a joke. "The gentleman said two steaks."

"He did. That's his order. I want two steaks, too."

§

The waitress brought glasses of water and Ingersoll nearly lunged for his and was three gulps in when he realized it wasn't water. The muscle ringing his throat pinched, and then he was sputtering moonshine all over the menu. Ham's thunder laugh and Jesse's too and Ingersoll was red-faced coughing and red-faced embarrassed and even the waitress was giggling and Jesse reached to give her fanny a pat. Through his tearing eyes, Ingersoll saw that their fingers clasped briefly before she pushed Jesse's hand away. He wondered if Jesse had a wife in some big house on Broad Street convinced her husband was at a prayer meeting.

Ingersoll held his napkin to his eyes and forced the cough to die in his throat. "Sorry," he croaked. "I thought it was—"

"We know what you thought," said the waitress. "Now, let me get this out of your way"—she dangled the menu so the whiskey dripped from the corner—"before we get another display of Yankee table manners." She pranced off, the apron bow framing her backside.

"I like a dumper with a little motion to it," said Ham. "Looks like a sack of puppies under that skirt."

Jesse laughed and Ham laughed and Ingersoll took another sip, and now that he knew what he was drinking, he drank with pleasure, the whiskey smooth as if it'd burbled out of the first spring thaw, between snowdrops and crocuses and little hopping birds. "Damn," he said, and holding the glass up to appraise its clarity, again, softer, "damn."

"I'm guessing if youda known 'bout this hooch, you'd a hurried on last night," Ham said. "Split a bottle," he said, nodding to Jesse.

Jesse lifted a roll form his bread plate. Ingersoll glanced around, hoping to see a waiter hustling toward him with tongs outstretched.

Ham lowered his voice. "I wouldn't mind knowing where a fella could get his hands on some more. Fella who's mighty thirsty."

Jesse looked at Ham as he brought the roll to his lips and bit.

Ham continued, "Mighty thirsty indeed. Thirsty enough to drink about a dozen cases."

Then the waitress's arm swooped around his face with a plate of ham omelet.

Merciful God, that was fast, thought Ingersoll.

"Ketchup, please, Connie my pearl," said Jesse, looking up, and Connie said "It's right here in my apron, gimme a sec." Her other arm held two plates, one in her fingers and the other balanced on her forearm, and she transferred that one to her free hand and began lowering Ham's heavy double steak.

Jesse reached into the apron and said, "Oh, I'll just help myself to what I want, don't mind me," and rummaged there as she squealed and shimmied, Ham's eyes gleaming as he watched the frisking, Ingersoll smelling his steak just out of reach and feeling saliva channel his tongue and thinking how strange it was when something you hear about your whole life happens: his mouth was watering.

At last Jesse got his ketchup and Ingersoll his steaks, decidedly smaller than Ham's. "I'll take two more," he nearly shouted at the waitress' back as she turned to bring more whiskey. Then he lowered his head and tucked in and didn't say anything for a long time. Which was fine: Ham might finally have met his match in terms of loquaciousness, a word Ham had taught him. The men watched as Ingersoll sawed a giant bit and forked it in.

§

Connie appeared to refill their glasses. "Drink up," she told them. "Somebody's got your check."

Jesse leaned slightly out of the booth to raise a finger in the direction of the police captain's blue hat.

Ingersoll's reach for his glass was a little off. *Lord Jesus but I am drunk*, he thought. *Shouldn't be, but I am*. He was thinking of the way the baby had lounged in his upended hat by the fire last night, leaning back to watch the flames. Mellow, like a tired old cowboy soaking in hot springs after rounding up cattle. And now Ingersoll was thinking how empty his hat must feel with nothing in it but the hook.

§

"I reckon it's time," said Ham, "to get back to bidness. Now this whiskey is the finest I've had outside Kentuck, bonded or no. And I'm thinking a man like you, who makes dinner bills vanish and pretty waitresses bat their eyes like toads in a hailstorm, might know how to get some more."

Jesse lifted the knife beside his plate and tilted it, smiled to inspect his white teeth. He flicked his thumb beneath the right wing of his mustache to curl it, then flicked the left. "Love to oblige you, boys," he said, lowering the knife to the table. "But I don't know nothing about nothing."

"That so," said Ham.

"That so. And even if I did why would I trust a fella won't tell me his real name?"

"All sorts of reasons to trust a fella."

"Such as?"

"A taste of the take."

"Thought you fellas were engineers."

"Engineers is what we be. But with expensive tastes."

"That right?"

"Got a blue-book octoroon named Sappho in a house of ill repute in Storyville. Smokes moota with her coochie."

Jesse leaned forward, eyes boyish and bright. "Liar."

"No lie. She opens her whorehouse window and lowers a basket and the banana vendor packs up a big bunch of those Chiquitas, and a little moota in the bottom, rolled up to smoke. My gal Sappho can French inhale, blows smoke rings with her coochie lips. It kills me, every time. Can't stay away. Even if her room always smells like rotting bananas." Ham shrugged philosophically. "But such talent don't come cheap. Costs me ten dollars. Wanna do her in the mirrored parlor? Costs extry. Wanna see her with her friend, Miss Carmen Brazilia of the Mule Skinner's Whips? Costs extry. So you see even a distinguished engineer got to have some extry extry."

Jesse nodded, removing the toothpick from between his lips and dropping it into the ashtray. "You have a point. Ten dollars is a lot."

"Yeah, well"—here Ham jutted his jaw out and scratched his sideburns—"she charges by the inch."

All three laughed, Ham the hardest.

"So if you find out the distiller of this here whiskey," Ham continued, "wants a partner with ties to vast engineered metropoli scattered across this great nation, you tell him to come find us."

"Oh, will do, will do." Jesse gave them a keen look with those queer eyes of his. "Gentlemen," he said, and pushed his chair back and stood, "this has been a most enlightening meal. We'll see each other soon, I trust."

§

At last Jesse, still chuckling, made his way to the door, passing the table Connie was wiping down. He leaned close and whispered something that made her laugh too. She straightened, and all three of them watched Jesse proceed to the coatrack and slip into the camel hair and place his hat on his black hair and flick the brim. He withdrew his umbrella from the stand and opened the door, the bells ringing. Under the awning, he dipped his head to open the umbrella, then pushed off into the blustery night.

Ingersoll was exhausted. It hit him just that fast. "Let's go," he said, thinking of the rooming-house bed, and Ham nodded.

Then Ingersoll leaned over and picked up Jesse's glass, a half inch of whiskey left, and he drained it. "Huh."

"Water?"

Ingersoll nodded.

REVIEW OF *THE TILTED WORLD*
By Kelvin Krill

Tom Franklin and Beth Ann Fennelly are the dynamic duo of contemporary southern letters: long married, parents, equally successful in their respective careers, and supremely entrenched figures at the MFA program at Ole Miss, where Fennelly serves as current Director and Franklin as Associate Professor of Fiction. Franklin, an Alabama native, is southern to his core, while Fennelly has lived in the South for so long—first Arkansas and then Mississippi—that her credentials as a southerner can no longer be contested. What they have not done—until now, with the creation of *The Tilted World*—is write together. It would seem on the surface to be an odd fit. Fennelly has proven herself to be a linguistically exacting and emotionally probing poet, with work that is clean, honest, and direct; a writer whose most profound subject, in both her poetry and prose, is parenthood, a subject she addresses with humor, honesty, and intelligence. Franklin has a well-earned reputation as a leader in the new southern gothic. His lurid historical-comical-fantastical novel *Smonk,* for instance, makes O'Connor's southern grotesques look like AV club geeks. There's not a gun he's met that he hasn't wanted to squeeze (literally and figuratively) into a novel; there's not a death so gruesome, or a smell so stinky that he doesn't revel in it. So how does Franklin's raucous and earthy sense of southern humor mix with Fennelly's seriousness, high intellect, and inborn sensitivity to women's rights?

Surprisingly well, actually. Cagily focusing *The Tilted World* on two equally significant protagonists—one male, one female—the two different writers develop the novel on separate tracks for most of its length, permanently bringing together the protagonists only about three quarters of the way through. (And fittingly with a powerhouse, nearly perfect scene that features a medical emergency with a child and some brilliantly calm parental nerves.) It's impossible not to imagine Franklin acting as the progenitor of Ingersoll, a twenty-something revenuer and former army sharpshooter who falls in love with the short, freckled figure of Dixie Clay, the young wife of a Mississippi bootlegger, or to imagine anyone but Fennelly as the originator of Dixie, who after a series of miscarriages and the disappointment of finding out her husband is a slick cad, discovers her real role in life after being given an orphaned child to raise as her own. Against the historical backdrop of the Great Flood of 1927—an event, the authors note in their engaging prologue, that not only displaced hundreds of thousands of people and came with a political fallout similar to that which followed Hurricane Katrina in 2005, but which permanently altered the social and political landscape of America—Fennelly portrays Dixie's struggles to align who she is with what she is allowed to do. Not merely a pretty, innocent woman done wrong, Dixie is a proud craftsman, a woman given the unusual job of running the still because of her bootlegger husband's frequent sales trips. She proves not just capable at making tasty moonshine but superb at it, so good her husband insists she sacrifice quality for quantity so that he can better keep up with demand and turn an even better profit. Dixie refuses to submit to this violation and comes up with a better plan: She increases the quality even more, so that her customers will be willing to pay many times what they would for ordinary moonshine, and in the process earn her husband the profit he seeks. This sly strategy to maintain her self-respect and pacify her husband fails in the end. But then again, everything is destined to fail in the light of the unprecedented natural disaster released upon Mississippi. Franklin's Ingersoll, meanwhile, is a loveable and even quietly heroic galoot. While he's a well-crafted and credible hero, what fascinates the reader is the world of revenuers and revenuing in an America very late into the experiment of Prohibition—in which revenuers can easily be bribed or made to disappear, where the revenuers themselves when off duty enjoy illegal whiskey as much as anyone, where things have gotten so bad Herbert Hoover has to create a special task force of select, honest revenuers, because so many in service are uselessly corrupt. In the Ingersoll chapters, Franklin's taste for the lurid, the off-color, and the folkloric rise to the fore.

Eventually, the two separate tracks of the novel merge, and half the delight of the novel from that point on is guessing which scenes and what lines and which character impulses one of the authors suggested to the other. It is a credit to them both that the latter chapters, when Dixie and Ingersoll are bound together, are as seamless and engaging as any in the book.

The *Tilted World* is a well-told literary novel set in the time of a notable historical event. It's no knock to the novel to say that one can imagine a movie coming from it. It is that tight of a creation. But as with any book there are flaws. One could wish for an even stronger emphasis on the flood itself and the resulting geo-political damage, or for a further exploration of the history of enforcement of the Volstead Act—but it's a novel not an academic treatise. One could wish that the inevitable pairing of Dixie and Ingersoll seem a bit less inevitable and the sex scene between them a little less ludicrous; one could wish for a few more characters who seem less like types we've seen in southern fiction before. On the other hand, when two writers of very different styles and sensibilities work together it is always a risk that they will cancel each other out, and that what makes each most idiosyncratic, even masterful, will be sacrificed in the name of compromise—the result being a muddled mess of competent but uninteresting writing. It's safe to say that this did not happen to *The Tilted World*. Rather than blunting each other's strengths, they have enhanced them. In fact, it seems as if it's the poet Fennelly who discovers and probes and solidifies the heart of the book, while it's the fiction writer Franklin who keeps the story humming along at a steady pace. That's a delicate dance few writing couples, to say nothing of married writing couples, can pull off. It's a pleasure worth the price of admission to see Fennelly and Franklin make it work.

LOVERS SPELUNKING SMOKE SCREAMING
By Doug Luman

EASTERN OREGON ALMANAC

Romans run wild
           among foothills of the Cascades
    through abandoned plywood mills
making sawdustballs
           from forgotten rosin
giggling with reckless abandon,
           teenagers learning
    that love and liquor
are kissing cousins.

Lovers are spelunking
           over Eastern Oregon,
    probing terrain with Richter's forefingers
reaching peaks in scales measured gasp
           by gasp
    cresting top soils
lithe tricks in the lithosphere
           hiding from morning under the mantle
    in crevasses rated for experienced climbers.

Local laws are no match
           for rules of these Saturnalian sports.
    Rustlers steal needles from haystacks
draw straws
    taking turns
           hiding innocence among covered bridges
throughout Clackamas County,
           alarming farmers' daughters
    parked in fathers' cars.

Bacchus watches his children
           from the crown of old Bald Peter,
    making boulders fall with raucous laughter
park rangers confuse with an avalanche,
           bellow so deep, folks hear it far as Corvallis–
    like the night in 1921 six boys from Bend
summited Three-Fingered Jack.

Folklore tells of a full laugh,
           so hard Bacchus fell from his perch in Olympia
    rolling down from Washington to the Willamette

where he settled
> causing shockwaves felt until 1927.

Even Ma and Pa couldn't fault 'em;
> in youth, they were busy
> blazing trails through Santiam Pass
driving livestock
> through to pastures on steppes for grazing,
> stopping long enough for child rearing
and barn raising.

Now, rivers are dry grails;
> locked up lochs
> abandoned railroads
hold these Olympic games in erotic escrow.
> Bacchus' players
> press wine to stay hydrated,
wear clothes, shameful of being naked.

Bacchus knows
> where vines are sown, lust ferments in oak
> new grapes will grow. He declares open season!
and at the drop of their hats
> shirts
> rest of their clothes,
runners resume the steeple-chase, jumping busted dams
> razing forests in their wake
> when the horizon sets fire to the landscape.

Listen closely to timber
> falling in the forest
> to hear cracking cackles
mistaken for the death rattle of trees
> or levees breaking under water's weight
> flooding the valley with passion
not seen since December of 1861
> when the Willamette River took
> hundreds in the undertow,
leaving Mr. and Mrs. John Chapman of Oregon City
> alone to wonder if they needed to repopulate the world.
That morning after,
> rapids went placid,
> marooned on the new island mill,
how Mr. Chapman wondered what his god had wrought,
> seeking a rainbow,
> only seeing his wife,
not realizing that his front yard
> was inundated.

ST. PULASKI'S FIRE

In 1910, French hearts were aflame

        from weeks of no rain and dry wood

scattering hundreds in all directions

        each man an ember

flagging surrender in the wind

        out of chimney—like canyons

with the sound of one thousand freight trains

        circling the mountains for supplies.

Of forty-five, seven did not survive high-altitude breathing lessons

        swept sky-high to Heaven

dropped down a mineshaft to Hell

        a world afire with foolhardiness.

It was a case of saving our lives

        and three horses

from the call of the wind conductor

        under seductive blankets of smoke.

We crawled to an abandoned mine tunnel

        we raced for it

one man claiming victory over death

        under a fallen tree, reduced to ash

to swim in the river of the dead with burnt bear and trout gods

        drinking flake for refreshment.

Another, finding the edge of the deforested world leaped

        off, into the heart of the mountain.
I brandished my pistol as a pointer

        on the black slate of smoke screaming

the first man who tries to leave this vein, I will shoot

        commanding the men to lay as lignite

while the mountain god smoked his own intestines.

        I would have gladly fanned the hammer

of the six-shot revolver

        to slap the hearts of mischievous men.

The mountain spoke a sermon of Pentecostal fire

        while we tended its mouth with woolen tongues

scavenged from supply carts, using holy water

        making a sleeping draught of soot.

The mountain begged us to sleep.

        As pious men of the pines we snoozed

waking up to the end of the end of the world —

        we were pioneers of the pyre, come to preach

cleansing chastity among heathen mountain men.

        I plead to stand, my legs refused to pray with me

hearing the funeral litany pronouncing,

        come outside, boys, the boss is dead.

I testified, using my lips to crawl from mountain's mouth

        calling out my own hosanna

like hell I was, but now I am saved

        though my eyes were blackened to the world.

I could not say the same for five men

> who practiced being coal too well.

We wandered down the mountain,

> I saw the baptized skeletons of the bear and trout gods,

joined by a husk of man

> fished from this world by bait of flame, each body a verse of gospel.

Now when I whiskey-dream, I see them;

> if the bodies hadn't been so fresh a burnt offering,

I wouldn't have been able to tell the difference

> between lumps of charcoal and prophets.

Borocho Xing, Nicaragua.

EARTH DAY, TEXAS
By David Taylor

In my backyard,
the henbit is wilting in the early April, 80-degree days,
purple flowers turn curled yellow to brown.
Above, a front of starlings
spills over the neighbor's white-shawled Bradford pears,
the greening privet leaf bundles
just beginning to open in the fence row.

Don't trust the weeds and city trees, my father says. *Mesquites
tell you when the last freeze is coming*,
opening their feathers
only when winter is past.
The closest is a mile or two away,
so I've held off
until I can go out to the country.

To the West,
    honey locust, hackberry on the fence rows,
    mockingbirds and cardinals dropping seeds there,
    by the creek banks box elder, sycamore, cottonwood,
    the faint redbud purples and serviceberry white in a clutch of
      brown tree trunks,
    and farther still, red yucca, more mesquite, sage, red dust.
East, too,
    pine-filtered, cypress swamps, dense cover, reed-lined,
      cattail-thick lake edges,
    white egret, blue heron, a pileated woodpecker keeping time
    to the passing songbirds, the steady reptiles,
    an orange blur of monarchs in the next few weeks.
South, as well,
    the rush of cold rivers Pedernales, Blanco, Guadelupe,
    deep pools and down through seeps and caves,
    limestone cliffs, live oaks, cedar and more cedar,
    even ringtails, white-tailed deer, a turkey buzzard feeding
      on roadside armadillo.
Only a few miles North,
    the muddy vein of the Red River twists and turns
    through the patchwork forests and prairies.
    a limestone ridge here, a rise in the black soil there,
    carrying water and red clay, the color of blood,
    to the beginning of the matter.

In a prairie near Sanger, late afternoon,
I'm resting my left hand near spring flowers of bluebonnet
and winecup as I write.

An early season, red-chested, scissortail
treads the wind, hunting grasshoppers.
Above Clear Creek, buzzards circle over

their rookery in the burr oaks.
Only small pools remain in the river, not much water—
    the carp and gar moved downriver days ago.

I jot down what I see,
the raccoon tracks in the creek bed,
coyote scat beaded with berries,
and a tuft of rabbit hair on the prairie above.

I try to write these pieces into my journal,
visceral things, black soil, prairie life, Cooper's hawk, blood moon,
post oaks upon post oaks,
scattered dried skulls and bones of cattle and deer,
red yucca sprouting bright flowers,
cockleburs stuck in my leg hair,
soft, white rain lilies after a good rain,
a copperhead hunting by night,
drunken cowboy songs,
Townes Van Zandt singing "High, Low and in Between,"
    ... answers don't seem easy
    I'm wondering if they could be.
a Shiner Bock on the wobbly plywood table
by the fire pit.

In a median outside the Flying Fish restaurant in Fort Worth,
a small, native pecan grows,
no more than fifteen feet high,
trunk the size of a grown man's thigh,
dried, black, quartered husks
clinging to the end of the stems.

Under the detritus of candy wrappers, drink straws, and leaves,
last fall's pecans idle away the winter,
and somehow it seems worth it,
filling the drink holder in the car
with all the thumb-sized pecans
it can hold.
They're more shell than nut, my dad says.
He holds three in his hand at a time
to crack them
and carefully picks and sorts shell from nut.
Five minutes for a teaspoon of pecan,
he laughs,
and damn if it ain't worth every second.

There's a note in what's worth noticing,
    a core, a past that is its presence, a place, a nod, a turn of
    color, a flash of wing, the uplift of rock, a sculpture of limestone
    fossil ammonites and sea biscuits, brown river, open sky,
    a canvas of wildflowers, dangling moss, perched mule ear
    cactus, coyote shadow,
that might be melody, this place.

FLOAT: A TEASER
By JoAnn Hart

God Help Us.

The words, writ large in the sand, appeared on the beach after Duncan Leland's attention had already drifted. It was in the pink of the afternoon, at the end of another trying day, when he should have been attempting something spectacularly proactive to save his sinking business, such as scrambling numbers on a screen or gathering somber consultants around him, but instead, as was his habit, he was looking for answers outside his office window. The sky was clear and blue, the water calm. The serenity of the day mocked the economic storm raging around him. He was now, as Harvey Storer of Coastal Bank & Trust had so coldly pointed out to him that morning, officially underwater. He owed more on Seacrest's Ocean Products of Maine, Ltd. than the business was worth.

"True that," Duncan had agreed, "but only at this very moment."

"What else is there?" asked Storer.

A leveling silence washed over Duncan as his mind slowly emptied of words. He was opening and shutting his mouth like a fish when Storer, sitting across from him at the loan desk, leaned in closer.

"Duncan? What else do you have that might secure this loan?"

Duncan shook himself out of his trance, realizing that Storer's was a fiscal rather than a philosophical challenge. "It's all here," he said, half-standing as he slapped pages of the loan application down on the mahogany like tarot cards. "Look, in the spring, our new line of fertilizer hits the market, opening a revenue stream so robust it'll be like drinking water from a fire hose!" He displayed a spreadsheet thick with projections, but this banker, like the ones who came before him, remained unmoved. Duncan's vision of rosy profits in the future failed to overcome the devalued assets of the present, and in that moment he saw his business begin to slide away.

He'd left Storer's sterile cubicle in a funk and gone back to his office, back to the warm embrace of his chair and the tranquilizing effect of the harbor view. He fixed his gaze on the beach, a patch of rust-streaked sand so inhospitable it did not even exist at high tide, and let his mind fix on a plastic bag caught on a submerged stick. He watched the bag, alive with water, wash gently from side to side until his own currents of thought slowed to a listless tempo. After an empty space of time, the retreating tide abandoned both stick and bag to the land, and his hypnotic amusement was over. Looking back, he was sure of one thing: There had been no one on the beach, and there had been no mysterious message written in the sand. That was two things, but still.

He wondered if he might have been a witness to the event if the music hadn't ended. He liked to keep an iPod playing on the factory floor, on the theory that if he was asking his employees to spend their days cooking fish skeletons down to a fine powder, then he had better give them some background music to divert their senses. If nothing else, managing the sound system was one of the few enjoyable duties left to him, so when a cycle of early Beatles ended, he turned his back on the water view to deliberate at length between PLAYLIST #8 (Miles, Coltrane, and Rufus Harley) and PLAYLIST #22 (Dylan, Joni, and Steve Earle) before abandoning hope of coming to any decision at all. He clicked SHUFFLE in defeat and returned to his chair. When he looked back down at the beach, there, scratched into the sand, were the three-foot-high wobbly letters spelling out *God Help Us*. The surface was still reflective from its recent brush with water. The message faced the harbor, not him, so it didn't appear to be a personal accusation, more like a random act of prayer. Or not. Worst case scenario, it was written by an employee petitioning God on behalf of Seacrest's. But no matter who wrote it or what the intention was, it was a desperate message and a bad one for potential investors, should he ever have any. It had to go.

Down, down to the sea he climbed, taking the two iron flights of the fire escape to avoid his factory workers, who seemed to want so much from him these days, most of all an optimistic face on Seacrest's future. Gone, gone, gone. It was low tide now, and his heels sank into the wet sand as he trudged toward the words, his footprints filling with water behind him. With the tip of his black rubber boot, he proceeded to rub out the message, erasing the *d* first, changing *God Help Us* to *Go Help Us*.

"Better," he mumbled. More ecumenical, more in keeping with his Unitarian ancestry. Then he contemplated *Us*, that sweet plural pronoun of marriage. He rubbed it out. It had been the middle of August when Cora had asked for a little air, and here it was after Labor Day and he still hadn't heard back from her whether she'd caught her breath. He stood very still, trying to quell the sour tide in his gut. How had the solid continent of *Us* become the scattered islands of *him* and *her*? They had just wanted what everyone else seemed to have. "Is a baby really too much to ask for?" as Cora would say. "They're everywhere!"

He should have known that to have expectations was to court disappointment. Two years ago they'd decided it was time to add to their fund of general happiness, but nature had not taken its usual course in the bedroom. Was it her? Was it him? Or were they just a bad combination? But Cora, even-keeled as she was, wouldn't let them go there. "No finger-pointing," she'd said. "Let's just get the problem solved." And in July they began to take deliberate steps toward in vitro. At the very first appointment, he was asked for a sperm sample to test for motility. He found the staff oddly humorless about the situation, and his jokes fell flat, but he got the job done. Afterward, it was he who fell flat. He froze in the hallway with the filled specimen cup in hand, locked in terror as if staring into a milky abyss. A nurse had to wrest the container from him, and from then on his marriage began to spiral down the drain.

The problem was this: Fertility treatment had led him to think about the dangers of replicating his family's genes, and those worries began to bloom like algae in a stagnant pond. The next thing he knew, he was debating whether it was right to bring children into the world at all, a world so overcrowded and polluted it sat on the brink of ecological extinction. This, in turn, led to questions about the meaning of life itself. "When we give them life, we give them death," he said. "What's the point?"

That had been it for Cora. "Enough thinking," she'd said through her tears. "It's time to act." Off to counseling they went, but they could not reach the line of salvage in that desolate terrain, with its boxes of tissues and anatomically correct dolls stored in a milk crate in the corner. Cora was particularly teary because she'd been getting estrogen shots in preparation for the egg harvest. Marriage counseling ended when he failed to follow through on scheduling an appointment, a chore the therapist insisted they take turns doing, a tactic that seemed like some kind of a test. He remembered the moment he stalled. He had been, as was his habit, gazing out of his office window, watching the Hood Dairy blimp hover in the air above a distant beach. ENJOY HOOD ICE CREAM was printed on the rounded sides, sending him into a smiling reverie of dripping vanilla cones, sand buckets, and other childhood joys. "Enjoy it *all*," he'd said out loud. He continued to watch until the blimp turned inland, but instead of majestically disappearing over the horizon as usual, it slowly—ever, ever so slowly—dipped too close to the treetops. The navigation bucket got stuck in the branches, and it could not move. Engine trouble, he'd found out later. No one was hurt, but how could he make an appointment after that?

"What kind of a world is this where a zeppelin can just fall out of the sky?" he said to Cora. It was the day when he'd gone to Portland to produce the specimen for the first attempt at implantation later that week, so he was particularly shaken up. "How can we bring a child into a world that hasn't even mastered nineteenth-century technology?"

Cora was as unmoved as the zeppelin. "Fuck the blimp," she said. She was a family therapist herself, and as far as she was concerned, his inability to make the appointment demonstrated not just his lack of commitment to the process but a lack of commitment to her and their future baby. Like a cruise ship, Cora was not easy to turn around once she was set on a particular heading. She started throwing ballast overboard. She sent Duncan away that very night. "Go to Slocum's for a few days to get your head on straight. You're too anxious to be around right now."

Their relationship had been sitting in dead air ever since. But that was not today's problem. His marriage would have to wait in a long line of tomorrow's problems because today he had to save his business. Seacrest's was letting in water at every seam, and it was all his fault. He had aimed too high. He should have opted for the cheapest solution he could get away with a few years ago when the EPA mandated the installation of pollution controls, but no—in the spirit of the careless prosperity of the times, he'd gone trolloping to where the woodbine twineth and borrowed too much money for a complete modernization of the plant, making it as clean and tight as a toolbox. The banks were crazy to loan him so much money. How much profit, really, could be had from fish waste? Seacrest's, whose business was to process marine waste into feed and fertilizer, used to be known, along with all the other gurry or dehydration plants on the coast, as the smelly stepchild of Maine's fishing world. Now the renovated plant was almost odorless. The industry had come a long way since his great-great-grandfather Lucius Leland's time, when gurry—the finny bones and entrails left over from cleaning the day's catch—was unceremoniously dumped into the harbor, only to wash up on shore later in the day. Lucius was originally from bustling New Bedford, but he'd dropped anchor in Port Ellery in the name of love for a local lass, and he soon saw wealth where others saw garbage. Using the money he'd raised touring the Midwest with a sawdust-stuffed whale in a boxcar, he built a factory to dry and grind up the fish scraps for livestock feed. The first thing he processed was his whale. The pet food industry soon became a major buyer as well, and business boomed for more than a century, but in the last few decades they'd had to branch out just to keep up. Duncan's father developed their unique fish fertilizer, and more recently Duncan had added kelp to the recipe after watching Cora gather seaweed from the beach for her garden.

Kelp. He looked at *Go Help* in the sand, then changed the *H* in *Help* to a *K* and added an exclamation point.

"*Go Kelp!*" he shouted, then looked around, but there was no one to hear. Not even the gang of seagulls patrolling the water's edge had paused to consider his outburst. As was too often the case these days, his words made sense only to him. Go Kelp! could be the name of his new retail line of soil amendments, if there was a future for them at all. Before the expensive renovations to the building, he'd always sold his fertilizer in barrels to companies who resold the powder in small bags under their own pricey labels, but as the bills came flooding in, some daft accountant said that the only way to recoup his capital expenditure was to leave the safe harbor of wholesale and set out into the deep waters of retail. Which meant more money out the door. His marketing investment had been huge, and the product was still not launched. Worse, competition was darkening the sky. A dehyde down in Massachusetts had contracted with key fish processors for their waste and was already selling eco-sludge directly to the planting public. Another company in northern Maine was peddling lobster-shell dust and getting as much play in the gardening magazines as a dazzling new rose. He hadn't acted fast enough in making the transition. The words he'd overheard in a bar ten years ago, soon after he took his father's place at Seacrest's, came back to him now: "Duncan Leland run a business? He couldn't run a bath."

One of the seagulls bounced closer with an eye toward a blue shell near his foot. Duncan kicked the mussel to the bird so it could see for itself that it was empty, then, with a start, he realized that there were no footprints on the beach other than his. How was that possible? Someone had written the words without walking on the sand? He looked around, then up. He was lost in troubled thought when a ship's horn sounded, frightening the seagulls into the air with hysterical shrieks and a slow flapping of wings.

All but one. There was always one.

The large black-backed gull had a loop of a six-pack holder stuck in its beak and around its neck, so that the sharp plastic dug into the sides of its face. The rest of the holder was bunched up around its head, and two of the loops formed glasses through which the bird stared at him with red, burning eyes. One wing hung limply by its side, dragging in the sand. The poor bastard could hardly move without making things worse, and Duncan knew that feeling all too well. The kindest thing to do was to let nature take its course, but when the bird opened its beak in mute appeal, Duncan realized he was screwed. He'd have to give it a fighting chance or never face his friend Josefa Gould again. Josefa ran Seagull Rescue out of her backyard, a cramped space where the birds went to linger in pain before dying. He looked up at the factory. He couldn't see anyone at the windows because of the harsh reflection of the sun. But even though he couldn't see his employees, he could feel their eyes upon him, and in his mind he heard them laughing.

Let them. Wounded animals had to stick together.

He held his arms out, fluttering his hands, and as he edged slowly toward the injured gull he felt himself to be the ridiculous figure his employees thought he was. He could hear Cora telling him in the measured cadence of her profession that he was being paranoid, that he had the love and respect of all his employees. But this was not paranoia; how he wished it were. Ever since his father died, forcing Duncan to move back from New York to take over Seacrest's helm—his older brother Nod having laughed it off—he felt he was not meeting the employees' expectations of a Leland boss. Duncan had arrived at the tail end of a long line of rugged, blond male specimens who were athletic, competent, and self-assured on land and sea. He was none of those things. Baby pictures showed him as a happy towhead, but the years had darkened his hair along with his mood, until both were mud-colored. Behind his back, he imagined that his workers made fun of his coordination (faulty) and glasses (eyes too dry for contacts). He was tall, yes, but tall in a gangly, loose-limbed sort of way. His image was not helped by the fact that at the moment he wore a business suit tucked into calf-high muck boots. After he'd returned from the bank with an empty begging bowl, he was too tired to change into his work clothes of jeans and a sweatshirt. He'd removed his tie and tossed it up and over the ceiling fan like a noose, then slipped off his leather shoes and put on the wellies he kept in his office for slogging around the factory floor, but he'd done nothing to protect his navy Brooks Brothers outfit. What did it matter? He saw no future that included a three-piece suit.

Taking care not to slip on the amber blobs of jellyfish that had been stranded by the tide, Duncan feigned left and the bird bobbed right. Back and forth they went, tangoing their way slowly to the crumbling seawall where the gull could be cornered among the debris. If the harbor of Port Ellery, Maine, was anatomical, they now stood firmly in the appendix. The town, all red brick and shadows, was neatly centered in the groin between two intertwining estuaries that flowed into the harbor like crossed legs. Protected coves formed armpits, and piney islands spread across the skin of water like raised hives. Seacrest's sat off the harbor's irregular belly, in a small unnavigable loop prone to collecting trash. Blue rubber gloves and pieces of yellow rope were dashed twice daily against the seawall, then fell behind the dark wet rocks. Twisted metal shrines of lobster traps had dug into the beach to become part of the natural landscape, but plastic water bottles and featherweight polystyrene coffee cups were the transient and windblown accessories. Some days the tide took it all away; other days it left it all behind.

The gull's options narrowed, and it turned its back to the wall, preparing to hold its ground. Duncan removed his jacket and held it aside like a toreador. The air blowing in off the harbor was cool, but the warmth of the sun on his back reminded him it was still technically summer. "It's not over yet," he said to the bird and moved carefully toward it, attempting a graceful drop of the jacket, but that required him to get so close that the gull was able to slash the tender part of his palm with the curved tip of his beak before trundling away.

"Damn!" Duncan squeezed his hand and looked up at the factory. He was sure he saw people move away. Would no one come to help him? Worse, would someone come to help and expose him as a leader who could not even catch an injured gull? It was equally unthinkable that they should see him walk away from a bad situation. He had to hurry. He took hold of his jacket and, with what he considered to be a superb show of agility, pounced on the bird. There ensued a whir of elbows and wings, and for a moment Duncan thought he'd lost him, but finally, kneeling in the wet sand with sea water seeping through the wool blend of his trousers, he managed to wrap the jacket over the bird's head. Darkness calmed it down while Duncan restrained its wings with the sleeves. He was breathing hard by the time he collapsed against a barnacled rock with the neat package of gull under his arm. "For a dying bird, you've got a lot of fight left in you," he said. He readjusted his glasses, then dug around in his pants pocket for his cell phone.

"Josefa, I'm on Seacrest's beach with a gull for you—bring a cage and a Band-Aid."

Note: Thanks to Ashland Creek Press for permission to publish the first chapter of this novel. *Float* is available through both online and local booksellers (if they don't stock it, just ask). It's a colorful, sophisticated read, so order the book and check out the rest!

WALKING TO LAOS
By Scott Ezell

> "I do not know much about gods; but I think that the river
> Is a strong brown god.—"
> —T.S. Eliot, *Four Quartets*.

I ripcorded north from Hanoi on a day train and sank into the bovine sentience of slow-train travel, looking out the window at nothing and into my own skull at nothing as girls in white blouses with long black hair glided by on bicycles. The land spread flat and red, stitched and awled with industry of various sorts, and traffic crawled insecticine and metal along the roads, precipitating its corresponding human consciousness. It's insect consciousness I guess that allows us to burn and burn for the sake of locomotion and convenience and damn the rising seas.

We arrived at the Lao Cai station in Vietnam's northwest mountains an hour before dusk. I sat down and drank a Hanoi beer while the tourists filed from the depot to the buses waiting for them. Then the station was empty and I walked out into the oblique slide of sun across the green slopes of the mountains and the cracked concrete parking lot, and hired a moto taxi to drive me the hour west to the hill tribe town of Sapa. I climbed on back and the driver exclaimed at the incongruity between himself and my two-meter, hundred-kilo self, as we putted off beneath a sky clear blue and streaked with silver clouds, shards of rainbow strewn all through. It was so gorgeous and alive that I couldn't help laughing aloud—there's so much laughter implicit in the earth even though it sometimes seems untappable, trapped below some bedrock sternness, but 360 degrees of light and mountains and color made each heartbeat an upthrust of risible joy.

In Sapa, it rained all night. The mountains were shrouded in gray when I woke early and drank a cup of coffee and walked up the hill to the town square, then took a moto taxio [sic] to the bus "stop" in literal terms, the place on the edge of town where the bus would pause long enough to take on a poet in the rain as it clunked on west. I huddled beneath a piece of tarp where a woman was making fried dough balls over a coal fire. The street was empty except for a Vietnamese woman hurrying through in high heels, and a few Hmong women in flip-flops carrying baskets of textiles to sell to tourists. I bought one of the fried globs, a bolus of grease layered with a crust of sugar flakes, and chewed it down along with the coal smoke from her brazier until a bus swung around the bend with a conductor hanging out the door and hollering "Lai Chau!"—my destination. It didn't stop, but slowed enough for me to run and jump aboard to join the movement and momentum of the hulking machine on yonder west, on into the hills, on to further higher peaks.

Freshets streamed down the jungle mountains in the rain. Forty of us were crammed in the midsize bus, plastic stools set in the aisle to fit more passengers. We ascended into fog and silver rain.

The mountains disappeared. We passed a tarp settlement on the side of the road, construction workers and market women, streams of fog blew off the side of the road into an abyss.

We jounced and swayed for ten hours, the road a series of potholes and ruts, a concatenation of debris. We lurched horribly over the worst areas, just a hair from tipping over. The whole road was a succession of landslides, some still rent and broken, just a narrow track bulldozed through, as if we were driving through a landscape where the world was perpetually falling. We wound up switchbacks for two hours, then down into a valley of emerald rice terraces, the rain so hard a curtain of water streamed down the windshield. Along the valley bottom a river thrashed like an angry ghost. A Flower Hmong woman walked along a path through the fields in an embroidered red and purple tunic, a piece of plastic held above her head against the rain. A woman in the bus became motion-sick, and stuck her head out the window to vomit. The local passengers, mostly hill tribe women, chuckled good-naturedly and made a chorus of retching sounds to help her.

We arrived in Lai Chau, a Vietnamese town in the middle of Hmong and Tai tribe settlements, a crossroad of cell phone shops and scrap metal collection lots. Hill tribe women in splendiferously embroidered clothes walked up and down streets alongside motorbikes and trucks. They had baskets of corn and squashes strapped to their backs with woven tump lines around their foreheads—but they were somehow not "of" the town, and seemed to melt back into the hills when their business was done. No "tribal" goods were purveyed here, as if, in the absence of tourist demand, the ethnic minority peoples produced only what they needed for their own use. By contrast, the tourist-glutted streets of Sapa are virtually paved with Hmong textiles. Aside from local-grown vegetables, the market in Lai Chau was nothing but manufactured goods from lowland factories, a mandala of polyester.

I sat down at a *bia hoi,* where fresh beer was siphoned out of barrels, for a dinner of steamed corn, mangoes, and beer, watching the slow revolutions of the streets where everyone called and waved to me, I was exotic as a circus bear on a unicycle pedaling through. A duck fell off the motorbike it was strapped to and the driver stopped and walked back to retrieve it. Its wings, legs, and beak bound with twine, the duck was unable to walk, fly, or even call out—its primary animal abilities neutralized and negated. As the owner strapped the duck back to the rack of his motorbike I couldn't help but feel there was something grotesque in this complete reduction of an animal to living, useable meat. Back on Tue Tinh Street in Hanoi two days before, I'd seen a dog howling and writhing with its back legs tied, a woman trying to pull a grain sack over its head. I couldn't even stay to see what they did to it.

The next day I went to the depot to catch a bus to Dien Bien Phu, the town just shy of the Lao border where the French lost their Indochina war in 1954. (By the time it was the Americans' war it was Vietnam, rather than with the tripartite French colony consisting of Tonkin, Annam, and Cochin China.) Five minutes after we pulled out of the Lai Chau station I realized that if I'd only gotten a mile out of town I would've transcended the provincial commercial blandness of Lai Chau, and arrived in a misty realm of hill tribe villages and terraced fields, but this realization came a moment too late, as with many things in life, when what I could have grasped was already beyond me.

It was another day of rain out the window of the bus, me still in love with the earth despite the rattle of the wheels and struts up into my brain and viscera. The bus had Korean letters on the doors from when it had run its normal life expectancy in Seoul or Busan before being sold on for a second incarnation in Vietnam. We followed a muddy river; along the valley walls wood stilt villages stood amid a cloud forest, and then suddenly we stopped where backhoes were clearing the landslide debris of a hill that had slid down across the road. The bus stood in mudpuddles so deep we passengers couldn't even get out of the bus to move around a bit while we waited. By some miracle, it took only half an hour for the earth machines to finish—it was only by chance that it didn't take days. Traffic started forward from both directions, creating a two-way traffic jam in the mud as earth and stones still trickled down the raw hill face. I looked up at the loose earth of the hillside dissolving above as the driver honked his horn at the vehicles in our way and revved the engine, but the soil held together long enough for us to squeeze forward out of the landslide's path and onto the open road.

We passed hill women walking through the mist in woven blue and red blouses and plastic boots, then over a pass and down to the town of Muong Lay in a flat valley. The surrounding hills were shaved and beveled into squares and angles, industrial red dirt shapes, with shanty towns along the riverbank and piles of gravel mounded everywhere. The machine geometry and concrete landscape seemed grotesque and even obscene after miles of jungle and thatch villages.

An hour later we stopped to take a break at a roadside restaurant-shack. The sky was dark and low though the rain had paused. I sat beneath the eaves in a plastic chair and ordered the fifty-cent set lunch. Across a table from me was a most beautiful seventy-year-old tribal woman in a maroon silk blouse with silver buttons, wearing swirling gold earrings and her hair pulled into a bun. We stared back and forth at each other with (apparently) the same thought in our heads, How did the world create a creature such as this?

Lunch was coarse rice, some fried greens, and a few scraps of rangy meat. The rain resumed, a metal percussion across the corrugated roof. Two six-year-old girls walked down towards the river, each holding a naked baby. Across from the restaurant a little girl about four years old squatted on the side of the road, shitting a yellow mound while holding an umbrella above her head. The driver jumped from beneath the eaves into the bus and started the engine. Everyone else followed suit, and we pulled off down the road. Just beyond the restaurant boys and girls held fishing lines from a bridge above the river, while other children herded water buffalo into the current to wash them. A road sign said "Dien Bien Phu 50 km," and two hours later we pulled into town in the twilight and the rain.

Golden sun gushed across the valley the next morning. I rented a motorbike and drove out beyond the lowland city grid into the Tai tribe villages on the outskirts of town. An old couple invited me in to their stilt house, and the man poured me homemade rice wine as he showed me photos of his grandchildren in army uniforms. My limping Vietnamese, which always seemed inadequate in Hanoi, was enough to share friendly sentiments and a few words about our families and occupations and where we came from.

Tai women wear their long hair (when unbound, it reaches to the ground) in large round buns on the tops of their heads. They perch their plastic motorbike helmets atop their hair, so the helmets never descend to the level of their actual heads, as if the helmets were levitating above them. I drove to the center of town beneath the same low ceiling of clouds that (along with Soviet anti-aircraft cannons) had prevented air support during the siege of Dien Bien Phu. I parked and walked into the earthen bulge of the ruined French fortress. Mud had collected at the mouths of its tunnel entrances. Plaques described the routing of the imperialists, an ironic monument to anti-colonialism in the midst of a place where all the original hill peoples are themselves colonized, engulfed into the nation-state of Vietnam. I drove over to the War Museum, the front of which was a vast lot crammed with piles of howitzers, missiles, rockets, stacks of bomb casings, and battered, greasy tanks with broken treads. The clouds thickened, and a heavy thundershower broke from the sky and swept across the town. I stood under the eaves of the museum and watched the rain crash down upon the rusted paraphernalia of war.

I woke at five the next morning and shuffled through a gentle rain to the depot for my seven-hour bus across the border to Muong Khoa, Laos. In the depot lot a man held out a piece of paper with a rough pen drawing of a landslide. "Too much rain," he said, "the road is washed out." He refunded my ticket money and told me I might as well take the express bus ten hours back to Hanoi; the road to Laos would be out for days.

I walked across the street in a stunned torpor as rain blotted the coming dawn, and sat down in a café for a cup of coffee. Returning to Hanoi and flying to Luang Prabang was as pusillanimous an option as I'd had to consider in all my traveling days. I couldn't stand the thought of disemboweling this journey *in utero*, leaving it bleeding and twitching in the greasy asphalt lot in the rain before I'd even passed out of Vietnam.

"Where you going today?" the proprietor asked me.

"To Muong Khoa, but the bus is out."

"It's the rainy season, it always happens. But if you want to go, I can give you a ride to the border on my motorbike."

"And there's a bus from there?"

He just shrugged. Who knew what would lie across the border? Not me, but I didn't care. Five minutes later my pack was wedged into the gap at the front of the moto and I sat astride the back behind the driver.

"Maybe you should take some bread for the road," he said, "in case you get hungry on the way."

"No, no, it'll be fine, let's go," I said.

This was some perverse recalcitrance on my part, a disregard or disinterest in what would be ahead, a determination to simply move forward and deal with the road moment by moment, mile by mile, to front the unknown, let it surround and saturate me, and either drown or succor me. I didn't care about any future hunger or need; I only cared that I was moving forward and the road was still alive beneath me and within me, and I was alive in it.

We drove down the main boulevard of the town, just rousing itself to the business of the day, and out into the countryside where rows of trees lined both sides of the road. We zoomed through the sparse traffic of ox carts and water buffalo and old-metal-colored motorbikes. The road curved gently through farmland, then into soft round hills that precipitated up and up into clouds and mountains. Soon we were driving through curtains of mist that fluttered and undulated all around, sun pouring through and Tai women walking down the road in purple and silver sarongs.

The driver gunned it all the way. We slalomed through like a ballerina on skis. After an hour he dropped me at the entrance to Vietnamese immigration. I slung my pack over my shoulders, paid him, shook his hand, and stepped inside. While I waited for an epauleted official to find the necessary stamp to let me through, a boyish officer chimed in in perfect English, asking where I was going. He then offered to arrange a moto ride for me all the way to Muong Khoa, insisting there was no other way I could go. No bus or any other kind of ride would be available once I crossed into Laos. But when the official handed back my passport I simply turned like an automaton and walked out the back door of the border post towards Laos.

There's a seven-kilometer no man's land between the Vietnam and Lao border checkpoints. I stepped into nothingness, and nothing greeted me, just the single-lane concrete road winding through mountains with no other vehicle or pedestrian in sight, the single-strand consciousness of walking into this stateless space, into a void of no governance, no jurisdiction, nothing to argue or explain. It was a geographic and political bivouac, a series of ridges suspended high between two countries, a lumpy hammock of hills strung between two border posts.

"*Sabaidee,*" said the mustachioed immigration officials when I approached the checkpoint. They were relaxed and friendly as they stamped my passport and offered me a terrible rate on the exchange of my Vietnam Dong for Lao Kip, which I had no choice but to accept.

"Where are you going today?" they asked me.

"Muong Khoa."

"Have a good trip," they said. No mention of the road being washed away, no question how I planned to get there. I walked down a graded roadbed with rain pooling in machine tracks. After two kilometers I reached a scrappy village, a few shacks serving as sundry shops, chickens scratching through weeds in a ditch, a Chinese lorry jacked up with two pairs of legs extending from beneath it. I pantomimed to the bedraggled villagers that I wanted to hire a moto ride to Muong Khoa, they made elaborate gestures of ambivalence or futility. I was barely able to keep the attention of an old woman with a basket of longan (dragon eye fruit) long enough to buy a handful of them from her. I got a couple of packs of peanuts from one of the sundry shops, and continued down the road.

I walked out of the village into ridge after ridge of cloud forest receding every direction. A sense of the implicit liberation of mountains heaved up out of my chest. I moved alone through the deep green of the jungle's swell and undulation, through alternating sun and rain, opening a cheap umbrella for the former, pulling on my hat for the latter. The sun was like liquid metal when it spilled through the clouds, and melted my skin where it touched me. I don't think I have ever felt such an absolute sense of isolation, though I've been alone in more remote places—but, with no idea whether the road would go through, or how far I would have to walk for food or a roof, and my only linguistic currency here the word "*sabaidee*," I was saturated with isolation. It seeped from my pores and ran down my arms and legs.

I walked through the red mud and stones of the road which had been scraped out of the mountainsides, a beveled gash of earth. A project was underway to rebuild the road, making it bigger and faster, *de rigueur,* and for now it was at the midpoint, neither old nor new, just a nascent roadbed waiting to be graded, compacted, fortified, stabilized and paved. Occasionally I passed big bulldozers or graders parked off the road with Vietnamese flags painted on their sides.

I loved the rhythm of my feet and bones moving down the road step by step, and the weight of my pack on my shoulders, my old Swiss infantry rucksack with leather straps which I'd bought second-hand in Seattle years before. But by the afternoon I began to be overtaken by exhaustion. My feet and back hurt, and my whole body was bloated with heat, like a hot welt covered the entirety of my skin. The road descended and crossed a stream. I sat down to rest, soaked my feet in the cool current. As I sat there a four-wheel-drive vehicle suddenly burst through and splashed across. It was the only chance of a ride I'd had all day, but it passed so quickly I didn't have time to jump up and try to flag it down—in fact I didn't even move, stunned by this mechanical apparition of an entirely other mode of locomotion, so alien to my propulsion of muscle and bone.

I walked two more hours, staggering a bit from fatigue and hunger, starting to feel the road like body blows, each step a fist to my ribs, when a flat valley opened outwards and a scattering of bamboo and thatch houses appeared. A sign on one house set back from the road said "*Com Pho*," Vietnamese for "rice and noodles." It was a restaurant for the Vietnamese engineers and workers on the new road, and the owner was half-Lao, half-Vietnamese. I ordered some food, not understanding what it was they offered to bring me and not caring. The boss said he could get me a free ride with one of the engineering trucks up to Muong May, ten kilometers ahead, the halfway point between Dien Bien Phu and Muong Khoa. It was late afternoon, Muong Khoa was beyond question now. Children played in front of their homes, and a lovely girl in a green and gold brocade skirt sat by a sundry stall in front of her hut.

The rain began to come down hard, running in rivers off the thatch roofs. This was no problem for the locals—in the houses near the restaurant everybody just went to sleep when the rain increased, either in hammocks or on cushions on the ground. The exception was an enormous young man with the physique of a weightlifter who walked around through the rain and the mud in a pair of white briefs, as if he were on some mission of discovery—he was an anomaly here where everyone else was thin as an eel. I imagined life slowly turning year after year in this place, villagers wearing seasons like a reincarnating soul wears bodies, as disinterested in them too, even in the year the planes flew overhead on bombing runs to Dien Bien Phu.

My food arrived, I ate it still not knowing what it was, watery meat and vegetables and coarse rice. The owner lazily took the bird cages down from the eaves where they hung and cleaned them, giving the encaged jungle birds bits of fruit to feed their songs. When a new white truck pulled up in front of the lot, the resto boss jumped up and said this was it, let him talk to these men and he'd arrange a ride for me.

It was a truckload of Lao engineers working on the road, and they were happy to give me a ride to Muong May for the fair and non-negotiable price of me sharing their bottle of "Lao whiskey," or rice liquor with them. Three of them were young and friendly, but the head engineer was a wispy waif of a man, barely five feet tall, who staggered out of the driver's seat already plastered. He insisted on toasting me repeatedly, but was so drunk he spilled most of his liquor onto his lap, making a dark hundred-proof stain on his groin. He collapsed forward onto the table, and when the others went into the kitchen to pick out something to eat, I said to myself, *Fuck this*, and picked up my pack and struck off down the road in a spitting rain, not caring that there was no way in hell I'd make Muong May by nightfall.

I strode ahead grimly, the sky already tinting towards dusk, refusing to think about what would happen when night fell, or about my aching body. I heard an engine behind me, and the pick-up pulled up—the driver's window scrolled down, and one of the young engineers sat at the wheel, asking me to get in while another opened the back door and made room for me. The asinine boss was passed out in the front seat. "Never mind, never mind," the young men said, indicating the boss. I slammed the door shut behind me and we bumped down the road to Muong May.

They dropped me at a guest house by a river at the edge of town. The boy in charge, about fifteen years old, apparently knew no English other than "fifty-thousand," the price of a room in Lao kip, about six dollars. I was half-drunk on Lao whiskey, and immediately stashed my things in my room and flopped into the river that ran right past the guesthouse door as twilight spread like marmalade across the sky. It was the village bathing hour. Upstream, men and women stood in mid-current, lathering themselves with soaps and shampoos, the men in dark-toned briefs, the women wrapped in sarongs that clung like sheets of sodden breath to their bodies. The guesthouse lad waded out into the river and set a plastic basket with his soap and toothbrush on a rock that protruded above the surface. He grinned and told me to help myself. We stood in the waist-deep river and I scrubbed off a layer of dirt and fatigue as the brown water flowed over us, while shopkeepers dumped the day's rubbish into the current. Chicken feathers floated past me as I looked up at the sky and let the silty water swirl across my skin.

Rain had turned the dirt streets to gray mud, with a fierce adhesive power, so everyone walked in their flip-flops like they were stalking prey—taking a step forward and freezing, slowly lifting the back foot so as not to tear the sandal flaps or splatter mud upon themselves. Candles lit stalls and shops, giving the streets the aspect of a wake. Strange shadow scenes flickered with orange light. The only electric light came from two Chinese electronics shops located side by side on the market street, where the merchants sat bundled in heavy overcoats watching tiny tv sets powered by generators that thrummed noisily in front of the shops.

By morning the river had swollen and was lapping at the steps of the guesthouse. The outcrops of rocks that had served as shelves for bathing accoutrements were now submerged. I sat on a bamboo veranda that extended from the guesthouse over the river on bamboo stilts. The rain came down in torrents like a wet bear hug as I sat and drank a cup of instant coffee and watched the river thrash by full of flotsam, foam, trash, whole trees. The river seemed to rise higher as I watched it, as the rain fell thick across its ridges and ribs like across some sprinting beast's back. I looked straight down onto the river through spaces between the bamboo slats of the floor, wondering how the stilts were holding up against the current. Across the river the rice fields received the rain into their lush deep green. Mountains were visible as shadows beyond the curtains of the downpour. A hundred meters downriver foot traffic still crossed over a suspension bridge that led onward to Muong Khoa.

I jumped from the guesthouse steps over the verge of the river where it was lapping up against them and propped my umbrella against the rain, a losing battle. In the market, beneath thatch roofed stalls, local women sold mushrooms, banana flowers, and herbs, so bored and soporific in the relentless rain they didn't even attempt to sell me the pieces of fried dough lined up on wet banana leaves. They watched me dully, as if certain I was like the rain, falling from some far place, and that I too would pass away and leave no trace. I had a bowl of *pho,* Vietnamese rice noodles, the noodles handmade and more delicious than any of the factory-made ones I'd ever eaten on the streets of Hanoi, with fresh sweet potato leaves and thick slices of chicken. No one spoke a single word to me and I passed through the village like a ghost. How many lifetimes are implicit in such a scene? Infinite, of course, just like in every scene.

I could have stayed forever, and yet, when the rain began to lessen I began to think of moving on.

The guesthouse was empty when I returned. I slung my pack up on my back, jumped from the steps over the foamy river lips, crossed the suspension bridge, and continued down the road.

There was less glory in setting out now. My shoulders were sore and my feet hurt too. I had managed little nourishment since leaving Dien Bien Phu, and didn't even know how far ahead Muong Khoa still lay. It was at least half-foolish to strike out exhausted and hungry into an unknown land, but foolishness may sometimes be the tithe that lets you enter the cathedral of the road.

The mud road was rutted and wrecked. From the suspension bridge it ascended above the valley floor into the jungle, a pullulation of exuberant green. The road was a scar dug out of the side of the hill, a red and bleeding gill in the songline of the upthrust earth. Now, in the heart of the rainy season, my footsteps sank deep into the nascent road, and I carried a thick layer of it along with me, caked on my shoes and pants cuffs. In some places the road had simply sloughed off over the edge of the slope and down to the oblivion of rivers, those strong brown gods.

A few motorbikes passed me, I hailed them and tried to hire them to drive me the direction from which they'd come (for none had embarked from my direction). But they all said no, just smiled and shrugged their helplessness.

I arrived at a bamboo shelter on the side of the road. A path ascended to a village at the top of a bluff. I already felt I couldn't walk any further, and knew I couldn't make it all the way to Muong Khoa by foot. I left my pack on the bench of the shelter and headed up the path. I had no fear any jungle bandit would steal my pack. No, it was too heavy and too meaningless, just a green army rucksack full of books in the middle of ten thousand miles of jungle.

The hilltop village sat a hundred feet above the road, a dozen or two bamboo shacks, all weathered gray, naked children standing in dirt yards which were not demarcated from each other. I thought of Laozi, and his ideal community of villagers who hear barking dogs and crowing roosters from neighboring villages but don't bother to walk over and see who's next door. A woman bathed by a well, raising water bucket by bucket with a rope. She was shrouded in a sarong which sometimes descended to reveal full lovely breasts with large dark nipples. Children stood and stared at me as if frozen, fingers in their mouths.

A motorbike sat parked next to a hut. A young man came out. I asked him if he or someone could drive me to Muong Khoa. He turned and called back inside, and an old man emerged, about sixty-five, shirtless and bony-chested, with wire spectacles and crude tattoos on his forearms. "No," he said in stern pantomime, "you can't make it. The bike would fall over on you along the way, too much rain." He turned back into the hut without any sign of farewell or curiosity. I waited for him to reemerge with some suggestion or advice about how to navigate the road ahead, but that was the end of the conversation. Big whitie walks in from the road and wants a ride, we don't give it to him, end of story. I was not even a speck of dust on the lens of this village looking up at the sky and back down upon itself. I cursed myself that I had not whipped out a wad of currency and waved it at the man, slapped it down on the dirt floor, but later I realized it wouldn't have made any difference.

I walked back through the village, past a sign saying the Danish Red Cross had provided medical aid to this village, and back down to the road. A dozen children silently followed me. They were so shy that with any movement from me they recoiled in fear, I was strange and alien as a space creature. The youngest children were naked, and carried by siblings six, seven, or eight years old. They followed me like an oracle back down to the shelter where I sat on the knobby bamboo bench next to my pack. It was the first place I'd ever been where no one even knew the word "hello." "*Sabaidee*," I said to them as gently as I could, and they whispered it back to me, as if afraid to respond, afraid not to. The little girls had the purest, loveliest faces I've ever seen, perfect in the composition of lips and eyes and cheeks, a dusky, milky color, with dusty sun-lightened hair all tangled and tied up at the napes of their necks. They wore ragged t-shirts with English slogans and images printed on them, and looked at me across a chasm of innocence, the innocence of childhood exponented by the innocence of this jungle settlement on a dirt hilltop with pigs rooting through the trash heaps and women bathing in the middle of the day and elders who know the difference between yes and no.

I walked on with defeat in my heart, my feet all punch-drunk and leaden. I passed a road construction site. Workers played cards and drank beer in a tarp shelter, four-wheel-drive trucks parked out front. I tried to talk to them about a ride to Muong Khoa, but they just laughed and swilled their beer. A hundred meters further up the road a woman washed a blouse in a stream where it ran across the road. "Muong Khoa?" she asked. "Yes," I said. But this elicited nothing from her. She just went back to scrubbing her shirt against a stone.

After another mile I reached the place that made everything impossible. A quarter-mile of the road had been dug out, turned into a trench as wide as the road itself and ten feet deep. Only a narrow ledge remained along the face of the hill that had been carved away. Sixty percent of the road from the border was nearly impossible for a bus to navigate, but navigate it they somehow did. Here, however, no four-wheeled vehicle could pass. Motorbikes could perhaps find some way along the sodden and eroding ledge, but it was hard even on foot, the wet sucking earth grasping my every footstep as if trying to pull me down, unwilling to relinquish me to the future, to arrival. I walked along the edge of the long, wide trench as the backhoes roared and belched and scooped huge bellyfuls of rust-colored mud to heap up on the verge. The thin edge along the slope ended and I had to scree-fall down to the bottom of the trench, the grave of the road, and hike back up and out on the other side.

The road went up and up, I couldn't believe it. I'd been sure for hours that it had to subside, decline, but it never did, at least in my perception. Where in heaven was it going? I didn't know, and I wondered, Why am I so insane, to trek off with nothing into nothingness? Why at age forty have I still not learned a better way to locomote myself across the face of earth? Why do I thrust myself into such uncertainty and exhaustion? There was no answer. There was no reason to be here, and no reason to continue except that there was nothing else to do.

Along the rise of a curving slope two enormous backhoes scooped and pushed hillocks of soil and stone over the edge of the roadbed into the declivity of the valley. They were fearsome machines—one dull yellow, one metallic blue, both scraped and dented from wrestling against boulders and trees, both with tinted glass enclosing their operators, no human presence visible. They roared and belched diesel exhaust as they swung their metal edges and angles in circles, snouting their teeth into the hillside, backhandedly cupping detritus and swinging it out to fall towards the river below. Each could have killed me with a single stray stroke of its double-jointed arm. I crept up towards the first, and sprinted past it when the arm extended away from me to push a tree over the slope of the hill. My "sprint" was laughable—I shambled like a bear, my feet cloddish and my shoulders sagging. I ran, too, past the second, fearing that any moment it would swivel for a scoop of earth exactly where I was, and would sever me from my blood and bones in a blind instant.

The road continued implacably up, looping around bends, ascending through clouds and green, dropping down at times only as a precursor to further climbing. I was alone, and felt so isolated it was as if rather than moving through a physical landscape I was navigating the topography of my own consciousness.

Ascending a long straight incline cut along the face of a hill, the machined geometry of the road was cracked and sagging, and seemed about to fall like a soufflé and tumble down. It was a spooky walk up that slope, like skating along a continental fault where vast plates could slip and bury me in a blink. But at the top of the hill, the apex of the road, was a village. At the convergence point between the village and the road I felt fear in my heart for this place and its people, certain the road would break asunder and take the village with it when it went. But with one more step the road and all that had constructed it was gone from my mind. The village seemed to be built on bedrock and I didn't believe this cluster of shacks could ever fall.

This village was one of the two great strokes of luck that saved me on this day's walk. Just as I crested the hill and saw the first thatch homes a furious rain began to fall. It had rained off and on since I left Muong May, but this was of a different order, a thunderous, bludgeoning roar of water. There was a communal shelter at the center of the village, and I simply walked from the downpour beneath its thatched bamboo roof and joined a dozen villagers who sat there chatting and watching the rain. Just as I eased my pack off and set it on the raised platform of the shelter a grinning man with a broad chest and thick arms, and with hair that looked like it'd been cut with a machete, thumbed himself in the chest and bellowed above the sound of rain in his language, cut with a few words of English, that he could moto me down to Muong Khoa for some number of dollars. Before I could try to discern any details he was gone, out through the thickening ropes of rain to a hut on the other side of the village, across a wide dirt space. It didn't matter. Having just arrived, I wasn't in a hurry. The rain, anyway, was a visceral impediment to progress. The sky to the west was a wall of mist and cloud, but across the valleys to the east (where I'd come from) the sky was still blue as a kingfisher, sharded with bright white clouds, and light poured down in gold gushes across the mountains. The villagers spoke a hill language (probably Khmu), with a gentle melodic quality and a preponderance of rolled Rs. The men were skinny as rails. Even the older ones had just a few horizontal wrinkles at their bellies, not even a bit of fat to fill them out. But there was no sense of hunger or bad health among them; all were fit and whole with the exception of a small boy who was missing three fingers on his right hand. Later this boy made a performance of lifting a bunch of bamboo shoots with just the pinky of this hand. Everyone exclaimed appreciatively.

The women beneath the shelter wore long embroidered skirts, the same as in Muong May, but here they were faded and caked with mud, along with completely random tops, t-shirts, terry cloth, crocheted lace—perhaps from the same donation pile as the children's t-shirts from the last village. Some by necessity or choice did not seek to remain dry. Girls carrying water in plastic jugs tied to bamboo shoulder yokes walked through the downpour as if it weren't there at all, their clothes plastered to their bodies like a second skin.

For small boys the rain turned the village into a playground, or maybe for them it had been one to begin with and the rain only changed its terms. They ran naked through the village center rolling motorcycle tires before them, whacking them with sticks to propel them along and steer them. Invariably, the boys lost control and fell into mudholes, where they looked momentarily disconsolate, on the verge of tears, covered with mud, then got back up and continued on laughing again, the rain washing them as they ran. Those with me in the shelter watched and commented on this frenetic motion, a Lao village version of spectator sport.

Sitting amid laughter and rain, with no explanation or invitation, and yet feeling perfectly welcome and at ease, I couldn't help but wonder if the very concept of civilization is not flawed. Here it seemed that the wealth of this remote, undeveloped village—time for children and friends, the leisure to interact as families and as a community—is exactly that which, in the hamsterwheel of civilization, we are ever striving harder for, and ever further from. Here there was no trace of "the odd combination of isolation and crowding that characterizes much of modern life." (Spencer Wells, *Pandora's Seed*) Will speed, efficiency, comfort, all those smug, easy gods, ever add up to the wholeness we have traded for them? And if not, why do we continue to sacrifice everything at their altar of industrial progress?

The rain lasted over an hour. As it lessened, the eastern and western skyscapes reversed. Behind me now was the silver-gray gauze of clouds and rain, and gold and green spilled across the sky and mountains up ahead. The villagers began bringing in clusters of bamboo shoots, stubby and cylindrical, tapering to a point, with triangular leaves shading from yellow to brown like patterns on a venomous snake. They mounded them high in front of the shelter where I sat, next to the motorbike of the man who'd approximated offering me a ride. That man returned from his hut, where he'd waited out the rain, and I asked if he was going to Muong Khoa. *Yes,* he gestured with a grin, *but now I've got to take all these bamboo shoots to the market down there, I don't have any room for you.* Which of course was obvious already, and in the wake of the downpour, the air and earth so fresh and alive, I only really felt like walking. I was restored by the hour of rest, and from this apex of the journey the road would finally subside. As the village woke from it's rainy somnolence and returned to the activities of the afternoon, I laced up my shoes and said "*sabaidee"* all around. The girls smiled and whispered the greeting back, and I walked through the village and down the hill on the other side.

The afternoon was drawing on as I walked through the mud, the road rising and falling over hills like swells on a green sea. A white pick-up truck passed me going the wrong way (not my way). I passed another construction settlement, where a dozen workers drank liquor and played cards in a gravel yard, and three women cooked dinner. A new four-wheel-drive truck was parked there, and a man standing next to it said, "Chauffer," pointing to himself. I thought he was offering his services to me, but when I said "Muong Khoa," he simply smiled blankly and shook his head. I walked a mile further to a large village shrouded in blowing mist. It was already twilight here within the fog, spittles of rain blowing in on the wind. From the side of the road a young man on a porch with a girl sitting on his lap laughed and called out to me, "*Mua*!" (Vietnamese for "rain.") "You'll never make it to Muong Khoa by walking," he said, "it's fifteen more kilometers." He was right, it was getting dark already, I'd never make it by foot.

At the far end of the village a crappy motorbike was parked in front of a shack. I called out, and a young Lao man emerged, smiling and friendly. I asked him to moto me to Muong Khoa. He said, "No, the road is too bad." I slapped my wallet against my palm, determined to lay some cash on the line in the negotiations this time. His wife emerged along with another woman. They all began debating the question, but in a slow and easy way, with no cutthroat bottom line-ism. He said he would do it for 150,000 Lao kip, about $20. It was a high price. I started trying to bargain, writing figures in my notebook, but I was in no position to do so. There was no place to stay here, nothing to eat, and I couldn't go any further on my own. He didn't seem to care whether he made the money or not, and I couldn't blame him. It was dinner time. Slightly exasperated, not with the man but with the whole situation, including my own intractability, I looked around at the other shacks. In front of the one next door there were two strange flower boxes, oblong and oval. I walked over to have a closer look—they were bomb casings that had been sheared open on one side, about four feet long and a foot in diameter, filled with earth and planted with blue flowers. I stood staring at them, stunned by the history of this place, of the "secret" bombing of Laos during America's Vietnam War (not secret to the Laotians, boy) suddenly precipitating in this moment and this metal before me. "Hey, come around here," my could-be moto owner motioned to me, and waved me to the back of his home. I followed him around to where a pyramid of bombs was stacked against his back wall. He'd "harvested" this unexploded ordinance (UXO), removed the explosives inside, and unscrewed the detonator caps. What remained were long hollow tubes, which would be sold to Chinese scrap metal merchants.

"From the Americans," the man said, and smiled.

At that moment I heard the sound of an engine. I said a quick prayer to the gods of the road, and ran from the stack of bombs to the front of the shack. A new white pick-up came churning down the road—it was the truck I'd seen earlier when it was going the other way. I waved my arms like a deranged marionette. The driver calmly pulled over. "Are you going to Muong Khoa?" I asked him. Yes. "Can you give me a ride?" He said yes again.

It was too much, too good to be true. This was the second great stroke of luck of the day. There was no room in the cab—the truck was part of an NGO health project, and there were two passengers up front already. So the driver got out and removed the tarp covering the bed. I ran over to the moto driver and shook his hand. His smile had not changed in the whole time since I'd arrived, calm and friendly. Behind him, behind his shack, the bamboo forest descended, wet with recent rain, lush with the swelling of cicada songs, into a wilderness still strewn with bombs.

I jumped in the back of the truck, my shoes immediately muddying everything. I sat on the spare tire, and we took off. I couldn't believe this luxury, a truck ride (the moto ride would have been a hell of mud and bouncing pain) combined with the 360-degree view usually restricted to motorbikes or walking. The truck engine roared and we pulled away. There were chains on the tires, but even so we slipped and fishtailed as I waved goodbye to this village and this long walk into Laos, and jotted in my notebook:

> I would not pull the trigger
> on a single bullet here
> though American bombers flew above
> and dropped millions of tons of war
> on this country of slow, brown rivers.

Just two hundred meters beyond the village, we exited the fog, and the late afternoon was spangled heaven across the earth and sky. The sun was beginning to descend through broken strata of clouds that glowed like shoals of coral. The hills and valleys were gorgeous, lush green, almost sexually beautiful. O if I were a god I would descend and make love with this earth, all the undulant breasts and thighs of hills and valleys, the smooth run of rivers curving through, all limned and sparkled by the recent rain.

At a curve in the road we passed a passel of boys playing with a rubber soccer ball, they waved and shouted *sabaidee* as they stood aside to let us pass. I couldn't fathom how I'd arrived here, in this open steel chariot driving through a Canaan-like beauty, how I'd been somehow embraced by the gods of the road exactly at the moment when I could no longer continue on my own. I felt like a sham for forgetting the holiness of life and possibility, and especially for forgetting it on the road, where I always set out to rediscover it, where I drop myself like a pinch of salt into the sea to see if I really will wash up on the other shore, or if I will just dissolve into nothing. All the protestations and curses I'd uttered when my feet and shoulders hurt, when I'd felt I'd made a false step that day from the border, now sounded tinny and dissonant to my ear. The road is the way I assay my love for the earth, and the more extreme the road the truer my heart feels at the end.

Halfway to Muong Khoa we stopped and took the chains off the wheels, and continued along a sealed macadam road, which was simply a smooth charcoal-gray miracle, nothing short of that. The villages became larger and more frequent, we passed a gravel-crushing plant with a Vietnamese flag hanging from the scaffolding (the road construction is a cooperative venture between Vietnam and Laos), and then the road ended at a broad river, the Nam Ou.

The tongue of the road ran down a slope into the strong brown current. The driver stopped, he and his passengers got out, I jumped down and paid him what he asked for, 40,000 kip. He grinned and put it into his pocket, a dragon tattoo on his shoulder twitched beneath his tank top. The driver and his companions stepped into a tea stall to wait for the ferry to take the truck across the river—a barge, essentially, pushed by a tugboat with throaty diesel engines. But I walked right down to the water and without breaking stride stepped into a long narrow boat right as it was pushing off, a motorized cross between a canoe and a kayak, which ferried me and two local men across the river. I stepped off on the other shore and walked up the sloping main road of Muong Khoa, the end of the road, in the last fading light of day.

YOU'RE KEEPING MY OXYGEN IN YOUR OXYGEN TANK, BUT EVEN THIS BORES ME TO TEARS

By Daniel Bănulescu
Translated from Romanian by Adam Sorkin and Lidia Vianu

If you went mad tomorrow
Nobody would walk out on you

Nothing can help you anymore
Except perhaps the pink of your ear or your nipple
Because in truth nothing can help you anymore

While I slept and my hot blood flooded the sheets
I felt it like nearness to a woman

I woke up and spoke your name but didn't see you
I opened my eyes but didn't see you
I reached my hand out and you'd have confessed
I was nothing more than a rag that wipes the dust off your cunt

I giggled and drew back my hands from between your knees
And they began to ooze
I drew them back and left you with them as if in a snake pit

I could dismantle you demolish you soften you
I could educate you and turn you toward me
I could teach you that in the end my better side will win

But I'm bored
My spirit is bored
My corduroy slacks are bored
My pocket change is bored I could drink a bored coffee with it
Yet even my boot's boredom is bored only of you

I could build a large window
That I'd open to the city every morning and call the stray dogs

I could come down and feed them and lure them with swift
    kicks in the tail

I could squeeze from their fur
A coat for a woman like you to see Paris in

I'd forget about the coffee
Together we'd drag the woman to the coffee doctor (a lunatic)
Who'd understand her and from her scales and claws
Make a warm holy beast for the belly

I'd enter there together with these bedmates
They'd lick my fingers and maybe learn to read

I'd calm myself for a while
I'd be foolish and kind
Until I felt your ankles again your calves on my hips
And your feet would grow out of my shoulders like angel wings

I'd calm myself and you as well
I'd divvy up your womb into two dozen squares
On which we'd scribble Gigel and Costel Confucius and Adelaide

But I'm bored
My hips are bored
My love of elevators is bored
And my boot's boredom is bored only of you

Why should I ask of you in bed when we're alone at night
Much more than I'd dare ask of God
Why should I force you to have just two arms two legs and one cunt
When you're part of a ball of women
Whom I've had an important coffee with in silence

I'm walking down a street hidden in the city
I've gone deep into the city and no one can take it away

If I ever were to assume some man's life I'd choose such a street

I carry with me a young slender body that time has turned
          into a warrior for your bed
Who'd dare provoke me
Who'd enjoy having his head smashed like a lentil
Who'd even now dare to smoke around me and let me fill my lungs
With the smoke of his name
No one

And I'm bored
And my boot's boredom is bored only of you

BIOS

Daniel Bănulescu, one of Romania's most prominent authors, writes from an ironic self-vaunting pose, as the titles of many of his books suggest. His poetry includes *I'll Love You to the End of the Bed* (1993), *The Ballad of Daniel Bănulescu* (1997), *The Federal Republic of Daniel Bănulescu* (2000), and *It's Good to Be Daniel Bănulescu* (2010). His novels are provocative and fantastical: *I Kiss Your Ass, Adored Leader!* (1994)—rewritten as *Flee from Your Revolting and Hideous Life into My Book* (2009)—*The Seven Kings of the City of Bucharest* (1998), and *The Best Novel of All Time* (2008).

Nicolas Bataille was a kid in France who forged Rimbaud and fooled the world.

Vicente Aleixandre was the winner of the Nobel Prize for Literature in 1977. Part of the "Generation of '27," he participated in a creative circle including Federico Garcia Lorca and Pedro Salinas. Staying in Spain during the course of the Spanish Civil War, he was a bridge between generations and mentored many young Spanish poets before his death in 1984, producing more than a dozen volumes of poetry and prose. The poems included in this volume are from *Poems of Consummation*, first published in Spain in 1968.

Banksy is the pseudonym of a controversial English graffiti artist, activist, and film director. He is most widely known for his subversive political graffiti art which is scattered across the globe. He has published several volumes of photography of his art and was also the director of the film *Exit through the Gift Shop* (2010).

William S. Burroughs was an American novelist, poet, essayist and member of the Beat Generation. Among his most notable creations are *Naked Lunch* (1959) and the cut-up method. Before his death in 1997, Burroughs was elected to the American Society of Arts and Letters (1984).

Joshua D. Bellins' writing has appeared or is forthcoming in such periodicals as *Permafrost*, *Snowy Egret*, *Bellow*, and *Terrain.org*.

Billy Cancel's work has recently appeared in *Barzakh*, *Horseless Reviews* & *Offcourse Journal*. He helps with Hidden House Press. His collection *The Autobiography Of Shrewd Phil* was published by Blue & Yellow Dog Press. Sound poems, visual shorts, and other aberrations can be found at billycancelpoetry.com

Christopher Citro lives in Syracuse, NY. His poetry is forthcoming or has appeared recently in *Third Coast*, *Salamander*, *Quarter After Eight*, *Cream City Review*, *Southeast Review*, and *Verse Daily*.

JJ Cromer's work is in numerous private and public collections, including the American Visionary Art Museum, the Intuit Center of Outsider Art, the High Museum of Art, and the Taubman Museum of Art. The Fall 2010 issue of *Raw Vision* features his work. His art has also been presented on *Diagram*, *But Does It Float*, *Lost at E Minor*, *Knee-Jerk*, and other places on the web and in print.

Michael Cuglietta is a Florida writer. His work has appeared in *The Gettysburg Review*, *Passages North*, *Saw Palm*, *The Hawaii Review*, *Gertrude Press* and *Deep South Magazine*. He can be reached at cuges57@yahoo.com.

Jacqueline Doyle's work has recently appeared in *South Dakota Review*, *Front Porch Journal*, *CRATE*, *California Northern*, *Thin Air Magazine*, and *Ninth Letter* (winner of their online meta-essay contest), and is forthcoming in *The Rumpus*, *Birkensnake*, *Sweet*, and *Vestal Review*. She teaches in the San Francisco Bay Area. Visit her at facebook.com/authorjacquelinedoyle.

Scott Ezell is an American poet and multi-genre artist. His books include *Petroglyph Americana*, *Songs from a Yahi Bow*, and *Hanoi Rhapsodies*. His current work explores landscapes and identity in border regions of China, Laos, and Myanmar.

Claire T. Field is an English composition instructor. She was born and grew up in Yazoo City, MS, the town where the hills meet the Mississippi Delta. Her most recent poetry book, *Mississippi Delta Women in Prism,* was published by NewSouth Books in Montgomery, AL. Portions of her memoir, *A Delta Vigil*, have been published in *Boston's Full Circle: A Journal of Poetry and Prose*.

M. John Fayhee earned his Tae Kwon Do black belt in 1995. He has hiked the Appalachian, Colorado, and Arizona trails, as well as the Colorado section of the Continental Divide Trail. In 2000, along with two partners, Fayhee helped re-launch the iconic *Mountain Gazette*, where he still works as Editor in Chief. After twenty-four years living in the Colorado High Country, Fayhee moved back to his old stomping grounds in Southwest New Mexico, where he lives in warmth and sunshine with his wife, Gay Gangel-Fayhee, his little dog Casey, and his very weird cat Tucker.

Beth Ann Fennelly is Director of the MFA Program at the University of Mississippi, and the author of three books of poetry, most recently *Unmentionables* (2009). Her poems have been published in *TriQuarterly*, *Shenandoah*, *The American Poetry Review*, *The Believer*, *The Georgia Review*, *Ploughshares*, *Poetry Ireland Review*, and several other leading journals.

Kyle Flak is from Grand Rapids, MI. He has two volumes of poetry out. His favorite poem is "trees." He's hoping to make a go of it in the moving pictures industry.

Tom Franklin teaches in the MFA Program at the University of Mississippi. His first book, *Poachers* (1999), a collection of short stories, earned the Edgar Award for Mystery Writing. Previous to the *The Tilted World*, he published *Hell at the Breech* (2003), *Smonk* (2006), and *Crooked Letter, Crooked Letter* (2010).

Greg Graham teaches writing at the University of Central Arkansas. He also serves on the leadership team of the Little Rock Writing Project. Greg's writing has appeared in *Quills and Pixels*, *Written River: A Journal of Eco-Poetics*, *Teachers & Writers Magazine*, and *The Chronicle of Higher Education*.

JoeAnn Hart is the author of the novels *Float* and *Addled*. Her short fiction, essays, and articles have been widely published, most recently in *The Sonora Review* and *Harpur Palate*. On a cross-country road trip in January 2011, she stopped for breakfast in Toad Suck, AR.

Matthew Henriksen's first book, *Ordinary Sun*, emerged from Black Ocean Press in 2010. He co-edits *Typo* and *Cannibal* and curates The Burning Chair Readings in Fayetteville, AR.

Jonathon Irpino is a writer and innkeeper. After abandoning the Catholic Seminary, he moved to Los Angeles to seek a career in partying, but later relocated to New Orleans to assist his brother after Hurricane Katrina. A proud member of the American Airlines Advantage program, avid fan of the continental breakfast, and reasonable shopper, Irpino now splits his time among homes in Chicago, New Orleans, and New York.

Sarah Katharina Kayß studied comparative religion and modern history in Germany and Britain. In autumn 2012, she became a PhD candidate at the War Studies Department of King's College London. Her artwork, essays and poetry have appeared in literary magazines, journals and anthologies in Germany, Switzerland, Austria, the United Kingdom, Italy, Canada, New Zealand, and the United States.

Stephen Kessler is a writer of poetry and prose as well as a translator and editor. His translation of *Desolation of the Chimera* by Luis Cernuda received the Harold Marton Landon Translation Award from the Academy of American Poets.

klipschutz is a San Francisco-based poet, songwriter and occasional freelance journalist. His latest collection is *This Drawn & Quartered Moon* (Anvil Press, 2013). He co-wrote Chuck Prophet's critically acclaimed *Temple Beautiful* (2012).

Kelvin Krill has recently migrated to the underappreciated state of West Virginia, where he works as a security guard at a cemetery and plays a mean blues harmonica for his captive audience.

Tom Lavoie is a retired book publisher, most recently from the University of Arkansas Press, now living in Portland, OR. He's a regular reviewer for the on-line magazine *Shelf Awareness*.

Douglas Luman is a poet and nonfiction writer whose work has appeared in journals including *Burningword*, *uCity Review*, *Epigraph Magazine*, and *Kenning Journal*.

Bob May holds an MFA in playwriting from the University of Nevada, Las Vegas, and teaches playwriting and screenwriting at the University of Central Arkansas. Twenty-two of his plays have been published. Mr. May is a member of The Dramatists Guild of America.

Bob Mielke is Professor of English at Truman State University in Kirksville, MO. He has published *Kirksville*, a book of poetry, and *The Riddle of the Painful Earth: Suffering and Society in W. D. Howells' Major Writings of the Early 1890s*, a study of the socialist phase of William Dean Howells' career.

Jennifer McGaha's work has been published or is pending publication in dozens of magazines and literary journals including *The Brooklyner*, *Switchback*, *Still*, *Portland Review*, *Little Patuxent Review*, *Lumina*, *Literary Mama*, *Mason's Road*, *Now and Then*, *Slow Trains*, *North Carolina Literary Review*, etc.

Dustin Nightingale lives in Fargo, ND. His poetry has been published in various journals including *Margie*, *Cimarron Review*, *Portland Review*, *Mudfish*, and *Stickman Review*.

Seth Pennington grew up in the minnow farm capital of Lonoke, AR, as the son of a mortician. He is the Associate Editor of Sibling Rivalry Press and the poetry journal *Assaracus*.

Simon Perchik is an attorney whose poems have appeared in *Partisan Review*, *The Nation*, *The New Yorker*, and elsewhere. For more information, including free e-books, his essay titled "Magic, Illusion and Other Realities," and a complete bibliography, please visit his website at simonperchik.com.

Charles Portis is an American author and native Arkansan who, after beginning his career in journalism, published five novels including *Norwood* (1966), *True Grit* (1968), and (most recently) *Gringos* (1991). Both *Norwood* and *True Grit* were made into feature films, the latter having been produced twice. He now lives in Little Rock.

Akakia-Viala Prasteau was a kid in France who forged Rimbaud and fooled the world.

C. Prozac is still kicking. Like a rabbit in the throes of death.

Sean Rabin is an emerging writer from Australia with stories published in *Permafrost* (US), *Wet Ink* (AUS) and *Best Australian Stories 2012* (Black Inc). He also has a story in competition for this year's Pushcart Prize.

Arthur Rimbaud was an iconic French poet born in 1854 who abandoned poetry and became a merchant in Abyssinia. Credited with being a founder of French Symbolism, his work is considered to have influenced the development of Surrealism.

Davis Schneiderman is the author or editor of more than ten books, including *Drain*, *Blank*, and the forthcoming *[Sic] and Ink*. He blogs for *The Huffington Post*, directs &NOW Books, and serves as Associate Dean of the Faculty and Professor of English at Lake Forest College.

Adam J. Sorkin is a translator of contemporary Romanian poetry. Among his recent books are Ion Mureșan's *The Book of Winter* (translated with Lidia Vianu—University of Plymouth), *A Path to the Sea* by Liliana Ursu (translated with Ursu and Tess Gallagher—Pleasure Boat Studio), and Ioan Flora's *Medea and Her War Machines* (translated with Alina Cârâc—University of New Orleans), as well as the anthology *The Vanishing Point that Whistles* (Talisman House).

Daryl Spurlock is a translator and devotee of international nineteenth-century poetry and prose. He teaches Spanish at the University of Central Arkansas.

Lidia Vianu, a poet, novelist, critic, and translator, is Professor of English at the University of Bucharest, where she serves as Director of the Centre for the Translation and Interpretation of the Contemporary Text. She has published numerous of books of translation with Adam Sorkin including Marin Sorescu's *The Bridge,* which won the Poetry Society (UK) Prize for European Poetry Translation.

Jeffrey Zable has been published in many magazines and anthologies throughout the years. He has five chapbooks, including *Zable's Fables,* with an introduction by the late great Beat poet Harold Norse. He has upcoming poetry in *Muse, Clackamas Literary Review*, and *Skive Magazine*.

JOIN A CUTTING-EDGE
LITERARY COMMUNITY

THE ARKANSAS WRITERS MFA WORKSHOP

A HIGHLY SPECIALIZED STUDIO PROGRAM WITH AN EMPHASIS ON PUBLISHING AND PEDAGOGY

CREATIVE WRITING FACULTY

STACY KIDD
GARRY CRAIG POWELL
MARK SPITZER
JOHN VANDERSLICE
STEPHANIE VANDERSLICE
TERRY WRIGHT

RECENT WRITERS IN RESIDENCE

CHUCK KLOSTERMAN
ANDREI CODRESCU
MICHAEL CHABON
ANNE WALDMAN
DAVID GESSNER
ED SANDERS
DAN CHAON
CD WRIGHT
NAOMI NYE
NEIL GAIMAN
PETER CAREY
RICHARD RUSSO
HEATHER SELLERS
KEVIN BROCKMEIER

"Central Arkansas . . . has become a kind of academic incubator for the arts."
—*Chronicle of Higher Education.*

"The University of Central Arkansas is now in the fine arts 'big leagues.'"
—*Arkansas Democrat-Gazette.*

GREAT BEAR
WRITING PROJECT

DEPARTMENT
OF WRITING

COLLEGE OF
FINE ARTS &
COMMUNICATION

BACK ISSUES AVAILABLE

Antler | Alfredo Benavidez Bedoya | Jose Perez Beduya
Marck Beggs | Teresa Bergen | Kevin Brockmeier
Perrin Carrell | Jack Collom | Cathy Day
Lawrence Ferlinghetti | Menachem Feuer | Mr. Stir Fry
David Gessner | Daniel Grandbois | Johnnie M. Gray
Jack Hirschman | Julee Jaeger | Xaviera Hollander
Toshiya Kamei | Kelvin Krill | Anna Leahy
Lyn Lifshin | Leticia Luna | William Lychack
David X. Machina | Myron Michael | Poetry Class
Jacques Prevert | C. Prozak | Bernard Reed
Norman R. Shapiro | Davis Schneiderman
Willie Smith | Timothy Snediker | Mike Topp
Stephanie Vanderslice | C.D. Wright

TOAD SUCK REVIEW #1 $10.00

Larry Betz | Dave Brinks | R. Crumb | Debra Di Blasi
Gretchen Henderson | Tyrone Jaeger | Steve Katz
Jan Kerouac | Bill Lavender | Bernadette Mayer
Elinor Nauen | Emil Niculescu | Pat Nolan
Gerald Nicosia | Andrei Pleşu
Kevin Peter Quigley Phelan | Ed Sanders
Jared Schickling | Hariette Surovell
Hunter S. Thompson | Mike Topp | John Vanderslice
Anne Waldman | Brook Wilensky-Lanford

EXQUISITE CORPSE ANNUAL #2 $10.00

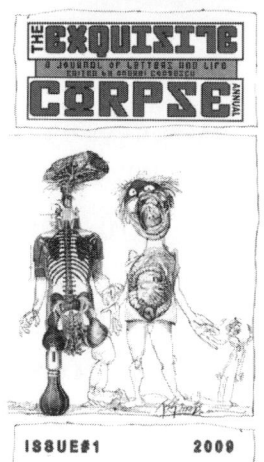

DAWN-MICHELLE BAUDE • ROBIN BECKER
BILL BERKSON • NICOLAS BORN • DAVE BRINKS
MEGAN BURNS • RUXANDRA CESEREANU
ANDREI CODRESCU • JOEL DAILEY • DIANE
DI PRIMA • KANE X. FAUCHER • SKIP FOX
OMER COKCUMEN • JIM GUSTAFSON • RADU
IOVITZA • ATTILA JOZSEF • JOEL LIPMAN
ADRIAN C. LOUIS • RICHARD MARTIN • BOB MAY
NOAM MOR • ALICE NOTLEY • ANDREI OISTEANU
LANCE OLSEN • GARRY CRAIG POWELL
JEROME ROTHENBERG • ARAM SAROYAN
DAVIS SCHNEIDERMAN • WILLIE SMITH
MIKE TOPP • ARLENE ZIDE

EXQUISITE CORPSE ANNUAL #1 $10.00

Just send check made out to "UCA" to Toad Suck Review/
Dept. of Writing/UCA/Conway, AR 72035 & indicate what
issue/s you want (add $20 for international orders)!!!!

GET THE AWARD-WINNING *TOAD SUCK REVIEW* #2 FOR ONLY $10!!!!

NO POSTAGE OR SHIPPING FEE!! JUST SEND CHECK MADE OUT TO "UCA" TO TOAD SUCK REVIEW / DEPT. OF WRITING / UCA / CONWAY, AR 72035 AND WE WILL SEND!!!

CHARLES BUKOWSKI / AMIRI BARAKA / SHEPARD FAIREY / LOUIS-FERDINAND CELINE / DAN CHAON
CRAIG PAULENICH / ANNE WALDMAN / PATRICK HICKS
RICHARD KOSTELANETZ / KATIE FALLON / TIM DARDIS
NAT HARDY / ANDREW HILL / CHRISTIAN BLADES
G. MCCULLOUGH / SHARON ANDREWS / C. PROZAC
VINCENT CELLUCI / ROY TRASK / CONOR WOODY
THOMAS COCHRAN / FRANK THURMOND / MIKE TOPP
JUNED SUBHAN / JOAO CERQUEIRA / FRANCIE BOLTER
DEBANGANA BANERJEE / KIRBY OLSON / DIRTY POET
KAREN LILLIS / BRENDA HAMMACK / M. BENEDICT
COURT MERRIGAN / KATE LADEW / TERRY WRIGHT
ALAN BRITT / ILEANA IOANA / ANGIE SPOTO
KAREN BENNETT / K. KRILL / B. FRANK

TOAD SUCK REVIEW 3D!!!!

THEY SAID IT COULDN'T BE DONE, BUT WE DID IT THE FIRST-EVER LIT JOURNAL WITH A 3D FRONT AND BACK COVER IN SMALL PRESS HISTORY!!

NO POSTAGE OR SHIPPING FEE!! JUST SEND A $10 CHECK MADE OUT TO "UCA" TO TOAD SUCK REVIEW / DEPT. OF WRITING / UCA / CONWAY, AR 72035 AND WE WILL SEND!!!

EDWARD ABBEY
GARY SNYDER
LEW WELCH

ED SANDERS	GERALD LOCKLIN	ANTLER
JEAN GENET	JESSE GLASS	REX ROSE
MOLLY KAT	TYRONE JAEGER	SKIP FOX
SANDY LONGHORN	DREA KATO	C. PROZAC
DENNIS HUMPHREY	MARK JACKSON	PETER LIU
CHRIS SHIPMAN	ANDREW HILL	JUST KIBBE
BEN McCLENDON	JAY LEVON	HEATHER COX
MARK DeCARTERET	EMILY EDINS	BRENT HOUSE
BRAD JOHNSON	DEVIN MURPHY	L. LEFKOWITZ
T. KERCHER	F. PETRUCELLI	M. MEKLINA
TRACY THOMAS	K. STEIGER	D. GOGIA
	& XU XI	

Made in the USA
San Bernardino, CA
30 December 2013